D1639532

FOOTBALL
AND
ALL THAT

FOOTBALL
AND
ALL THAT

AN IRREVERENT HISTORY

Norman Giller

Hodder & Stoughton

Copyright © 2004 by Norman Giller

First published in Great Britain in 2004
by Hodder and Stoughton
A division of Hodder Headline

The right of Norman Giller to be identified as the Author of
the Work has been asserted by him in accordance with the
Copyright, Designs and Patents Act 1988

1 3 5 7 9 10 8 6 4 2

A CIP catalogue record for this title
is available from the British Library

ISBN 0340 83588 5

Typeset in Rotis Serif by Hewer Text Ltd, Edinburgh
Printed and bound by
Clays Ltd, St Ives plc

Hodder Headline's policy is to use papers that are natural,
renewable and recyclable products and made from wood
grown in sustainable forests. The logging and manufacturing
processes are expected to conform to the environmental
regulations of the country of origin

Hodder and Stoughton Ltd
A division of Hodder Headline
338 Euston Road
London NW1 3BH

CONTENTS

ACKNOWLEDGEMENTS

Norman Giller wishes to thank Hodder's legendary Roddy Bloomfield for commissioning the book, and trusting me to tell the story of the Beautiful Game. Marion Paull has performed her usual thorough and conscientious editing role, and I am indebted to Ian Allen for his safety-net work on the hundreds of facts and figures that have been knitted together to make *Football And All That*. Thanks in particular to Mark Ecob for a perfectly tailored jacket, and to Ian Blackwell and Vito Ingelese at Popperfoto for their help on picture research. Thanks, too, to Natasha Laws for her valued support, and Clare Smith for help on an all-encompassing index that will be invaluable for historical points of reference. For the facts of the book, I have dipped copiously into works of many authors and I give them the full recognition they deserve in the Bibliography and Webography at the back of the book. I was also given considerable help by the staff of the Colindale branch of the British Library, who kindly allowed me time and space in their archives section. Finally, my gratitude to my son and right-hand man, Michael, who is a sports factician like his old dad but, thank goodness, strengthened and steadied by the common sense he inherited from his mum.

PHOTOGRAPHIC ACKNOWLEDGEMENTS

All photographs are published by courtesy of popperfoto.com

To the memory of my old friend Bobby Moore,
who was quite a footballer and all that

FOREWORD
by Jimmy Greaves

Football has always been a funny old game!

This unique football book explodes the theory that I was the first to come up with the line, 'It's a funny old game'. You don't have to get far into the compelling story to discover that it has *always* been a funny old game.

From the time Adam first kicked the apple to Cain, the Far East warriors hoofed a decapitated head around the battlefield and the second-century Chinese played the takeaway version of keepy-uppy, football has been game for a laugh.

You are in good company with Norman Giller, whom I have known and tried to avoid for more than forty years. He is a walking, talking record book and shares stories in the following pages that are often funny, always fascinating and, he assures me, completely factual. He bet me I'd find more than a hundred facts about the game that I didn't know but I gave up counting at twenty-five, and that was after just two chapters!

Norman has six *Carry On* novels to his credit, which makes him eminently qualified to write this often humorous history. It could be called *Carry On Football*. For a start, it should be dedicated to the memory of the woman who virtually gave her life so that we could have better balls. I won't spoil it for you – it's just one of the amazing stories in a book that heaves with facts, figures and anecdotes. I particularly liked the fact that England's first captain, rejoicing in the name of Cuthbert Ottaway, was a classics student at Oxford who later became a barrister. Contrast him with David Beckham who has, so I believe, an 'O' level in woodwork – but I bet Becks has a better educated right foot.

As the tight git Norman Giller is not paying me a penny piece for this foreword, I feel entitled to share a story about him. In the days back in the 1960s and '70s when he was earning his daily bread as a football writer on the *Daily Express*, he filled so much space with graphs and features about the history of the game that the newspaper's legendary columnist, Des 'The Man in the Brown Bowler' Hackett, used to taunt him with the nickname 'Giller the Filler'. Now Norman has the last laugh. All that record gathering has paid off with this engrossing book on the greatest game of them all.

Take the same test that Norman gave me. Count the facts you didn't know about the game – it's bound to be more than a hundred. You'll need an in-depth grasp of football not to be beaten by know-all Norman, who shows off his knowledge every week as the argument-settling Judge of the *Sun* and teases readers of *The Times* with a daily sports crossword.

I strongly recommend this book to anybody who loves football. I promise you will be enlightened and entertained. Giller the Filler strikes again.

AUTHOR'S INTRODUCTION

I N THE BEGINNING was the word – and the word was 'football'. Adam kicked an apple to Cain (or it might have been Abel) and was the first to utter the immortal words, 'On me 'ead, son.'

I wish I could claim this historic gem as my own, but the credit has to go to no less an authority than the late, hilarious Eric Morecambe. This, Eric assured me, was the start of football.

He was, of course, joking for a column we used to write together for the *Daily Express* back in the 1970s. This collaboration got me thinking about how the game really started and, as a result of much rigorous research into its origins, I have gathered together an enormous number of facts and figures, many of which I have had published in various forms over the last thirty years. Collecting little-known football gems has become something of a habit, a continuing process, and the master file has got fatter still during the compilation of this informal and, I hope, entertaining history of the Beautiful Game. My aim is to be as accurate as possible – irreverent but not irrelevant.

This is not so much a who-won-what-and-when football book as a who-did-what-and-why, with the emphasis whenever possible on the main characters who have given the game the kick of life since the modern form of football was invented in England in the 1880s. It is essentially about this domestic football world, with nods and bows to the international gods of the game in the appropriate places.

I apologise in advance for making occasional appearances in a story that is a personalised history of the game. It was my good fortune to have a pitch-side seat for many of the magical moments that feature in the following pages, particularly during the golden age of the 1960s when English football was on top of the world.

For this compelling tale of football and all that, we travel from where the ball first started rolling with the Chinese in the second century BC right up to date with the exciting emergence of Wayne Rooney on the international stage in the Euro 2004 finals.

An estimated two billion people tune into the World Cup finals on television. No other game on earth can match this for pulling power. So fasten your safety belts for the story of the Beautiful Game so far – warts 'n' all. We could be in for a bumpy ride.

CHAPTER 1

FROM ADAM
TO THE VICTORIANS

T HE ERIC MORECAMBE theory that it was Adam who started the ball rolling has almost as much sense and credence as the dozens of other claims about who first put the emphasis on *kicking* rather than *carrying* a ball. You will find Egyptians, Assyrians, Persians, Chinese, Japanese, Mexicans, Greeks and Romans with folklore that focuses on them as the founders of football.

I tend to side with the Chinese, who have dug up evidence that a form of football was played as far back as 255 BC and even earlier. The game was called Tsu'Chu, which may sound like a forerunner of the Paul Whitehouse 'Suits You' comedy catchphrase but, loosely translated, means 'kick with feet' (Tsu) and 'stuffed leather ball' (Chu).

Military manuals dating back to the Tsin Dynasty (255–206 BC) provide details of how Tsu'Chu – or cuju, depending on where you are orienteering in China – was part of the physical training programme for foot soldiers to help build their stamina and co-ordination. The goal, just 15ins (40cm) in diameter, consisted of a hole cut in the middle of a large silk backcloth that was strung between two 30ft (9 metres) high bamboo poles. It took extra-ordinary skill to kick the ball – made of leather stuffed with feathers and fur – through the hole, and teams could play for a day without scoring a single goal. It must have been a bit like watching George Graham's Arsenal – although my good friend George would never concede that Arsenal were ever boring-boring.

The game became a favourite pastime throughout China during the Han Dynasty (206 BC–AD 220). Emperor Wudi (156–87 BC) was such a disciple of the game that, in celebration of conquering Central Asia, he ordered all the best ball players to move to the capital so that he could watch them play. He was the Roman Abramovich of his time. To add a little spice to the games laid on for the Emperor, the losers were executed. And Rio Ferdinand thought he was hard done by with a suspension!

Various forms of Tsu'Chu, including playing with a hollow, air-filled ball, remained popular in China until the Qing Dynasty (1644–1912) when western-style football began to take over. A resurgence of interest in Tsu'Chu in recent years has not been accompanied by any forfeiting of lives.

Another contender for the foundation of football comes from the battlefields of Burma, where the decapitated heads of warriors were kicked to and fro. The game survives to this day with a wickerwork ball in place of the human head. It is also claimed, and indeed a matter of record in both Kingston-on-Thames and Chester, that the Anglo-Saxons were first to play football, using the severed heads of vanquished Viking invaders as balls. This invokes a whole new picture of the Great Dane Peter Schmeichel screaming at his team-mates from the back of the Manchester United defence, losing his head so to speak.

But much earlier than the Anglo-Saxons, in AD 43 to be precise, the Romans had brought their version of football, *harpastum*, to Britain, along with their roads and defensive walls. They adapted the game from *episkyros*, a form of kick-catch-and-rush football they had witnessed when invading Greece back in 146 BC. The Greeks included the game in the Ancient Olympics. The Roman version involved two teams on a rectangular field trying to kick or carry a ball over their rivals' goalline. It was more rugby than football, and involved crashing tackles and mass mauls as teams of as many as a hundred players took part in what was the brutal transportation of a small round ball – 8ins (20cm) in diameter – from one end of the field to the other.

The Brits and Celts adopted the game with a fervour bordering on fanaticism (and many years later fanatics became shortened to fans, which captures the extreme passion of football supporters).

William the Conqueror and his invading army brought with them the French game *choule* (or *soule*), another variety of the violent Roman pastime of *harpastum*. The Brits married the two games and over the following centuries the sport spread like a rash, appearing under different banners from 'hurling over country' and 'hurling the goal' to 'knappen' and 'foeth ball', then 'fute balle'. Finally, in the fifteenth century, somebody came up with the bright idea that it should be called 'football'. The game, played in one form or another throughout England, Scotland, Ireland and Wales, was still more of a carrying than a kicking game, and the name referred to the fact that it was played on foot rather than horseback – most sports of the time involved horses.

Just about every version of the game involved vicious physical contact and huge scrums of people, usually peasants, pushing and heaving against each other as they tried to move the ball – normally a stuffed pig's bladder – towards goals that were often miles apart. They not only played the game across fields, but through entire villages and towns. This truly was football for the masses.

The tradition lives on in half a dozen English towns, most notably in Ashbourne in Derbyshire, where every Shrove Tuesday and Ash Wednesday two halves of the town battle each other in an annual gathering that dates back to AD 217. The town splits in half – those born north of Henmore Brook are the Up'ards, and those born south, the Down'ards.

Up to 2,000 players take part and few get to see, let alone touch, the cork-filled ball as it is forced back and forth between goals three miles apart and through streams running off the River Henmore. Few know the rules apart from two regulations that have survived following some early catastrophes, when it was deemed necessary to declare that murder and manslaughter were not allowed. Either would certainly be a red-card offence today.

From as early as 1280, daggers and swords were banned. This followed the death of one Henry de Ellington after he had been accidentally stabbed by a dagger worn by David Le Keu as they battled for the ball in a Trinity Sunday match at Ulkham, Kent. Another death was recorded during a match between the villages of Lavenham and Brent Eleigh in Suffolk in the 1490s.

One school of thought suggests that the mass-maul game was pagan in origin, played to herald the arrival of spring, while other historians maintain that the kick-and-chase battle was the medieval ancestor of modern English football. It is reasonable to assume that, in many cases, pagan customs, especially fertility rites, played a major role in the early development of the game. According to legend, the ball symbolised the sun, which had to be conquered in order to secure a bountiful harvest. It needed to be propelled around, or across, a field so that the crops would flourish and the attacks of the opponents had to be warded off like evil spirits. Perhaps the early creators of crop circles?

The games were generally confined to male contestants, but in the Scottish town of Inveresk, for example, married women took on maidens in what was the forerunner of women's football. It was an unwritten law that the married women always won.

Another of the traditional Shrove Tuesday matches is staged at Sedgefield, County Durham – Tony Blair territory – where on the village green a ball is passed through a small ring, known as the Bull Ring, and then thrown to a gathering of anything up to 1,000 players. The 500 yard pitch stretches between the two goals – an old duck pond and a stream – and the game comes complete with its own traditional chant, in best north-east tones:

> When the pancakes are sated,
> Come to the ring and you'll be mated,
> There this ball will be upcast,
> May this game be better than the last.

The annual Ashbourne festival has been given royal patronage, with two Princes of Wales – Edward in 1928 and Charles in 2003 – starting the ball rolling by throwing it to the hordes of players, a ceremony known as 'turning it up'.

This helped make up for the mean spirit of their ancestors Edward II, Edward III, Richard II and Henry IV. They each took turns banning mass football games because, apart from causing street riots and public disorder, they were costing vital archery practice time during the Hundred Years war with France (seasons 1338 to 1453). Edward III went to the extreme of commanding the local authorities to ban all sport and enforce archery practice. There are those in the here and now who would like to see a similar proclamation made banning the playing of computer games, so that the youths of Britain can get back to learning how to control a ball with their feet rather than surrendering playing fields to foreign invaders.

A fifteenth-century monk at Caunton, Nottinghamshire, had his daily meditation interrupted by 'much baying and shouting'. He looked out of his window to be greeted by the sight of a mass football match in progress, and recorded, 'The players propel a huge ball, not by throwing it up into the air, but by striking and rolling it along the ground, and not by their hands but by their feet, a game, I say, abominable enough . . . and rarely ending but with some loss, accident, or disadvantage of the players themselves.'

The anti-football feeling spread to Scotland, where a succession of fifteenth-century Scottish kings considered the game – mob football – the curse of the working class. James I decreed in 1424 'that na man play at the Fute-ball'. This decision made King James so unpopular that it might well have inspired the famous saying that is a precursor to a head-butt, known affectionately as a Glasgow kiss, 'I'll gie ye the heid, Jimmy.'

While busying himself with six marriages, building up the Navy and dissolving the monasteries, Henry VIII apparently also found time to become the first monarch to follow football. The proof emerged in early 2004 with the discovery of a royal shopping list, suggesting that Henry was a mix of the sixteenth-century versions of Imelda Marcos and David Beckham.

His 1525 order to a cordwainer called Cornelius Johnson, 'Cobblers to the King', for ten pairs of English-leather boots and forty-five pairs of velvet shoes included a payment of five shillings for a new pair of footie boots, or as the invoice put it, 'one pair sotular [suitable] for footeball'. That entire order cost £100, which would have been more than two years' salary for most of the king's servants. There is no record of Henry actually playing the game, and it is hard to picture him in the mass mauls of the time, unless he was surrounded by a scrum of bodyguards. Following widespread complaints, he turned against the game and banned it in 1548 because it was inciting riots across the country.

Henry's daughter, Elizabeth I, also considered the game a heathen practice. She passed a decree in 1572 – 'no football play to be used or suffered within the City of London' – and threatened a week's jail followed by church penance for anybody caught playing the vulgar game that was causing havoc among City market stallholders.

A scribe of the time known as William Shakespeare provided written proof that football was well established in Elizabethan times. In *Comedy of Errors* (Act II, Scene 1) Dromio of Ephesus has this exit speech:

> Am I so round with you as you with me,
> That like a football you do spurn me thus?
> You spurn me hence, and he will spurn me hither:
> If I last in this service, you must case me in leather.

In *King Lear* (Act I, Scene IV) Shakespeare has the Earl of Kent taunting Gloucester's steward, Oswald, as he trips him up, 'You base football player'. It was a sign of the times that this was the most insulting phrase the Bard could come up with, and an indication that football players were the lowest of the low. Just think, if Will the Quill was around today, he would no doubt be writing the Birmingham City programme notes – 'TV or not TV, that is the question as Sky continue to monopolise our football', or words to that effect.

The Puritans of the 1600s tried to outlaw football because 'it is a devlishe pastime' and 'more a bloody murdering practice than a fellowly sport'. Oliver Cromwell, a keen player when at Cambridge, banned any form of football on the Sabbath, a law that was largely ignored for many years.

That great chronicler Samuel Pepys described in his famous diary how, in the great frost of January 1665, 'the streets were full of footballs'.

While the genteel game of cricket was being claimed as an acceptable sporting pastime by the aristocracy and educated classes, mass football was considered the territory of thugs and tearaways and the unacceptable face of the common man.

The game was played throughout the country, usually to tie in with religious festivals and seasonal holidays, and ruffians took it as a licence to maim and mangle. Windows of houses and shops were smashed, high streets trashed, fields, fences and hedges wrecked and bones broken as drunken louts joined in the lark of getting the ball from one goal to another.

Teams used to get up to all sorts of devious tricks to try to win the games, which carried huge local prestige. The most ingenious scam occurred in one of the annual Shrovetide battles in Derby when a scrum of players hid the ball out of sight while it was unstuffed. Once pulled into pieces, it was smuggled under the dresses of village women and then put back together again in front of the rival's goal. That trick gave a whole new meaning to the idea of skirting the rules.

The Derby matches were notorious for their aggression, and a French observer wrote in 1829, 'If Englishmen call this play, it would be impossible to say what they call fighting.'

Over in Italy, particularly in Florence and Venice, they were carrying out similar violence in the name of sport with a brand of football called *Calcio* – 'I kick'. This was a much more colourful spectacle than that produced by the English yobs, with teams dressed in coloured livery so that everyone would know which side they were on, the prototype of football kits – tribal instincts were alive and well.

So how can England, having borrowed the idea of the game from the Romans and the French and turned it into a feast of fighting and feuding, claim to be the birthplace of football? The fact is that England is the home of *organised* football, played exclusively to and from the feet. That is what England gave to the world, a beautifully rounded game that many across the globe have learned to play better and more imaginatively than its founders.

The first sign of a wind of change had blown, as far back as the late sixteenth century, from the direction of a highly respected educational pioneer called Richard Mulcaster, Carlisle-born headmaster of two of London's most prominent day schools, Merchant Taylor's and then St Paul's.

The nobility, so anti the thuggery of football, sat up and took notice when the Old Etonian published his belief that football had many educational benefits as well as improving health and strength. It was, he believed, a character builder. He was the first to make the case for a reorganisation of the game, including limiting the number of players and the need for a referee to settle arguments and disputes. Until the rise of the dreaded referee, the unwritten rule was that, if reasoned argument failed, the participants settled disagreements with fists.

In his 1581 publication succinctly entitled *Positions Wherein Those Primitive Circumstances Be Examined, Which Are Necessarie for the Training up of Children*, the visionary Mulcaster wrote of the many benefits of the game under the sub-heading 'The handball, the football, the armball'. (You can read an extract in the appendices at the back of this book – sexed up with modern language.) The Mulcaster musings struck a chord with succeeding generations of young student teachers, who were about to play a key role in an educational revolution, as public schools became part of the fabric of English society. In the early nineteenth century, football was borrowed from the peasants by the privileged few in what was class-divided England.

The centuries-old Wall Game still flourishes at Eton, played on a pitch 120 yards long and just six yards wide and with little movement either way as bodies push and pull to little effect. The Duke of Wellington said that the Battle of Waterloo was won on the playing fields of Eton. Napoleon just might have been buried alive had they used Wall Game tactics.

The Eton Field Game was closer to what later became known as football, played on a large outside pitch, with goalposts. The rules described 'offside' – a player trying to get ahead of the ball – as 'sneaking'. Similar games became part of the tradition at such schools as Charterhouse, Harrow, Winchester, Shrewsbury and Rugby, where the groundbreaking educationalist Dr Thomas Arnold encouraged discipline and fitness through team sport.

The mention of Rugby school cannot pass without reference to a Manchester-born boy called William Webb Ellis who, according to legend, broke all conventions by catching the ball during a game of football in 1823, tucking it under his arm and running with it to the opponents' goalline. So rugby football was born to rival the developing kicking game.

What the public schools did was make use of facilities in their grounds rather than running roughshod through towns and villages. Thus began the practice of confining the game to a relatively small, defined space, and the numbers of participating players came down to a manageable level.

Each public school had its own rules and this led to confusion when the pupils went on to the universities of Oxford and Cambridge. Prolonged arguments about which rules to follow were the norm, most of the disputes centring on the kicking or catching of the ball.

Enter one J.C. Thring, who found on arriving at Cambridge that he was spending more time arguing about the rules than playing the game he had grown to love at Shrewsbury school. Thring, later an assistant master at Uppingham School before becoming a chaplain, decided that everything was too complicated and, in 1848, having consulted with representatives of students from fourteen public schools who had gone on to Cambridge, he produced the first set of rules. With his religious calling, it could have been called *The Ten Commandments of Football.* These rules were pinned up on posts surrounding Parker's Piece, the historic grounds where Cambridge students played their games, and it is Parker's Piece that can be pinpointed as the birthplace of football as we know it today.

The Cambridge influence cut even deeper into the game when the University set up a committee to build on the foundation of the Thring commandments, and in 1862 *The Winter Game: Rules of Football* was published.

Meantime, 'oop north' in 1857, the world's first football club – Sheffield FC – was being formed by army officers Colonel Nathaniel Cresswick and Major William Prest, who were based at Hillsborough Barracks. Within five years, fifteen different clubs had sprung up in the Sheffield area, and in 1861 the first organised club football match, between Sheffield and Hallam, drew 600 spectators. So Sheffield can share with Cambridge the honour of being the springboard for football almost as we recognise it today.

Old Etonians Cresswick, later a solicitor and chairman of a Sheffield steel company, and Prest, a wine merchant, studied the rules of public schools football, and came up with a version of their own. A cocktail of the Cambridge and Sheffield Rules eventually formed the bedrock of football. England now had a game to give to the world.

CHAPTER 2

ALWAYS PLAY TO THE HANDKERCHIEF

T HE YEAR 1863 was a significant one. Recently widowed, Queen Victoria was into the twenty-sixth year of her reign, Abraham Lincoln was the US President in the second year of the Civil War, Charles Dickens' *Great Expectations* was into its second print, and The Football Association was about to be formed. Never refer to it as the English Football Association. It is always *the* Football Association because it was the first in the world. Ah, sweet, sweet FA.

An upstairs room of the Freemasons' Tavern in Great Queen Street in the heart of London's legal eagle land was booked for the first meeting on 26 October 1863 to discuss the formation of 'an association of football clubs'. Great expectations, indeed.

There may well have been blood as well as beer staining the carpet of the Freemasons' Tavern at the end of the first and subsequent meetings. Two major points of discord emerged. The first was that the public schools of Eton, Harrow, Winchester, Rugby and Westminster turned down invitations to the first meeting. They did not take kindly to what they saw as outside interference with their own jealously guarded rules. The Harrow secretary sent a terse message that read, 'We cling to our present rules, and should be sorry to alter them in any respect whatsoever.'

The second, and much more contentious, point of disagreement focused on just how physical the game should be. To kick or not to kick, that was the question – and it was the body not the ball that was at the centre of the heated argument.

The battle was between the codes of rugby and the new foot-controlled game, the main divergence being over the issue of 'hacking'. Rugby supporters argued that it was both manly and courageous to be allowed to tackle an opponent and kick him across the shins. Those speaking up for the new-fangled dribbling game considered this unnecessary violence. They had to face taunts of being 'cissies' and even, when tempers flared, 'physical cowards'.

The Blackheath club argued most vociferously for a heavy mix of rugby rules to be included in regulations being considered by the proposed association of football clubs. Blackheath secretary F.W. Campbell claimed at the peak of the dispute, 'If you do away with hacking, you will do away with all the courage and pluck of the game, and I will be bound to bring over a lot of Frenchmen who would beat you with a week's practice.' These words will echo through Stamford Bridge and the marble halls of Highbury.

Following a bitter, gloves-off meeting on 1 December 1863, the rugby supporters left in a huff after being outvoted by thirteen votes to four. From then on, Rugby Union and Association Football were at daggers drawn.

Seven days after the rugby supporters had been kicked out – hacked out, even – the rules of the newly formed Football Association were passed. The last one, Rule 13, which stated that 'no player shall be allowed to wear projecting nails, iron plates, or gutta percha on the soles or heels of his boots', was added to stop the practice of players turning their working boots into weapons. The banning of gutta percha – a resin used in the making of golf balls – was aimed at those footballers who were using the gluey substance to get extra grip on slippery turf.

Following a merger with Sheffield Rules in 1877, all references to rugby conventions – making a mark, for instance – were removed, and it was agreed that only the goalkeeper could handle the ball, apart from for the throw-ins.

It was also decided that teams should be restricted to eleven players a side, and that the size and weight of the ball should be standardised, with a circumference of from 27 to 28ins (68–70cm) and weighing between 14 and 16oz (410–450gms). All those of a certain age who remember heading the heavy old leather balls will be surprised to learn that today's ball is an ounce heavier, but because it is rain and mud resistant it seems much lighter. The leather balls were often twice as heavy at the final whistle as at the beginning of the game. Ouch!

Here is an appropriate place to remember Mrs Lindon and her contribution to the development of footballs. Her husband, H.J. Lindon, made a living manufacturing footballs and she died from a lung disease caused by blowing up hundreds of pig bladders using her mouth. This tragedy inspired Mr Lindon to find an alternative to pig bladders and he developed the first inflatable rubber bladder in 1862.

Bootmaker William Gilbert, who made his reputation manufacturing rugby balls for his local Rugby school, exhibited both an oval ball and a round ball 'for dribbling' at the Great Exhibition at Crystal Palace in 1851. American Charles Goodyear designed the first vulcanised rubber football in 1855, all of which Greavise might describe as a load of balls.

London played Sheffield in the first representative match on record, at Battersea on 31 March 1866, and it was following this game that the playing time of ninety minutes became standard. London won 2–0, with the first goal being scored by E.C. (Ebenezer Cobb) Morley, the Barnes forward who had helped draw up the first set of FA Rules. C.W. (Charles) Alcock, who was to become known as the 'Father of Football' long before Sir Matt Busby's era, got himself into the history books by becoming the first player in a representative match to be ruled offside. That much-changed law has caused more argument throughout the history of the game than any other, and continues to do so.

Despite the outlawing of hacking, the London–Sheffield game continually bordered on physical violence and the *Bell's Life of London* reporter recorded, 'The game was a very hot one, and though Sheffield were overmatched, many of the Londoners were badly knocked about.'

The game started to take a shape recognisable as modern football with the introduction of corner kicks and free kicks in 1871. The crossbar replaced tape in 1875, the two-handed rather than one-handed throw-in was introduced in 1883, nets were used for the first time in 1890, a referee and two linesmen replaced umpires in 1891 and, in the same year, came the controversial addition of the penalty kick.

A new sound was heard during a match between Nottingham Forest and Sheffield in 1878 – the referee's whistle. Until then, umpires (later, referees) made their decisions by a wave of a handkerchief. 'Always play to the handkerchief' somehow does not have the same ring to it as 'always play to the whistle'.

The whistle – an Acme Thunderer – was invented by Birmingham toolmaker Joseph Hudson for use by the Bow Street runners after they complained that the rattles they used to carry were too cumbersome. The Thunderer and its successors have since been heard on football pitches across the world, with more than 160 million manufactured by the company formed by Hudson.

Once the Football Association had formulated the rules, the game spread like a forest fire – or perhaps a Notts County fire would be a more appropriate analogy. County were formed as early as 1862, and would become the oldest of the founder clubs of the Football League.

Using *the* Football Association as their model, the Scottish FA (1873), the FA of Wales (1875) and the Irish FA (1880) were formed, and willing disciples carried the gospel of football around the world. Young Victorian businessmen, teachers, construction workers, soldiers and men of the cloth – spreading what became known as 'muscular Christianity' – packed footballs in their luggage as they set off on their world travels.

In South America, the building of the railways attracted British workmen who arrived with footballs almost literally at their feet. Their enthusiasm lit the passion for the game in Argentina, and the memory of an English Victorian schoolteacher, Isaac Newell, has been preserved in the name of a prominent Argentinian club, Newell's Old Boys.

The ball was set rolling in Brazil by Sao Paulo-born Charles Miller, the son of a Scottish banker and an English mother from Hampshire. He was sent home to study at Banister Court School in Southampton, where he learned to play football so well that he was selected for Hampshire and Southampton. On his return to Brazil in 1894 at the age of twenty, he brought with him shirts, balls and boots and within a short time several clubs had been formed and the conveyor belt of the world's greatest footballers had started.

The English cannot take all the credit for good distribution. Former Paisley professional Archie McLean brought the Scottish passing game to Brazil at the start of the twentieth century, and Argentina's very first cup final featured St Andrews against Old Caledonians!

The next countries to follow the lead of the English and form football associations were the Netherlands and Denmark (1889), New Zealand (1891), Argentina (1893), Chile (1895), Switzerland and Belgium (1895), Italy (1898), Germany and Uruguay (1900) and Hungary (1901).

The United States, apart from a few European-dominated pockets, stoutly resisted the contagious spread of the game. They preferred to take the English game of rugby and twist it to their own design until it emerged as American Football.

Down under in Australia, the Irish influence was so strong, particularly in the Melbourne area, that they took to Gaelic football, mixed and matched it with an indigenous Aboriginal game and came up with Australian Rules Football.

Italy was greatly influenced by English football pioneers. Their first club, Genoa Cricket and Football Club, was founded by a group of English technicians and engineers, and Milan Cricket and Football Club was set up on the combined initiative of some English and Italian sportsmen – hence the name Milan rather than Milano. Napoli was created by the local Italian-British Society (and was initially named 'Naples'), and Juventus – the 'Grand Old Lady' of Italian football – chose their famous club colours after one of their members acquired a Notts County shirt on a visit to England.

Meantime, back at the birthplace of football, newly appointed Football Association secretary Charles Alcock realised that the game needed a competitive edge to give it a spark. He recalled how an annual football competition, the Cock House Cup – the winners were lauded as the cock house – had always caused excitement when he was a pupil at Harrow School. This triggered the idea for football's oldest club competition, the FA Cup.

Alcock called a meeting at the offices of *The Sportsman* in London on 20 July 1871. His proposal 'that it is desirable that a Challenge Cup should be established in connection with the Association, for which all clubs belonging to the Association should be invited to compete' met with unanimous favour and was finally approved three months later. The competition was simply named the Football Association Challenge Cup, quickly shortened by the headline writers to the FA Cup.

Fifteen member clubs answered the call, including Alcock's own Wanderers club, a team made up of ex-public schoolboys and university graduates. More than 600 teams take part in the modern competition. The original entrants were: Barnes, Civil Service, Clapham Rovers, Crystal Palace, Donnington School, Hampstead Heathens, Harrow Chequers, Hitchin, Maidenhead, Marlow, Reigate Priory, Royal Engineers, Upton Park, Wanderers and Queen's Park (Scotland).

If a tie was drawn, both sides would progress to the next round. Queen's Park of Glasgow were given a bye through to the semi-finals purely because of the cost of travelling to London, where the FA decreed all ties must be played. Donnington School created their own piece of bizarre history when they scratched from the competition without kicking a ball, and they never entered again.

The first round developed into something of a farce, with both eventual finalists progressing without playing a game. Harrow Chequers scratched before their scheduled match with Wanderers, while Royal Engineers earned a walkover against Reigate Priory. In the second round, Alcock's Wanderers beat Clapham Rovers 3–1, and the Engineers eliminated Hitchin 5–0.

There were just five teams in the quarter-finals instead of the expected eight. Wanderers and Crystal Palace drew and both went through. Queen's Park again progressed thanks to their agreed bye, while Royal Engineers accounted for Hampstead Heathens 2–0.

On paper, the semi-finals looked correct with four teams, but on the pitch it became extremely complicated. Queen's Park, then regarded as the finest team in Britain, made the trip to London from Glasgow to play the Wanderers. The game finished in a hard-fought goalless draw and a replay was ordered, but the Scottish amateurs, with jobs to go to, could afford neither the time nor the money to stay over, and they returned to Glasgow unbeaten.

So Wanderers had a walkover into the final despite having won just one tie on the way. Meanwhile, Royal Engineers were comfortable 3–0 winners against Crystal Palace, not the current club at Selhurst Park but a side representing employees of the London exhibition centre and park.

A crowd of 2,000 spectators, each paying a shilling entrance fee, gathered at the Kennington Oval for the final on 16 March 1872. Watching it today, the game would be unrecognisable, as though it was being played on another planet. The pitch had no penalty area or centre-circle markings. In the goal, there were no nets, and tapes were used for crossbars. The players wore knickerbockers, the goalkeepers had on the same jerseys as the outfield players and spectators exhibited no distinguishing colours to show which team they were supporting.

Wanderers, captained by the competition's creator Charles Alcock, were considered second favourites, but the Royal Engineers from Chatham were handicapped from the tenth minute after defender Lieutenant Edmund Cresswell fell and broke a collar bone.

The only goal of the match was created by eighteen-year-old Westminster pupil Robert Vidal. He was known as the 'Prince of Dribblers' after scoring three goals direct from the kick-off in one match, without an opponent touching the ball. The future England international and vicar turned the Engineers defence inside out before releasing the ball to a player calling himself A.H. Chequer, who had the simple task of steering the ball into the goal.

Chequer was later revealed to be Morton Peto Betts, who played under an assumed name because he had originally entered the competition with Harrow Chequers and switched to Wanderers after Harrow Chequers scratched. Five years later, he won an England cap as a goalkeeper, and he also played cricket for Kent and Middlesex.

Skippering the Royal Engineers was Captain Francis Marindin, who played in goal. Later he played as an outfielder, by which time he had been promoted to major, and he went on to become a leading referee, President of the Football Association and, for good measure, the Board of Trade representative in charge of the expansion of British Railways. Yes, you could say he was the first of the great all-rounders.

Three weeks after the final, at a special celebration dinner in Pall Mall, Alcock was presented with an 18in silver Cup. The trophy, which cost £20, would eventually finish up in the hands of thieves. It was stolen from a Birmingham jeweller's shop window, where it was on display after being won by Aston Villa in 1895. Many years later a man confessed that the silver trophy had been melted down and converted into hundreds of half-crown coins.

The world's oldest football competition was up and running after a shambolic start. Then Alcock the visionary had another idea that was every bit as ambitious as the FA Cup competition. 'How about,' he wondered, 'an *international* match?'

This, remember, was before most countries had even heard of football let alone games between nations, and five years ahead of the first cricket Test match between Australia and England. But it was the back end of the Industrial Revolution when, if you were British, you automatically thought internationally. Victorian Britain was the workshop of the world, mining nearly half the world's coal and exporting more manufactured goods than the United States, Germany, France and Italy combined.

When Alcock looked around for another football-playing country, his gaze, naturally, fell on Scotland. In 1870 he organised a series of four matches billed as between England and Scotland. To be more accurate, they were between London and exiled Scots based in London. 'England' won three and drew one.

They were not best pleased north o' the border to be represented by exiles, and they challenged England to bring a team to Scotland for an *official* international match against *bona fide* Scots. The challenge came from Queen's Park, far and away the finest of Scotland's ten established teams and a law unto themselves a year ahead of the forming of the Scottish FA.

The Football Association accepted the challenge, and on 24 October 1872 Alcock wrote to all the member clubs requesting donations to help pay for eleven players and officials to make the rail journey to Glasgow. Alcock selected himself as team captain but had to withdraw because of a shoulder injury and travelled as England's umpire.

Alcock had first proposed Monday, 24 November for the match. Back came a letter from the Scots requesting that the game be switched to the Saturday, and pointing out as politely as possible that 'many of those who would play or might witness the encounter would be engaged upon their businesses.'

It would not have occurred to Alcock and his Football Association colleagues that the little matter of work might get in the way of the fixture. They were from an élite rank still clinging to the vision that football was for the upper classes. Meanwhile, in Scotland, the game was developing as a sport of the 'common' man.

International football was born at the West of Scotland Cricket Club ground in Hamilton Crescent, Partick, on St Andrew's Day, 30 November, 1872. The game kicked off at 2.20 p.m., twenty minutes late while the Scottish referee William Keay and his two umpires waited for a heavy downpour to stop.

A crowd of more than 3,000 spectators paid gate receipts of £102 19s 6d to watch a game of vastly contrasting styles. The Scots wore blue shirts with a single lion crest, white knickerbockers, blue-and-white hooped socks and red woolly head cowls, while England had white shirts with a three-lions crest, and an assortment of multi-coloured knickerbockers and socks depending on the player's club team.

England lined up in a 1–2–7 formation. Their tactics were to dribble at the opponents and hoof the ball upfield before being tackled. One of the six forwards, following closely behind the man in possession, would then race after the ball.

Scotland had devised a 2–2–6 system, with all the players paired off so that they could play what would today be known as one-two passing movements. This was then a revolutionary tactic of 'passing and running' or 'give and go'. The Scots, strongly influenced by their captain Robert Gardner, called it 'the combination game'. England's players had never seen anything like it.

The Scots, the original wee blue devils, were dwarfed by the hefty England players, who weighed, on average, two stones more. Sadly, there is no photographic record of the teams. The players refused to guarantee buying prints and so a photographer was not booked to take team pictures.

The *Bell's Life of London* correspondent wrote an eyewitness account of the game, which had everything but goals. Ninety-eight years were to pass before England and Scotland played another goalless draw:

> *It was a splendid display of football in the really scientific sense of the word, and a most determined effort on the part of the representatives of the two nationalities to overcome each other.*
>
> *The only thing that saved the Scotch team from defeat, considering the powerful forward play of England, was the magnificent defensive display and tactics shown by their backs.*

It was naturally thought that the English players, although showing fine individual play, would be deficient in working together, belonging as they did to so many clubs. But the game had not proceeded far when this illusion was dispelled like mist at the approach of the sun, for the magnificent dribbling of the England forwards was greatly admired by the immense concourse of spectators, who kept the utmost order. L128,595/

Most of the Scotland team were from Queen's Park, a club formed in July 1867 at a time when Clydeside was producing one quarter of the world's ships and railways. There were no class divisions in their football, and manual workers played happily alongside bankers and lawyers.

James and Robert Smith, operating side by side as link men for the Scots, were the first brothers to play international football together. Both were domiciled in England with the South Norwood club, but kept their affiliation with Queen's Park. In the second half, Robert Smith switched positions with Scotland captain Robert Gardner, who had been playing in goal. England also switched their goalkeeper, Barker and Maynard changing roles after half-time. In those early days, goalkeepers were more like sweepers and would often come upfield, safe in the knowledge that they could handle the ball anywhere in their half of the pitch.

There were no match programmes. Had there been, the pen pictures of the eleven England players would have read something like this – with updates and Christian names added although, in the style of the privately educated class at the time, they would have referred to each other by their surnames:

1. R.C. (Robert) Barker
Born Wouldham, Kent, 1847
Clubs: Hertfordshire Rangers and Wanderers
A surprise choice in goal as he usually plays as a forward for his club teams. A late convert to association football. He played rugby at his public school.

2. Ernest Harwood Greenhalgh
Born Mansfield, Notts, 1849
Club: Notts County

Tackles like a lion in the Notts County defence, and can hoof a clearance the length of the field. The former Midlands public schoolboy is from a distinguished Mansfield business family and is the highly respected captain of Notts.

3. Reginald de Courtenay Welch
Born Kensington, London, 1851
Clubs: Harrow Chequers and Wanderers

Equally efficient as an outfield defender or in goal. A member of one of England's noblest families, the Old Harrovian was in goal for Wanderers when they became first winners of the FA Cup. (Later, he had a distinguished military career.)

4. Frederick Patey Chappell
Born London, 1850
Club: Oxford University

Noted at his club for his speed of foot and strong tackle, Chappell is a forward who likes to attack from a midfield base. (Shortly after this game, Chappell changed his name to Frederick Brunning Maddison.)

5. William John Maynard
Born Camberwell, London, 1853
Club: 1st Surrey Rifles

The baby of the side, Maynard is a utility player who is equally at home as a forward or goalkeeper. He is a professional soldier from a distinguished military family and on an officer's course. (Maynard was the first teenager to play for England.)

6. John Brockbank
Born Whitehaven, Cumbria, 1848
Club: Cambridge University

Brockbank, who plans to become an actor when he finishes his studies at Cambridge University, is a fine dribbler of the ball. He is also an excellent middle-order batsman who has attracted the interest of the MCC.

7. Charles Clegg
Born Sheffield 1850
Club: Sheffield Wednesday

A constructive attacking player with good ball control, Clegg is highly regarded at Sheffield Wednesday both for his football prowess and his intelligent views on the way forward for the game. (His barrister brother William played in the next match against Scotland, making them the first brothers capped by England. Both were knighted for their administrative services to football. Sir William became Lord Mayor of Sheffield, and Sir Charles was FA President from 1923 until his death in 1937.)

8. Arnold Kirke-Smith
Born Sheffield, 1850
Club: Oxford University

Kirke-Smith has taken time off from his theological studies at Oxford to play a linking role in the England attack. He is noted for the accuracy of his passing and the power of his shooting. (A year later he helped Oxford reach the FA Cup final. He played in goal until deciding to join the attack, leaving the goal unguarded for the last moments of the match, which was won 2–0 by the Wanderers. He was ordained in 1875.)

9. Cuthbert Ottaway
Born Dover, Kent, 1850
Club: Oxford University

A law and classics student at Oxford University, Ottaway is the England captain and one of the country's leading all-round sportsmen. The Old Etonian also represents Oxford at cricket, athletics and racquets. (He later played for Middlesex and Kent as a batsman-wicketkeeper, and tragically died at the age of twenty-eight soon after being called to the bar.)

10. Charles John Chenery
Born Lambourn, Berks, 1850
Club: Crystal Palace

Chenery is the star forward of the Crystal Palace team, which plays in the grounds of Joseph Paxton's famous Exhibition centre. He was an outstanding public school footballer and specialises in kick and chase. (The present Crystal Palace club was founded in 1905.)

11. Charles John Morice
Born Kensington, London, 1850
Club: Barnes

A dribbling player who likes to operate on the right wing, Morice stars with Barnes alongside the club founder Ebenezer Morley, who drew up the original draft of the Football Association rules. (Barnes played Richmond in the first game to test out the rules.)

William Kenyon-Slaney had the honour of scoring the first goal in international football, and he was also the first to score two goals in one game when winning his only cap for England against Scotland on 8 March 1873. Captain Kenyon-Slaney of the Household Brigade, and later an MP, completed a hat-trick of firsts by being the first player born overseas to be capped by England. He was born in Rajkot, India, where his father was an officer (and, of course, a gentleman). England won this second international 4–2 at The Oval, and the teams changed ends after every goal.

The uppercrust amateur players and administrators of England had the new game of football almost completely under their control, certainly in the south where public school, Old Boys, university and army officer teams were shooting up as quickly as daisies in a spring meadow.

They had also come up with a new name for the game – soccer. The credit for conjuring up the word is usually given to Charles Wreford-Brown, a player with England, Oxford University, Old Carthusians and, the most famous of all amateur clubs, the Corinthians. As he left his Oxford digs one day, dressed in playing togs, he was asked where he was bound.

'I'm off to play football,' he replied.

'Rugger or Association?'

'Soccer, of course,' said our hero, with an abbreviation of Association that could have come out of the mouth of a modern tabloid headline writer.

The name was popularised by the Victorian football cognoscenti, but gradually went out of use during the twentieth century until being revived in the United States to distinguish the game from American Football.

Even in these early years, football was seeing the light. Two teams drawn from the football hotbed of Sheffield and captained by the visionary Clegg brothers played a match at Bramall Lane on 14 October 1878 that stands out like a beacon in the history of the game. It was the first floodlit match.

Four huge electric lamps powered by portable generators stood on 50ft wooden towers erected at each corner of the ground and provided the light to play by. That was the good news. The bad news was that the near 20,000 crowd attracted to the spectacle stumbled around like drunks in a fog as they attempted to leave the darkened ground at the end of the game.

A repeat of the experiment at the Kennington Oval the following month was a total disaster as high winds played havoc with the lights, and all the spectators could see were the shadows of players. Football remained largely a daytime game for the next seventy-five years.

The first of the 'superstars' bred by the game appeared in the impressive shape of London-born Scot the Hon. A.F. (Alfred) Kinnaird. He played in nine FA Cup finals with Wanderers and Old Etonians from 1873 to 1883, finishing on the winning side five times. Later the eleventh Baron of Inchture, he was distinctive on the football field because of a red beard, an imposing physique and a warrior-like approach to a match in an era when fierce tackling was part and painful parcel of the game.

The oft-attributed story of the broken leg may well have originated with him. The story goes that his mother once said, 'I do so worry that Alfred will one day come home with a broken leg.'

'Aye,' responded one of his team-mates. 'I wonder whose.'

No doubt apocryphal, anyway, that tale gives a splendid whiff of the way his Lordship played the game.

Kinnaird, working in tandem with Charles Alcock, became the main driving force behind the early rise of the Football Association, and in 1911 his fifty-five years of service to the game were marked in an extraordinary way. He was presented with the FA Cup and a new trophy was ordered. Now there's one for a trivia quiz – who was the first Scot to win the FA Cup outright?

Kinnaird was a larger-than-life character, celebrating his fifth FA Cup winner's medal by standing on his head in front of the main stand after leading Old Etonians to victory over the provincial upstarts of Blackburn Rovers in the 1882 final at The Oval.

Oh, what a hoot it was for Kinnaird and all his amateur colleagues as they swanned around playing football, or soccer, to their heart's content. But waiting in the wings, so to speak, and about to spoil the party were – don't look Ethel, a dirty word coming up – the *professionals*.

CHAPTER 3

TAKE THE
MONEY AND RUN

S IR WALTER SCOTT wrote 'O what a tangled web we weave . . . when first we practise to deceive' in the nineteenth century. The irony of the sentiment coming from a Scot would have been lost on those Englishmen who originally brought football into disrepute by tainting it with money – by bribing the best Scottish players into moving south.

The subject of professionalism was the most contentious of all issues in the 1880s and led to a bitter north/south divide. Most of the Midlands clubs, not wanting to be caught in the middle so to speak, sided with the north.

Northern clubs considered football to be a working-class sport, while down in the south, true-blue, frock-coated amateur officials and administrators had a velvet-gloved stranglehold on the game. In the north, the clubs were generally financed by wealthy, self-made businessmen, busy making their brass from mills, mines and metal manufacturing. They kept their footballers – and their workers – happy by slipping the players under-the-counter cash payments. Money-in-the-boot shamateurism was to revolutionise the new game of football while it was still in its infancy.

Today's top players, many of them earning in excess of £50,000 a week, should raise a glass of champers to one Fergus 'Fergie' Suter, who was the first unofficial professional footballer.

Suter and his Partick team-mate James Love were persuaded to leave Scotland for the delights of Darwen in Lancashire, where they had impressed during a friendly match on New Year's Day 1878. Both were given jobs in Darwen, but Suter – a stonemason by trade – was never seen to do a day's work. His only appearances were on the football pitch, where he and Love became local heroes.

Suspicions were raised in the south when Suter and Love helped Darwen take the leading team of the time, Old Etonians, to two replays before losing a fourth-round FA Cup tie in 1879.

The Old Etonians, heaving with 'Hons' and full of noble intent, were far too gentlemanly to say anything publicly, but in private the question was being asked, 'What has encouraged two exceptional players from Partick to up sticks and move to Darwen?' The view was that it could only have been the promise of payment.

Suter and Love were in the forefront of a mass exodus as Scottish players were enticed across the border to take up jobs in the mines, mills, steelworks and shipyards of the industrial (and industrious) north. Money in their boots for playing 'fitba' was a great incentive. Suddenly, for Scots, the playing fields of northern England were paved with gold.

The best of the English players were generally to be found down south, having perfected their skills while at public schools and universities. The northern clubs went hunting in the Highlands, returning with what were known as 'Scotch professors' – players with educated feet who had developed close ball control and along-the-ground passing prowess that contrasted sharply with the kick-and-rush style of many of the English players.

A Football Association inquiry was launched in 1882, with a sub-committee set up to investigate the unsavoury topic of professionalism. Accrington were expelled from the FA Cup in 1883 on evidence that they had paid a player, and all-powerful Preston North End were next on the list to undergo FA scrutiny. Preston North End had emerged from the North End Cricket Club in 1881 and become known as either 'The Invincibles' or 'Proud Preston'. The committee summoned North End's manager to a disciplinary hearing but instead of interrogating one of the *nouveau riche* 'where there's muck, there's brass' northern brigade, they found themselves talking to one of their own – Major William Sudell, who was also the chairman of Preston.

Rather than denying the charge of paying the players, Sudell bluntly told the committee, 'Of course I pay them. If I don't, another club sure as hell will and we'll not be able to compete with them on the football field.'

The Football Association hierarchy huffed and puffed and blew Preston out of the FA Cup competition as punishment. Sudell laughed in their faces and set about helping to form a breakaway *British* Football Association, which had the support of twenty-eight clubs, all of them far north of Watford.

As a matter of interest, Major Sudell eventually left Preston to chase his fortune in the business world, and in 1895 suffered the humiliation of being jailed for three years for embezzling £5,000 from his employers. When he came out of prison, he emigrated to South Africa and became a sportswriter. There are those who will say he could sink no lower.

Under the threat of the breakaway movement, the Football Association quickly capitulated. They called an emergency meeting at Anderton's Hotel in Fleet Street in 1885 and gave the green light for professional football.

Surprisingly, the loudest protests came from north of the border, where the Scots were determined to keep the game amateur. They kicked up such a furore when nineteen-year-old Blackburn half-back Jimmy Forrest became the first professional to play for England in 1884 that what had become the annual fixture between England and Scotland was in danger of being called off. Forrest was allowed to play only when he agreed to wear a different style shirt that made him stand out like a leper.

All this must be taken in the context of the 'upstairs, downstairs' world of sport at the time. For example, professional cricketers were not allowed to use the same dressing room, or even the same entrance to the field, as the amateur 'gentlemen' cricketers – a divisive tradition that was maintained well into the twentieth century. In this era of hysteria and hypocrisy, you can imagine a Basil Fawlty type attending the strictly amateur Football Association council meeting and demanding, 'No riff raff.'

So what happened to those pioneer professionals Fergie Shuter, James Love, Jimmy Forrest and the Darwen Football Club?

Shuter, shunned by Scotland for taking the English shilling, moved on to Blackburn and collected three FA Cup winners' medals as a defender renowned for his attacking skills. His only league appearance for Rovers was as a stand-in goalkeeper and he returned to Darwen in the 1890s as a publican. In 2000, his 1884 FA Cup winners' medal fetched £6,500 at auction.

Jimmy Love gave up football to join the Royal Navy and was killed in the bombardment of Alexandria during the war with Egypt in 1882. Darwen, the club where he helped make history, slipped ignominiously out of the League in 1899 at the end of a season in which they set an all-time record of eighteen successive Second Division defeats. Their flame continues to flicker in the North West Counties League.

Jimmy Forrest picked up a record-equalling five FA Cup winners' medals with Blackburn before winding down his career with, yes, Darwen. He was carried shoulder-high round the town like a conquering hero when he agreed to join the club from near neighbours Rovers in 1895. But while his spirit was willing his flesh was weak and he retired after one season and settled for talking about the game to customers at his pub, the County Arms, on Darwen Street. He later returned to Blackburn as a club administrator and nominal director.

While the arguments raged over whether players should be paid, an exiled Scot in the Midlands was quietly convinced that professional football was the future. Aston Villa director William McGregor believed that more money would be needed to finance football, and that extra competition was needed to boost income, which came exclusively from FA Cup ties and friendly fixtures.

McGregor, born in Braco, Perthshire, in 1847, had come to England in the footsteps of his brother, Peter, at the age of twenty-three to seek his fortune. He and his wife, Jessie, ran a draper's shop at 301 Summer Lane, Aston, in the heart of England, and it was here that he secretly planned the revolution that was to change the face of English football forever.

He had been drawn to the newly formed Aston Villa club by the presence of three Scottish players, including club captain George Ramsay, who was 'a demon dribbler'. In March 1888, after seeing how a crowd-pleaser such as Ramsay could attract huge attendances, McGregor composed the following historic letter.

Handwritten copies were delivered to four carefully selected club chairmen, plus his Villa colleagues:

Every year it is becoming more and more difficult for football clubs of any standing to meet their friendly engagements and even arrange friendly matches. The consequence is that at the last moment, through cup-tie interference, clubs are compelled to take on teams who will not attract the public.

I beg to tender the following suggestion as a means of getting over the difficulty: that ten or twelve of the most prominent clubs in England combine to arrange home-and-away fixtures each season, the said fixtures to be arranged at a friendly conference about the same time as the International Conference.

This combination might be known as the Association Football Union, and could be managed by representatives from each club. Of course, this is in no way to interfere with the National Association; even the suggested matches might be played under cup-tie rules. However, this is a detail.

My object in writing to you at present is merely to draw your attention to the subject, and to suggest a friendly conference to discuss the matter more fully. I would take it as a favour if you would kindly think the matter over, and make whatever suggestions you deem necessary.

I am only writing to the following – Blackburn Rovers, Bolton Wanderers, Preston North End, West Bromwich Albion and Aston Villa, and would like to hear what other clubs you would suggest.

I am, yours very truly, William McGregor (Aston Villa F.C.)

P.S. How would Friday, 23rd March, 1888, suit for the friendly conference at Anderton's Hotel, London?

McGregor confided in his good friend Joe Tillotson, who ran a small café close to his draper's shop and was a keen Aston Villa supporter. Together they worked out how a league could be run on similar lines to the baseball league that had been up and running with huge success in the United States since 1876.

A teetotaller and deeply religious, McGregor had a demeanour that acquaintances variously described as 'trustworthy', 'inspirational', and 'deeply sincere'. He was portly, looked benevolent and had a bushy white beard that gave him the appearance of Father Christmas. The present he gave to English football was a structure that provided the foundation for the game as we know it today.

Again, Anderton's Hotel in Fleet Street was the watering hole selected for the momentous meeting, and the turnout exceeded McGregor's expectations. He found himself preaching to the converted, his rich Scottish tones carrying the sounds of Perthshire through the Victorian hotel and going on to reverberate throughout the land.

Representatives were present from Aston Villa, Burnley, Blackburn Rovers, Derby County, Notts County, Stoke, West Bromwich Albion and Wolverhampton Wanderers. It was agreed to hold another meeting at the Royal Hotel in Manchester on 17 April 1888, with Accrington, Bolton, Everton and Preston North End invited to take part.

These, then, were the twelve clubs who agreed to launch the Football League in September 1888, and it all took place against the backdrop of one of the most sensational stories of the century. As the first games were being played, Jack the Ripper was at large on the gas-lit streets of Whitechapel. There was no room on the front pages for the little matter of the first Football League matches.

McGregor argued against calling it the English League because, deep down, he wanted the competition eventually to embrace clubs from his homeland, too. This did not seem such a distant dream because, as already mentioned, top Scottish club Queen's Park had been leading challengers for the FA Cup.

McGregor, 'Father of the Football League' and its first President, had not bothered to invite any southern clubs to participate because the opposition to professionalism emanating from London was so strong. Quiet rage smouldered in the corridors of power at the Football Association over what was seen as the spread of a poison that could prove contagious.

While all the talking, arguing, plotting and progress was being made off the pitch, the game was gathering momentum where it really mattered, on the field of play, where some remarkable feats were taking place. For example, John Petrie helped himself to thirteen goals as Arbroath thumped Aberdeen side Bon Accord 36–0 in a Scottish Cup tie in 1885. The half-time score was 15–0.

Arbroath goalkeeper Jim Milne had so little to do on that rainy day that he borrowed an umbrella from a woman in the crowd to keep dry. The result remains a world-record score for a senior match, and Petrie's individual contribution is still recognised as the highest by one man in a single game.

The final tally could, however, have been much more had referee Dave Stormont taken a harder line with the Aberdeen team. Many years later, he revealed that Arbroath could actually have won the game 43–0. 'My only regret,' he said, 'was that I chalked off seven goals for what I ruled as offside. On reflection, I think I was showing sympathy for Bon Accord and the goals were probably legal.' There were no goal nets in those days and eyewitnesses claimed Arbroath could have notched up a few more goals had it not been for the many minutes lost in retrieving the ball after every goal was scored.

It later transpired that Bon Accord had been formed at the last moment to play the fixture after being invited to take part in error. The players were members of the Orion Cricket Club – the invitation from the SFA was intended for the Orion Football Club. The Bon Accord players did not possess a pair of football boots between them and had sketchy knowledge of the rules of the game. Several had never even seen a football before!

Incredibly, on the same day that Arbroath rattled 36 goals past Bon Accord, less than twenty miles away, Dundee Harp thrashed Aberdeen Rovers 35–0. The Dundee side could have claimed the world record for themselves – at the end of the game, the referee said that it had been difficult for him to keep count of the goals, but he thought it was 37. The Dundee men admitted, however, that they had recorded 'only' 35 goals. The referee accepted their version and telegraphed the official result through to the SFA as 35–0.

In the modern game, it is taken for granted that many teams in England will include several black players, but a black face in British football in the 1880s was as rare as snow in the Sahara. So it was a surprise to the England players in 1881 to find themselves confronted at the Kennington Oval by a Scotland team captained by the first black footballer in the world to play the game internationally.

His name was Andrew Watson and he was born in Georgetown, British Guyana, in 1857 of a white Scottish father and black mother.

His merchant father, whose name was apparently Peter Miller, sent him to Rugby School where he would almost certainly have been the first black player to take part in the oval-ball game.

Details of Watson's life and times are patchy. No reference to the fact that he was black appears in match reports of the time. We were into the twenty-first century before archivists at Hampden Park's splendid Scottish Football Museum, under the direction of curator and fount-of-all-things-Scottish Ged O'Brien, treated old team photographs and were able to see that he was clearly a black man. Then a researcher stumbled on a Falkirk newspaper report referring to Watson being 'a coloured gentleman'.

Watson moved to Glasgow after leaving Rugby and started to develop his footballing skills at the newly formed Maxwell FC before joining Parkgrove, where he became a player and match secretary.

He studied at Glasgow University's arts faculty for a year, and started to play regularly at full-back for the famous Queen's Park club, helping them win the Scottish Cup with a 4–1 victory over Dumbarton in the 1882 final. In all, he won three Scotland caps.

Watson set two more firsts. He was the first black footballer to play in the FA Cup when turning out for the London Swifts in 1882, and he was the first foreign-born and only black player to be invited to tour with the élite Corinthians amateur team, in 1885–86.

Little is known of his later life, except that he moved to Australia. He is buried in Sydney.

For the record, before the discovery of Watson it was always believed that the first black man to play in British football was an extraordinary all-rounder called Arthur Wharton. Born in Accra in Ghana in 1865 into the royal family, he was sent to London to be educated and excelled at cricket and rugby, proved himself the quickest sprinter in the land, and also set a fastest-time record in the Blackburn to Preston cycling race. He was certainly the world's first black professional footballer when he signed for Preston from Darlington in 1886, and he later played for Rotherham, Sheffield United and Stockport County.

His choice of position – goalkeeper – was an odd one for an athlete who was the first man in the world to run 100 yards in ten seconds flat, which he did when winning the Amateur Athletics Association title at Stamford Bridge in 1886. He later ran as a professional, taking on and beating all-comers on a national tour.

Arthur liked a drink, and putting him in charge of the Sportsman's Cottage pub in Sheffield did him no favours at all. He became an alcoholic, scratched a living as a colliery worker and died penniless in 1930. In the following year, former Welsh miner George Parris became the first black British-born international player when he was selected by Wales to play against Northern Ireland in Belfast on 5 December 1931.

For nearly seventy years, Wharton's body lay buried in an unmarked grave in Edlington Cemetery in Doncaster. He was finally given the dignity of a headstone in 1997 and the acclaim he deserved as a great pioneer for black sportsmen. The 'Football Unites, Racism Divides' movement got on his case and Arthur Wharton was finally heralded as Britain's first black footballer – until in Scotland they realised that in the sepia photograph of their 1881 team, their captain, Andrew Watson, was black not white! It was 123 years before Scotland's second selection of a black footballer at full international level. Portsmouth midfield player Nigel Quashie was summoned into the Scottish squad in the spring of 2004.

International matches involving the home countries started to become common from the early 1880s, and the Football Association invited the associations of Scotland, Wales and Ireland to discuss the formation of a board to settle their differences over rules and to organise an international championship. Scotland at first declined the invitation, relenting only after the Football Association threatened to end the annual international match with England, which was their main source of income.

At a meeting in Manchester on 6 December 1882, the four associations adopted a uniform code and established the International Football Association Board to approve changes in the laws, the first and oldest of international football governing bodies.

England began playing Wales in 1879, and in 1882 they took on Ireland for the first time, winning at the Knock ground by a runaway 13–0. The hapless Irish captain that day was John McAlery, who had introduced football to Ireland after discovering the game while honeymooning in Scotland. Wales played Scotland for the first time in 1876 and Ireland in 1882. Scotland's first match with Ireland in 1884 was the opening game in the newly launched Home International Championship tournament. The Scots won 5–0 in Belfast.

After losing seven out of eight annual matches against Scotland, England introduced a heavily criticised defensive formation for the 1884 game at Glasgow's Cathkin Park. Instead of the customary two full-backs, two half-backs and six attacking forwards, they played with two full-backs, three half-backs and only five forwards. They lost 1–0, but this signposted the formation of the future.

On 15 March 1890, England showed their strength in depth when they played two international matches on the same day – team one winning 3–1 against Wales in Wrexham, and team two hammering Ireland 9–1 in Belfast.

On the club front, Blackburn Rovers – including history-makers Jimmy Forrest and Fergie Shuter – won a record twenty-three FA Cup matches in succession from 1884 to 1886, equalling the Wanderers feat of capturing the FA Cup three times on the trot in the process.

On their official professional debut, Preston suffered a 16–0 trouncing by Blackburn but recovered to take over from Rovers as the masters. In 1887–88, they scored fifty-one goals in six FA Cup ties, including a Cup record 26–0 defeat of Hyde (who clearly missed the contribution of Jekyll). This bred such confidence – some would say arrogance – in the Preston players that, come the final, against West Bromwich Albion, they insisted on having their team photograph taken with the FA Cup before the kick-off so that their kit was not muddied. They lost 2–1.

The following season they made no mistake, completing the perfect double by winning the inaugural league championship without a single defeat and the FA Cup without conceding a goal in the tournament.

All the major league sides in these formative years had the tartan touch, and Preston certainly had Scotland stamped all the way through them. The Ross brothers from Edinburgh, Nick and Jimmy, were the heart and soul of the team – Nick was a defender who could kick the ball the length of the pitch, and Jimmy was a right-winger with a crashing shot. George 'Geordie' Drummond, another Edinburgh man, scored thirty-six goals in 139 league games for the Deepdale club.

Glaswegian Jack Gordon is credited with the distinction of scoring the first goal in the Football League on the opening day of the first season, 8 September 1888. He scored for Preston North End against Burnley although some record books claim his can't have been the first goal because the match kicked off later than the other fixtures.

Attacking centre-half David Russell, born and raised in Airdrie, put the punch into Preston with performances that earned him six Scottish caps and the reputation of being the hardest man in the League. He tackled like a clap of thunder, and was described by one Victorian sportswriter as charging upfield 'like a wild, hungry and ferocious animal in search of a meal'.

Aston Villa surpassed Preston in the trophy-winning stakes, motivated by the former 'demon dribbler' George Ramsay – in charge as manager-secretary – during what were golden years for the Birmingham club. The quiet Scot, a former clerk in a brass foundry, guided Villa to six FA Cups and six league championships between 1884 and 1920. He oversaw their development from a small club playing on the sloping pastures of Aston Park to kings of the castle at Villa Park, where at the turn of the century they were one of the most famous and feted clubs in the world. 'Mr Loyalty' Ramsay served Villa for an astonishing stretch of fifty-nine years.

Ramsay (be sure to spell it differently from the man the Scots loved to hate, Sir Alf Ramsey!) put much of his faith on the sturdy shoulders of fellow Scot Jimmy Cowan, from Jamestown. He was a driving centre-half, like Preston's David Russell but more composed on the ball, and a supreme passer in the true Scottish style. A single-minded character, he was once suspended by the club for taking time off to prepare secretly for the 1896 New Year's Day Powderhall Sprint, which was then the most prized professional handicap sprint race in Europe.

Not noted for his speed on the pitch, he went home to the Highlands to train after telling Villa that he had damaged his back. He worked on perfecting his start and stride pattern, and kept everything quiet so that he would be allowed as big a yardage advantage as possible over the off-scratch professional sprinters. The handicappers awarded him a $12\frac{1}{2}$ yard start to a race run over a flat grass course of 130 yards. The only people who knew of his secret preparations were a small group of gamblers from Birmingham, and they travelled to the Powderhall meeting in Scotland to see him win the race with a yard to spare over his nearest rival. They took the bookmakers for several hundred pounds, of which a percentage was paid to the canny Cowan.

One of the Birmingham betting syndicate failed to get paid out because the bookmaker took off quicker than Cowan had finished the race when he realised he was on the wrong end of a sting.

Aston Villa's biggest rivals during this golden age were Sunderland, who leaned heavily on the skilled contributions from Scottish players after they had replaced relegated Stoke in the League at the start of the 1890–91 season. They had been formed as the Sunderland and District Teachers' Association Football Club by Scottish schoolmaster James Allan in 1879, but quickly became Sunderland AFC when players from outside the teaching profession clamoured to join.

The north-east club made mass signings of Scots, promising them work in the local shipyards to supplement their football wage of twenty-five shillings a week. They were also paid a £10 signing-on bonus and were given club houses in which to live rent free. Ironically, James Allan disagreed with this form of recruitment. He led a breakaway group in 1888 and founded a rival amateur club, Sunderland Albion.

However, it was the club Allan left behind that prospered and flourished. Boosted by the powerhouse performances of centre-forward John Campbell, the trickery of inside-right Jimmy Millar and the midfield drive of captain Hugh Wilson – all Scots, of course – Sunderland were almost unbeatable at home, giving second best to a visiting team just once in their first six seasons in the League. They won the league championship three times in four years in the 1890s and again in 1902, always with sides packed with Scots.

Following one of their victories over Aston Villa, 'Father of the Football League' William McGregor told the Sunderland chairman, 'Your team have all the talents.' The newspapers latched on to this quote and from then on the Sunderland side became known as 'The Team of All the Talents'.

Best known of the Sunderland Scots was goalkeeper Edward – 'Teddy' or 'Ned' – Doig, who was rated as having the safest pair of hands in the game. When signed from Arbroath along with his brother, Robert, he played before his seven-day registration had been cleared. Sunderland were fined £50 and had two points deducted.

Doig, who had previously played one game for Lancashire giants Blackburn, became a much-loved personality at the back of the Sunderland defence across a span of fourteen seasons and 417 league games before winding down his career with Liverpool.

He was quite a character. When he was being chaired off after a series of match-winning saves in an international against England, a female spectator from his hometown called out, 'Gie me a lock o' your hair, Ned, tae tak hame tae Arbroath.'

Doig removed his goalkeeper's cap to reveal his bald dome. 'I'm awfu' sorry I canna oblige, madam,' he said. 'Ye will have tae make do with taking ma best wishes tae them at hame.'

The starkest evidence of how English clubs relied on Scottish players came when Liverpool made their debut as a league club in 1893 after Everton had famously walked out on Anfield landlord John Houlding. He responded by forming Liverpool Football Club, and kicked off with a team containing ten Scots and a Blackburn-born goalkeeper by the name of McOwen!

A Scottish visionary, William McGregor, pioneered the Football League, and now Scottish players were decorating and dictating the English game with their artistry and, let's be frank, their aggression and not a little arrogance – a wonderful cocktail that brought the scent of the heather to English football.

The Scottish Football Association looked on in growing fury and frustration as the English clubs continually raided their clubs for players to help them make an impact in the new Football League. A procession of top Scottish players were tempted down to England by offers of jobs to go with cash payments for playing on Saturdays. The Scottish press were unmerciful with their criticism of anybody taking 'the English bribes' and accused them of being 'traitorous mercenaries'.

The Scottish FA punished the players by refusing to select them for international matches, but eventually gave in after a run of six matches against England without a victory. They started to have annual trial matches between Scottish-based players and Anglo-Scottish teams to find the best combination with which to face the auld enemy.

In a bid to stop their best players being poached, several Scottish clubs resorted to the sort of under-the-counter payments that had been rife in England for some years. When Hibernian won the

Scottish Cup in 1887, runners-up Dumbarton hired a private detective to probe what they were convinced was professionalism by their opponents. He uncovered the fact that Hibs had paid one of their players a £1 broken-time payment for missing three days from his work as a stonemason, for which his weekly wage was ten shillings.

Faced with such disclosures, the Scottish FA slowly capitulated and finally gave a reluctant green light for professionalism in 1893, but by then many of their best players had emigrated south of the border where their cultured, all-on-the-floor passing style was much in demand.

An example of the bribery being used to attract the Scottish players south is that in 1889 England's oldest league club, Notts County, offered Third Lanark centre-forward James Oswald not only a salary of £160 a season but also a tobacconist's shop with £500 of stock. As he was on a wage of 36 shillings for a 54 hour week as a fitter, he took the bait and scored 55 goals in 95 league appearances for Notts County before returning to Scotland in 1892 to play for St Bernard's and then Rangers.

A great Anglo-Scottish tradition had started, and a conveyor belt of exceptional players and unmatchable managers carried it on.

For the record, these were the eleven clubs that formed the first Scottish League in 1890: Abercorn, Celtic, Cowlair, Cambuslang, Dumbarton, Hearts, Rangers, St Mirren, Renton, Third Lanark and Vale of Leven. Dumbarton and Rangers shared the first championship, each finishing with 29 points and drawing a play-off decider 2-2.

When Scotland beat England 4-1 at Parkhead in 1900 their players were wearing the primrose and pink racing colours of Lord Rosebery, prominent racehorse owner and president of the Scottish FA and Hearts. He later told team captain Jacky Robertson, 'I have never seen my colours so well sported since Ladas won the Derby,' and that was in 1894.

Three of Scotland's goals were scored by R.S. McColl, who was the last amateur in the side and the only representative of Queen's Park. The professionals were at last in charge north as well as south of the border.

In England, the game was developing so quickly that a Second Division was introduced to the Football League in 1892, with twelve

founder member clubs who transferred *en masse* from the rival
Football Alliance. They were, in the order they finished the inaugural season of 1892–93, Small Heath (later known as Birmingham
City), Sheffield United, Darwen, Grimsby, Ardwick, Burton Swifts,
Northwich Victoria, Bootle, Lincoln, Crewe, Burslem and Walsall.
Nottingham Forest and Newton Heath (later Manchester United)
finished first and second in the final season of the Alliance, and
were promoted to the Football League First Division to bring the
number of clubs enjoying the top-table banquet to sixteen.

The new Second Division admitted its first club from the south in
1893 when Woolwich Arsenal, despairing of the London-domi-
nated Football Association's head-in-the-sand reaction to professional football, applied for election to the League. A year later more
clubs from the south jumped on the bandwagon, with Millwall the
motivating force behind the forming of a Southern League.

For those who think that play-offs in the Football League are a
relatively new innovation, it can be recorded that a similar system
was in operation as far back as the 1890s. They were called Test
matches, and played at the end of the season to decide promotion
and relegation issues after the English Second Division had been
introduced. The top three teams from the Second Division played
the bottom three from the First. An automatic two-up two-down
system was introduced after a suspicious goalless draw in 1898
between Stoke and Burnley kept both clubs in the top flight.

A blatant handball on the goalline by a Notts County player in an
FA Cup quarter-final led to the introduction of penalties in 1891, a
law change originally proposed by the Irish FA. Wolverhampton's
John Heath had the distinction of being the first player to score
from the penalty spot in a league match, against Accrington on 14
September 1891.

In that first penalty season, Stoke were given a spot-kick in the
final minute of a game against Aston Villa. The Villa goalkeeper
hoofed the ball out of the ground and by the time it was recovered
the referee had blown the whistle dead on ninety minutes, as
stipulated in the rules. From then on, referees were allowed to
add time for stoppages.

Extra-time periods had been added as far back as 1875, when the
Royal Engineers and Old Etonians drew 1–1 in the FA Cup final.
That game was still deadlocked after the extra time and the

Engineers won the replay 2–0. Not every club took kindly to the added time to break deadlocked matches. When a crucial 1880 match between Nottingham Forest and Sheffield ended in a draw after ninety minutes, the Sheffield players refused to carry on into extra time and the game was awarded to Forest.

Penalties were not universally welcomed, either. Corinthian Casuals, the epitome of amateur gentlemen, considered them crass, unsporting and against the spirit of the game. Their players would deliberately shoot the spot-kicks wide of the goal, and their goalkeepers would make no attempt to save them.

Another first in this Victorian age was women's football, launched at Crouch End in 1895 with a North v. South match, arranged by the newly formed British Ladies' Football Club. The person behind the movement to get ladies playing the game was an energetic organiser delighting in the name of Nettie Honeyball. The match drew an attendance of 10,000, but was sneered at and snubbed by the élitist and sexist Football Association.

The *Manchester Guardian*'s report of the match reads like something out of a fashion magazine:

> *The ladies of the North team wore red blouses with white yolks, and full black knickerbockers fastened below the knee, black stockings, red beretta caps, brown leather boots and leg pads.*

The Northern ladies won 7–0 and a combined team under the management of Lady Florence Dixie later toured Scotland. The response from the Football Association was to instruct their member clubs not to allow matches involving 'lady teams'. You could almost hear them saying in the gentlemen's clubs of Mayfair, 'Gad, next thing they'll be wanting the vote.'

The leg pads referred to in the *Guardian* report were actually shin pads, which had been introduced in 1874 by Nottingham Forest and England centre-forward Sam Widdowson when he cut down some cricket pads and wore them on the outside of his socks. Mocked by team-mates and opponents alike, Sam nevertheless patented the idea. Before the season was out, most players were wearing them and Sam had done very nicely thank you.

While all these big clubs were falling over themselves to embrace professionalism, an explosion of interest in football at amateur level was led by the churches. Having been vociferously anti the game when it was mass football, they now saw it as a way of attracting young people, and hundreds of teams were formed. One of them, Southampton St Mary's formed in 1885, is now a Premiership club playing their home matches at a grand new stadium fittingly called St Mary's.

Another first raised its ugly head in the form of hooliganism. During the days of mass football, most of the participants could reasonably be classed as hooligans. For example, a game in Derby in 1846 got so out of control that two brigades of dragoon guardsmen were called in to restore order, and the riot act was read after the Mayor – pleading for an end to the brawling game – was viciously attacked.

Preston are not so proud of the fact that their successes of the 1880s were accompanied by the unacceptable face of hooliganism. Following their 5–0 victory over Aston Villa in a bitterly contested friendly, supporters of both sides – described by newspaper reporters as 'howling roughs' – fought each other and then turned on the teams. The players were stoned, attacked with sticks, punched and kicked, and a member of the Preston team, one of the Ross brothers, was carried unconscious into the dressing room.

The following year, Preston fans were involved in the first railway station battle, attacking travelling Queen's Park supporters after another 'friendly'.

Anybody who believes hooliganism was a hell child of the 1960s will be surprised to learn that police records show that between 1894 and 1914 there were, astonishingly, more than 4,000 reported cases of violence at football matches. That violence was transferred to the bloody killing fields of the First World War.

Incidentally, the word hooligans began to appear frequently in newspaper reports at the turn of the century, taking over from the word vandals as a popular way of describing thuggish behaviour. Some claim it's derived from the rowdy conduct of an Irish family named Hooligan, or Houlihan, living in South London in the 1890s. When Londoners started to act wildly, usually driven by drink, they were said to be 'behaving like the Hooligans'.

At the back end of the nineteenth century, the game's stars became household names. There was William (Bill) Townley, for example, the 'quick as a whippet' Blackburn outside-left, who scored the first FA Cup final hat-trick, against Sheffield Wednesday at The Oval in 1890.

Down in the south, there were the Walters brothers – the Charltons of the time – whose initials were A.M. and P.M. They were Old Carthusians, Cambridge University and Corinthian full-back partners, and became the first brothers to captain England. They were persuaded to hang up their boots when another brother, H.M., died after being injured in a game in 1890.

The early superstars did not come any bigger than Billy Foulke, the larger-than-life Sheffield United goalkeeper who played for England in the 1890s when hitting the scales at a mere 20 stone. He was affectionately known as 'Fatty' Foulke. Big Billy was famed and feared for picking up rival forwards and dropping them on their heads. His weight went up to a reported 24 stone when he became the redoubtable last line of defence for Chelsea.

Penniless at the end of his playing career, he scraped a living in a Blackpool fairground, offering twopence to anybody who could beat him with a penny-a-go penalty. He died of pneumonia at the age of forty-two after catching a cold diving for pennies.

The fact that a player of Foulke's fame could end up in such dire circumstances was just the sort of sorry situation that hastened the formation of the first football trade union in 1899.

The twentieth century stretched ahead of the new professionals like the Promised Land. They were not to know that for many years the pastures would be poisoned, and that they would become known as 'Soccer Slaves'.

CHAPTER 4

STOP THE WORLD, WE WANT TO GET OFF

QUEEN VICTORIA died in the first year of the twentieth century, and her passing coincided with the beginning of the end of England's short-lived claim to be leaders of world football. The Victorian times were the Golden Age. The Bronze Age was just around the corner.

England gave the game to the world, but sniffily surrendered the chance to lead it into the new century. The idea of having an *international* association was the brainchild of a Frenchman, who rarely gets the credit he deserves for coming up with the concept that eventually led to the launch of the most compelling of all football competitions – the World Cup.

His name was Robert Guérin, President of the French Football Federation, and he was a journalist employed by the French daily newspaper *Le Matin*. Out of respect for the founders of the game, he made two trips to England to invite the Football Association to lead a campaign to bring the football playing countries of the world together under one umbrella. Here's the story in Guérin's own words, as recorded for his readers:

First of all, the secretary of the Netherlands Association went to London to say what we had in mind. Then I, in person,

outlined my idea to Frederick Wall, the secretary of the
Football Association. His head in his hands, Mr Wall listened
to my story. He said he would report back to his council, but
his distinct lack of enthusiasm did not fill me with optimism. I
waited a few months. Nothing. So I travelled back to London,
and this time had a meeting with the esteemed President, Lord
Kinnaird. That, too, was of no avail.

Tired of the struggle, and recognising that the Englishmen,
true to tradition, wanted to wait and watch, I undertook to
invite delegates myself.

While the FA prevaricated during interminable committee meetings – considering whether they should lower themselves to mix with foreign associations – Guérin got down to business. He contacted all the associations that had been formed on the lines of the English original, and invited them to send representatives to the French Athletic Sports Union headquarters at 220 Rue St Honore in Paris on 21 May 1904. Today it is a shoe shop but one hundred years ago it was the birthplace of what was to become the most influential body in world football.

The new controlling power, known by its French title *Fédération Internationale de Football Association*, had seven founder members – France, Belgium, Denmark, the Netherlands, Spain (represented by Madrid FC, later Real Madrid), Sweden and Switzerland. The German Football Federation cabled its intention to join on the same day.

Guérin was elected president and within a year the Football Association were finally persuaded to join FIFA, a world organisation they could and should have been governing. Austria, Italy and Hungary also signed up and Scotland, Wales and Ireland followed close on English heels. By 1912, twenty-one associations were affiliated and the number steadily increased to today's total of 204.

The visionary Guérin quit in a cloud of disillusion after his proposed international tournament, scheduled for 1906, failed to get off the ground. He was ahead of his time. It would be another twenty-four years before the first World Cup tournament took place, and by then the home associations had fallen out with FIFA and gone into a sulk that lasted until the middle of the century.

The major cause of the break with FIFA had echoes of the

problem that caused the north/south divide. FIFA demanded that amateur players should be compensated with broken-time payments to make up for lost earnings when they took days off from their jobs to play for their countries in Olympic and amateur internationals. The home associations were appalled, and saw it as an open invitation for shamateurism to poison the game again. They withdrew from FIFA in protest in 1928 and stubbornly sat out the first three World Cup tournaments of 1930, 1934 and 1938.

The nearest there was in these formative years to a peaceful co-existence between the upstarts of FIFA and the supercilious officials of the Football Association was when a Blackburn accountant, Daniel Burley Woolfall, was elected president of the new organisation in 1906. He had helped draw up the original laws of the Football Association in his role as treasurer and during his reign as FIFA president from 1906 to 1918 he tried to bring the British associations into what he liked to consider 'the football family fold'.

During his tenure, the Olympic football competition came under FIFA jurisdiction and Great Britain – represented by the England amateur team – twice won the title. The first triumph came in London in 1908 and the second in Stockholm four years later. This followed victory by a Great Britain side – actually, a thinly disguised Upton Park Football Club – in the first Olympic football final in Paris in 1900.

The team that won back-to-back Olympic titles was captained by centre-forward Vivian Woodward, arguably the greatest player of his generation. In 67 international matches, amateur and professional, he scored an extraordinary total of 86 goals, a record output challenged only by Pele and Gerd Muller. Woodward skippered the full England team 13 times and was on the losing side just once in 23 appearances, contributing 29 goals. Woodward once scored eight goals in an amateur international, against France in 1906, and three years later found the net six times playing against Holland at Stamford Bridge.

Born in Kennington in 1879, within goal-kicking distance of The Oval, he learned the football arts on the Essex coast at Clacton. He was a prolific goalscorer with Tottenham when they first joined the League in 1908, seven years after becoming the first non-league team to win the FA Cup. He later notched 34 goals for Chelsea in 116 league games before the outbreak of the First World War.

Chelsea reached the FA Cup final in 1915 and Woodward, who had not played all season, was given special leave from the Army in order to take part. On arriving at the ground, he discovered he would be taking the place of Bob Thompson, who had been a regular in the Chelsea attack in the earlier rounds. Woodward stepped aside and insisted that Thompson play. It typified the sportsmanship and fair-play attitude of a player who was never known to commit a foul – this in an era when forwards needed to be tough and physical to survive against defenders who tended to forget that hacking had been outlawed. Playing against Finland in the 1912 Olympic tournament, Woodward deliberately hoisted a penalty kick over the bar because he thought it had been harshly awarded. Yes, a true sportsman.

Wounded while fighting with the Middlesex Regiment late in the war, Woodward played his final game at the age of forty in the 1919–20 season before retiring to run a dairy farm and milk-delivery business in Essex. He died lonely and virtually forgotten in a London nursing home in 1954. What a way to treat a hero.

Rivalling Woodward as the finest player of the period was Cradley-born Steve Bloomer. He averaged an amazing 1.22 goals per match over a span of 12 years, including an all-time record goal in every one of his first 10 games for England. His final tally was 28 goals in 23 international matches, plus another 394 goals in league and Cup football for Middlesbrough and Derby County, the club where he kicked his first and last shots.

He was a slender, bony man, with skin as white as chalk, and he looked like a ghost when haunting defences from his favourite inside-right position. Bloomer was the first player to hold the record for most England caps and most England goals simultaneously, later equalled by Bobby Charlton.

He was sent off just once in his career and was so anguished on that occasion that he wrote a four-page letter to the Football Association pleading his innocence. The autocratic FA disciplinary officials were unmoved and he was suspended for two weeks. Yes, sweet, sweet FA.

Injury kept 'Paleface' Bloomer out of the 1903 FA Cup final in which Derby got a 6–0 drubbing from Bury, who did not concede a single goal throughout the whole tournament. Derby blamed the defeat on a gypsy curse that had been placed on the club when a

Romany camp was forced off the ground earmarked for their new Baseball Ground stadium. When first built, the stadium was meant for football and baseball but the anticipated baseball revolution failed to materialise and it became exclusive to soccer. Forty-three years later, when Derby reached their next FA Cup final, they had the curse lifted by a Romany chief and went on to beat Charlton Athletic 4–1 in the final.

At the outbreak of the First World War Bloomer was coaching in Berlin, and he spent the war years in a German internment camp. He later coached in Holland and, after a spell on the Derby training staff, in Spain. His legend was so great that when the original *Queen Mary* was launched in 1936, twenty-two years after his retirement, he featured in a huge mural in one of the lounges. He died just two years later at the age of fifty-four, but his name lives on at Derby's new Pride Park stadium where the team run out to the special anthem, 'Steve Bloomer's Watching'.

When he started his professional career Bloomer's weekly earnings were 7s 6d (37$^{1}/_{2}$ p), and by the time he retired they had risen to £5 10s (£5.50p). It was this appalling treatment that breathed life into the first footballers' union, which was so despised by the ruling Football Association.

One of the best known and most outspoken founder members of the union was Welshman Billy Meredith, the 'Prince of Wingers', who challenged even the exceptional duo of Woodward and Bloomer for the mantle of the greatest player of the era. These days 'Welsh Wizard' is a description that sits comfortably on the hunched shoulders of Ryan Giggs, but a hundred years earlier Meredith was producing even more dazzling performances in both the blue of Manchester City and the red of United.

Like Stanley 'Waiting in the Wings' Matthews, Meredith was a dribbling outside-right who put together a career of astonishing longevity. The former coalminer from Chirk, near Wrexham, won the first of his Welsh caps in 1895 and made his final bow on the international stage in March 1920 at the age of 45 years 229 days – when Wales beat England for the first time in their history!

Four years later, approaching his fiftieth birthday, he was called into the Manchester City side for their FA Cup semi-final despite the fact that he had made just three league appearances in the previous two years.

Meredith, who always played with a toothpick in his mouth – it was originally a wad of tobacco until he kicked the habit – was a continual companion of controversy.

He signed for Manchester City from Northwich Victoria in 1894 and quickly established himself as the quickest and trickiest winger in the League. In 1904 he skippered the City side and scored the only goal of the match in the FA Cup final against Bolton.

Just over a year after lifting the FA Cup, Meredith was caught in the middle of a bribery scandal. He was accused of offering the Aston Villa captain £10 to throw a game, and in defending himself he revealed cash inducements that indicted the Manchester City directors. After an FA inquiry into what were described as 'illegal payments', the entire City team along with several club officials were suspended.

The sentence was later quashed but by that time Meredith had made the stunning decision to cross the city to deadly rivals Manchester United. 'Old Skinny', as he had become known, was a major force in helping United win the league championships of 1908 and 1911 and the 1909 FA Cup final.

However, it was his off-the-field activities that were claiming attention and causing concern among football's rulers. On 2 December 1907, after several doomed attempts at forming a union, Meredith chaired the inaugural meeting of the Professional Footballers' Association. More than 500 players, mostly from the north and the Midlands, attended to voice their grievances over a maximum wage that had been set at £4 a week in 1901. They wanted a rise and the freedom to move to a club of their choosing at the end of their contracts.

Meredith and his Manchester United skipper Charlie Roberts were the main spokesmen. Paraphrasing Napoleon, Meredith said of the officials running the game, 'They are nothing but little shopkeepers and they are governing our destiny.' There was bold, threatening talk of strike action if the new union's demands were not met but it all came to nothing as the administrators attacked the weakest links with divide and rule tactics. The clubs drew up lists of players not supporting the union, with the plan to select them if the threatened strike went ahead in the 1909–10 season.

It ended with a compromise, and the revolt collapsed. Meredith and Roberts were among a group of Manchester United players –

known as 'Outcasts FC' – who refused to sign loyalty clauses that clubs were adding to contracts. Their victory was that the union was allowed to function, albeit with pulled teeth, but the players were shackled for another fifty years before a bearded saviour called Jimmy Hill came along, shooting from the lip.

Meredith wound down his long playing career with Manchester City, the club where he had first made his name as a player of exceptional skill and tinderbox temperament. Over a span of thirty years he had played around 1,200 matches, so there was a lot to talk about to customers at the Manchester pub that he ran after spells of coaching and scouting.

William Isaiah (Billy) Bassett, the pride of West Bromwich Albion, was a right winger almost in the Meredith class. Quick and clever, he specialised in pin-pointed centres from the touchline, and also had a powerful shot that brought him 61 league goals. He won 16 England caps in an era when the only chance to win one was in the home internationals. Appointed a director and then chairman of Albion, he later joined the establishment as a member of the FA Council and the Football League Management Committee. Not many players managed to get a foot in both camps. Bassett worked in harness at Albion with Fred Everiss, who served the club as secretary-manager for the little matter of forty-six years from 1902.

This was the age of the all-rounders, when there was a clear corridor between the end of the football season and the start of cricket. Many footballers doubled up on the two games, but few as successfully as R.E. (Reginald) Foster of Oxford University, the Corinthians and Worcestershire, who remains the only man to have captained England at both sports.

He scored six goals for England amateurs when they trounced a touring German team 12–0 at Tottenham in 1901–02. Four days later a professional England team hammered the Germans 10–0 at Manchester City's Hyde Road ground. The following year, the elegant Foster, one of seven sons of a Malvern clergyman, all of whom played for Worcestershire, scored what was then a Test record 287 for England against Australia in Sydney.

An even more extraordinary all-rounder than Foster was the dashing C.B. (Charles Burgess) Fry. Best known as a leading Test batsman and captain of England in the Edwardian golden age, Fry was also famous on the football pitch, playing soccer and rugby at the highest level. He equalled the world long-jump record in 1893, the same year that he got a First in classics at Oxford University, and after playing football for Southampton in the 1902 FA Cup final, declined an offer to become King of Albania (as you do!). At the end of the First World War and after teaching at Charterhouse, he became India's representative at the League of Nations, later settling down to a prolific writing career as an author and journalist while fulfilling the role of Commander of the Royal Navy training ship HMS *Mercury*. Wow!

What sort of man was he – apart from being remarkable? At the party after a 'This Is Your Life' tribute to the greatest of post-war cricketing/football all-rounders, Denis Compton, (which I scripted) the conversation got round to other outstanding all-round sportsmen and, inevitably, the name of C.B. Fry came up. The distinguished BBC radio commentator Rex Alston was among the guests and he recalled, in his distinctive public schoolmaster voice, 'When the Indians came to The Oval in 1946, Fry was invited by the BBC producers to join me in the commentary box as a summariser. He was in his mid seventies by then, but still upright and immaculate in his appearance. At the end of the first over, I brought him in, saying, "Well, Charles, what did you think of that?" We were live on air, remember. He raised his voice and snapped, "Charles? I will thank you not to be so familiar, sir. To you, my name is *Commander* Fry." Oh dear, it was the frostiest commentary I was ever part of and it was the only time we used him as a summariser.'

Legend has it that Fry had a domineering wife who made his life hell. You can't win 'em all, but old C.B. – the Commander – got damned close.

Football was considered to be going off its head in 1905 when Middlesbrough bought hefty centre-forward Alf Common from Sunderland in the first £1,000 transfer deal. *The Times* thundered: 'Whatever next? Footballers earning £1,000 a year? The game is heading for financial ruin, which is exactly what was forecast when professionalism was first allowed to pollute the sport.'

Common, built on the same stocky, hip-heavy lines of future goal-hunter Gerd Muller, was bought to shoot Middlesbrough out of relegation trouble. Charles Clegg, the chairman of the Football Association, was incandescent with rage over the transfer. Perhaps there was something personal in his undisguised anger. Just months earlier, his own club, Sheffield United, had sold Common to Sunderland for £375 after the player had said he was home-sick for his native north east. You could have measured Clegg's wrath on the Richter scale when Common scored the goal that beat Sheffield United at Bramall Lane in his debut for Middlesbrough. It was the first away win in two years for the Teesiders.

The way Middlesbrough were splashing money around to buy their way out of trouble brought them under the searchlight scrutiny of the Football Association, and they were later fined and censured for making irregular payments to players.

By the time he moved from Middlesbrough to Woolwich Arsenal for a nominal fee in 1910, the 5ft 8ins tall Common was a bulky caricature of the player who at his peak had won three England caps. With a paintbrush moustache and weighing around 15 stone, he was carthorse slow as he failed to stop Arsenal being relegated with just 18 points from 38 matches. Arsenal's end-of-season balance sheet showed they had just £19 in the bank. That would not even pay for Thierry Henry to have a haircut. The fact that Arsenal somehow reinvented themselves as a First Division club without *winning* promotion is a story to startle you in the next chapter.

After hanging up his once golden boots, Alf Common took the well-trodden ex-footballers' path into the licensing trade. For eleven years he was mein host at the Durham Alam Hotel in Cockerton, living off tales of when he was football's first £1,000 player – the Common man who started the transfer ball rolling.

Football grounds, with few seats but lots of terracing, were sprouting like mushrooms. The fairly new Ibrox stadium was chosen to host the annual Scotland-England game on 5 April 1902. In the opening minutes of the match, a section of the terracing collapsed. Twenty-five people were killed and more than 500 injured as they plunged through gaping holes to the concrete ground below. Many in the capacity crowd did not realise anything was wrong, and it was decided to continue the match rather than risk causing a panic. The game, which finished 1-1, was declared unofficial and a replay was held at Villa Park the following month, with the gate receipts going to the disaster fund.

From then on, Scotland's home matches were generally staged at Hampden Park. Football's first 100,000 crowd gathered there in 1906 and witnessed a 2–1 victory over England.

The Scots were proving to be more passionate about their football than the English, and pitch invasions became a cause for concern. Spectators got completely out of control at the 1908–09 Scottish Cup final replay at Hampden when hundreds of fans rioted at the end of the match. It was the second time that bitter rivals Rangers and Celtic had finished all square, and most of the spectators, plus some of the players, assumed there would be extra time. The SFA rules, however, stated that there had to be a replay if the final was deadlocked after ninety minutes. On seeing the referee calling the players off the pitch, the crowd erupted with fury. Many among the 60,000 paying spectators considered the two draws had been stage-managed to bring in additional revenue.

Angry fans raced on to the pitch, tore down the goals, dug up the Hampden turf and set fire to the turnstile pay boxes, using whisky to fuel the flames. Police, battling to maintain control, made matters worse with their aggressive methods, and when the fire brigade arrived they, too, came under attack, and their hoses were slashed. More than a hundred people were injured in the riot.

The Cup and the medals were withheld, and Rangers and Celtic were ordered to pay compensation to Queen's Park, the famous amateur club who used Hampden as their home ground.

Celtic had the edge over Rangers as twentieth century football got into its stride. They were close to back-to-back league and Cup doubles in 1909 until the 'riot final'. In their inside-forward trio of Jimmy McMenemy, Jimmy Quinn and Peter Somers they had a famed and feared attacking force.

Quinn plundered a hat-trick in the first Scottish Cup final staged at the new Hampden Park in 1904, helping Celtic to a 3–2 victory over Rangers – this was during a period when Celtic won six league titles in succession. While Celtic's manager, Willie Maley, was lifting the Scottish Cup, his brother, Tom, was steering Mere-dith-motivated Manchester City to the FA Cup – a remarkable family double.

Among all these tales of success, spare a moment's sympathy for Loughborough Town. They came into the new century with just one Second Division victory in the 1899–1900 season, losing all seven-teen of their away games and disappearing from the League with a flash and a bang after a 12–0 defeat by Woolwich Arsenal. Their meagre haul of 8 points from 34 games was an all-time record low.

The legend – or should it be the myth – of England being the 'Old Masters' gathered momentum in the summer of 1908 when a strong team made a first overseas tour. In the space of eight days they beat Austria 6–1 and 11–1, Hungary 7–0 and Bohemia 4–0.

At the end of the following season, 1908–09, another investigation took place into a dubious result – Leicester Fosse's 12–0 home First Division defeat by Nottingham Forest, for whom three players scored hat-tricks. Deep suspicion was aroused because Leicester were already relegated, while Forest needed to win to stay up. After interviewing everybody involved, the league committee reached the verdict that the main reason for Leicester's poor performance was that most of the players had spent the previous night celebrating a team-mate's wedding.

Goalkeepers became the focus of attention in 1910. Following a game between Third Lanark and Motherwell in which both goalkeepers scored after controlling the ball with their hands, the rule was changed and goalkeepers were restricted to handling the ball in their penalty area only. This was also the first season in which goalkeepers had to wear distinctive jerseys rather than the same colours as their team-mates.

The amateurs versus professionals row continued to rumble, and it came to a crisis point when the London, Middlesex and Surrey Associations – amateur to a man – broke away from the FA and formed the Amateur Football Association. The walk-out followed an FA resolution that professional clubs should be allowed to become affiliates.

Leading the breakaway movement was Nicholas Lane Jackson, known to everybody as 'Pa'. Honorary assistant secretary of the FA, he was the founder of the Corinthians and vehemently opposed to professionalism in any shape or form. Many amateurs would claim that Jackson was the *real* father of football, with his creed that sportsmanship and fair play should be paramount.

The Corinthians refused to play competitive matches, and it was an unwritten rule that only ex-public school or university graduates could play for the team. 'Football,' preached Jackson, 'is a game for gentlemen that should be played by gentlemen.' Their short passing game, copied from the Scots, was in sharp contrast to the dribble-and-hoof game of many of the English teams of the 1890s. The Corinthians toured the world playing exhibition football and made such an impression in Brazil that a Sao Paulo club was formed using their name, and remains a power in Brazilian football.

Proof positive of their standing and success is that in two international matches, the England team was composed entirely of players connected to the Corinthians. Their finest player was generally thought to be G.O. (Gilbert Oswald) Smith, a centre-forward who was the first England player to appear in ten consecutive international matches, the first to win twenty caps and the first to score a hat-trick while captaining the side. What makes his performances all the more astonishing is that throughout his life he was a chronic asthmatic.

The split with the Football Association engineered by Jackson lasted until 1914 before peace was made, with the FA's authority not only restored but reinforced. The fallout was that many public schools switched away from soccer to rugby union, which they saw as the only true amateur game of football.

The unashamed professionals of Sunderland, so prominent in the 1890s, made a bright start to the new century by reclaiming the championship in 1901–02, but suffered a self-inflicted handicap the following season. Some of their fans stoned the referee's hansom carriage after a 1–0 home defeat by championship rivals Sheffield Wednesday and, as a result, Sunderland were ordered to shut Roker Park for a week.

In the final match of the season they needed to win at, of all places, Newcastle to retain the title. They were beaten 1–0 and the championship went to Sheffield Wednesday for the first time.

Newcastle were going for the league and Cup double in 1904–05, but fell at the final fence in the Cup against an Aston Villa side with two-goal Harry Hampton in rampant mood. Nicknamed 'Happy Harry', he was one of the finest centre-forwards in the first period of the twentieth century, when physical strength was as important as skill and speed.

Newcastle took the League, though. On the last day of the season they won at Middlesbrough to capture their first major trophy. Everton fans could be forgiven for feeling misty eyed. They were in touching distance of the title until losing 2–1 to Arsenal in their penultimate game. This was a replay. The original game had been abandoned because of fog – with Everton leading 3–1.

The surprise team of the new century were Bristol City, driven by a remarkable player who gloried in the nickname of 'The Rubber Man'. Billy Wedlock was a legend in his own lifetime in the West Country. Despite standing just 5ft 4ins tall, he played at centre-half and astounded taller centre-forwards by propelling his rotund body above them to make wonderful clearances. Billy 'The Fatman' – he collected nearly as many nicknames as he did goals – was an attacking centre-half who was effective in both penalty areas, and was the first player to win 25 consecutive England caps, between 1907 and 1914. He was the human dynamo who powered Bristol City to the Second Division championship in 1905–06 – including a record 14 successive victories – and to the runners-up position in the First Division the following season.

There has never been a north-east derby quite like the one that was played in 1908–09. Newcastle, chasing the league championship, were beaten 9–1 at St James's Park by a Sunderland team that scored eight goals in 28 second-half minutes! Newcastle won 10 of their next 11 matches to pip Everton to the title.

The FA Cup gave Newcastle fans their greatest excitement – and frustration. The Geordies reached five out of seven finals between 1905 and 1911, but won just one, against Barnsley in 1910.

Their 1–0 defeat by Everton in 1906 brought the first Merseyside double, Liverpool having captured the league championship a year after being promoted from the Second Division. One of their stars was goalkeeper Sam Hardy, bought from Chesterfield for £500 to replace the veteran Teddy Doig. Hardy was to become a Liverpool legend.

In 1910–11, a new FA Cup was ordered from a Bradford silver-smith to replace the one awarded to Lord Kinnaird. The Cup stayed in Bradford when City beat Newcastle 1–0 in a replayed final at Old Trafford, Manchester United's new home. Three days later, United beat Sunderland 5–1 at their new ground to clinch their second league championship in four years – with Billy Meredith in full flow.

Barnsley kept the FA Cup in Yorkshire in 1912, after an amazing run to the final during which they played six goalless ties. They set a record by becoming the first Second Division club to reach two finals in three years, having gone down 2–0 to

Newcastle in 1910 in a game in which the Geordies were accused of using thug tactics.

No team has ever worked harder than Barnsley to win the FA Cup. In 1912, the first match against West Bromwich Albion was yet another goalless draw and in the replay at Bramall Lane, Harry Tufnell scored their winning goal with a great solo effort in extra time. The Tykes of Barnsley had played twelve Cup ties, of which three went to extra time, and they conceded just four goals. It was difficult to work out who were the most exhausted at the end of it all, the players or their supporters.

In 1912–13, Sunderland were involved in another nail-biting finish when locked in a head-to-head race for the title with Aston Villa, their great rivals of the 1890s. The Wearsiders had started the season with five defeats and two draws in their first seven matches. That was relegation form. Then they put together a run of five successive victories, and lost just one of their last 17 matches after Christmas, as their stylish inside-forward Charles Buchan produced the scintillating form that made him a legend in the game.

Sunderland met Villa in the FA Cup final at Crystal Palace on 19 April 1913 in front of a then world-record attendance of 120,081. Villa's Charlie Wallace, the only Sunderland-born player on the pitch, sliced a first-half penalty ten yards wide. It was the second penalty awarded in a Cup final, and the first miss.

Villa inside-left Clem Stephenson had dreamt the night before the game that his team-mate Tommy Barber headed a winning goal, and his dream came true fifteen minutes from the end when the Villa right-half nodded in a Wallace corner.

Four days after the final, Sunderland had to go to Villa Park, where a defeat would have let the Midlands club in for the league and Cup double. They battled to a 1–1 draw and three days later beat Bolton 3–1. So, five months after the *Titanic* went down, fourteen months after Scott had been beaten to the Pole by Amundsen, and twenty-one months after the 1911 coronation of George V, Sunderland won the championship, a target that had seemed impossible following their atrocious start to the season.

In 1914, George V became the first sovereign to attend an FA Cup final when he watched Burnley beat Liverpool 1–0 at Crystal Palace. The era had begun with the death of Queen Victoria, followed by the reign of Edward VII, and during it the age of the glorious amateurs had started to dwindle and die. It closed with football, now the people's game rather than a pastime for the toffs, at last getting the royal seal of approval. Just four months after the king presented the FA Cup, a shooting of a different kind shook the world.

CHAPTER 5

THE FOOTBALL WORLD AT WAR, ONE

T HE DAY war broke out – 4 August 1914 – football clubs were preparing for the coming season. The trigger for hostilities had been the shooting of the Austrian Archduke Franz Ferdinand in Sarajevo, but there was widespread optimism that the conflict would be over by Christmas. The Football League programme went ahead as planned but the customary 'we know best' arrogance of the football authorities boomeranged on them in explosive fashion. Parliament, the press and many members of the public were outraged that the game played on while volunteer soldiers were dying by the thousand on the bloody battlefields of Belgium.

Football's hierarchy, despite insisting they had decided to carry on only after consulting with the War Office, were shown no mercy by the newspaper leader writers and columnists. *The Times*, living up to its nickname of 'The Thunderer', gave it to them with both barrels:

We view with indignation and alarm the persistence of association football clubs in doing their best for the enemy. Every club that employs a professional football player is bribing a much-needed recruit to refrain from enlistment, and every spectator who pays his gate money is contributing so much to German victory. There is no excuse for diverting from the front thousands of athletes in order to feast the eyes of crowds of inactive spectators, who are either unfit to fight or else unfit to be fought for.

The Football Association responded to the devastating criticism by utilising the enormous power of the game as a recruiting tool, using it as a platform from which to preach patriotism and the need to put the war effort above all else.

Military bands played at football grounds and there were stirring speeches and poster campaigns aimed at the players as well as the spectators. At Chelsea, for example, players queued at a desk placed in front of the main Stamford Bridge stand and publicly signed up for military service. At the end of the 1914–15 season, the FA claimed their 'your country needs you' campaign had persuaded 500,000 men to enlist.

A Richmond-based Footballers' Battalion of the Middlesex Regiment was set up and one of its commanders, Major Frank Buckley, survived battleground wounds to become famous as the eccentric but successful manager of Wolverhampton Wanderers.

Everton won the controversial 1914–15 First Division championship, while Sheffield United beat Chelsea 3–0 in the FA Cup final, staged at Old Trafford. It became known as the Khaki Cup final because so many of the spectators were in uniform.

Matches could not be staged near munitions factories following a debate in Parliament. Shells being fired at the front were not exploding, it was alleged, because workers were being distracted by football and not concentrating on the job. This led to the second round FA Cup tie between Bradford City and Norwich being played behind closed doors at neutral Lincoln.

When Lord Derby presented the FA Cup at Old Trafford, his short speech reverberated right through the nation: 'You have played with one another and against one another for the Cup. It is now the duty of everyone to join with each other and play a sterner game for England.'

The story of the first professional footballer to sign up is worth recording as a mark of respect for the hundreds of players who gave their lives during the senseless conflict that raged over the next four years. His name was Donald (Donny) Simpson Bell, a Yorkshireman born in Harrogate on 3 December 1890. Educated at St Peter's School, Harrogate, Knaresborough Grammar School and Westminster College, Bell was a superb all-round sportsman who was equally outstanding at rugby, cricket and football.

While teaching as an assistant master at Starbeck School near Harrogate, he decided he needed to supplement his meagre income and signed as a professional footballer with Bradford Park Avenue after amateur experience with Crystal Palace, Bishop Auckland and Newcastle United. He made his league debut against Wolves at Molineux in 1913 and had established himself as a resolute full-back by the time war broke out. In November 1914, he signed up as a volunteer with the West Yorkshire Regiment.

Bell quickly moved through the ranks and within seven months had been promoted to Second Lieutenant in the 9th battalion of the Yorkshire Regiment, later the renowned Green Howards.

Five weeks after marrying his sweetheart, Rhoda Bonson, in a hurriedly arranged ceremony at Kirkby Stephen in the Lake District, he joined his battalion on their journey to the Western Front in preparation for the Battle of the Somme. This is how it is reported in the official Yorkshire Regiment records:

Nine battalions of the Yorkshire Regiment – each of approximately 1,000 men – fought on the Somme. There were 3,500 casualties by the time it ended on 18 November 1916. Four Victoria Crosses were awarded, one of which was to 2nd Lieutenant Donald Bell for a supreme act of gallantry on 5 July 1916.

To the south east of La Boiselle, the objective given to 69 Brigade was to capture a position known as Horse Shoe Trench. It was about 1,500 metres long and stood on high ground in a slight curve between La Boiselle and Mametz Wood.

A German machine gun began to enfilade the 9th Battalion of The Yorkshire Regiment. On his own initiative, 2nd Lieutenant Donald Bell, supported by Corporal Colwill and Private Batey, tried to destroy the gun position. They crept towards it along a communication trench and then suddenly made a dash towards it across open ground.

Bell, who was a superb athlete, moved with incredible speed and surprised the occupants of the machine-gun position, shot the gunner with his revolver and blew up the remainder with Mills bombs. He then threw bombs into the nearby trench, killing over 50 of the enemy.

This very brave act saved many lives and ensured the success of the attack. The citation for Bell's Victoria Cross recorded that it was for most conspicuous bravery.

Just five days later, the incredibly heroic Bell made a similar attack on another German machine-gun post and was killed. The place where he fell was named Bell's Redoubt in his honour.

In the first year of the twenty-first century, a 5ft high Yorkstone monument – jointly financed by the Green Howards and the Professional Footballers' Association – was erected close to the French village of Contalmaison in memory of Second Lieutenant Bell, VC, and his Yorkshire Regiment colleagues who lost their lives on the Somme. It is a corner of a foreign field that will be forever England.

Another footballing Second Lieutenant who died on the battle-fields of France was Walter Tull, the grandson of a slave, who had the distinction of being the first black officer in the British Army. Born in Folkestone in 1888, he was the son of a West Indian who had arrived in Britain from Barbados in 1876 and married a Kent girl.

His mother died when he was seven and his father soon after, and Walter was brought up along with his brother, Edward, in a Methodist-run orphanage in Bethnal Green in London's East End. A Tottenham scout spotted him playing amateur football for Clapton (not to be confused with the professional club Clapton Orient) and in 1908 he signed for Spurs. Walter was the first black footballer of the twentieth century to play in the League, following in the footsteps of Arthur Wharton.

A quick and powerful inside-forward or wing-half, he spent two seasons with Tottenham during which he was involved in an unpleasant and unsettling racial incident while playing at Bristol City. He was verbally abused by ignorant City fans who, according to one report, used 'language lower than Billingsgate'. It led to a loss of confidence and in 1910 Tull was sold to Northampton where he played 110 games. He was good enough to attract the interest of

Rangers, a move that appealed to him because Edward was working in Glasgow as a qualified dentist. Just as a deal was being discussed, war was declared. Walter enlisted with the 1st Football Battalion of the Middlesex Regiment and was quickly promoted to sergeant.

Tull served on the Somme until being invalided back to England in December 1916, suffering from trench fever. On his recovery, he was sent to officer's training school at Gailes in Scotland and received his commission in May 1917. This was an astonishing achievement at a time when the British Manual of Military Law specifically excluded 'Negroes from exercising actual command' as officers. It was Tull's superiors who recommended him for officer training, a remarkable testimony to his charisma and leadership qualities.

Second Lieutenant Tull was sent to the Italian front and was mentioned in dispatches for his 'gallantry and coolness' following the Battle of Piave. The war was into its last months when he was transferred to France where a push was on to break through the German Western Front defence.

He was ordered to make an attack on a heavily fortified German trench at Favreuil on 25 March 1918. Soon after entering no man's land, leading from the front, Tull was hit by a German bullet and fell mortally wounded. His men risked their own lives against heavy machine-gun fire in a bid to retrieve his body – an indication of how highly he was thought of by those to whom he had to give orders. Walter was twenty-nine.

His commanding officer broke the news to Walter's brother. 'He was so brave and conscientious and popular throughout the battalion,' he told Edward in extraordinarily emotional terms. 'The battalion and company have lost a faithful officer, and personally I have lost a good friend.'

It was 1999 before Tull, a hero on the pitch and in the trenches, received long overdue recognition with the opening of the Walter Tull Memorial Garden next to Northampton Town's Sixfields Community Stadium.

There are so many legends about how footballs were used to inspire soldiers to go over the top from their trenches during the First World War that it is difficult to separate fact from fiction, but one Blackadder-style event was verified by witnesses.

On 1 July 1916 the 8th Battalion of the East Surrey Regiment launched an attack on Prussian guards defending a ridge on the Somme. Captain W.P. Nevill produced four footballs that he had brought to the front with him after a spot of leave. He gave one to each company, and said there would be a reward for the men who were first to drive the ball across no man's land and through enemy lines.

As they chased after the footballs, the soldiers came under heavy machine-gun and mortar attack. Many of them, including Captain Nevill, were killed. Amazingly, the ridge was captured.

The following verse, inspired by Henry Newbold's '*Vitai Lampada*' poem ('Play up, play up and play the game'), appears in an undated field concert programme preserved in the Imperial War Museum:

> On through the hail of slaughter,
> Where gallant comrades Fall,
> Where blood is poured like water,
> They drive the trickling ball.
> The fear of death before them
> Is but an empty name.
> True to the land that bore them,
> The Surreys play the game.

The best known of all the football-entwined First World War stories – the 1914 Christmas Day truce match – has also been authenticated. British troops came back from the front with tales of how they had taken part in a football match with German soldiers on 25 December 1914 during a lull in the fighting.

A diary kept by Kurt Zehmisch, a twenty-four-year-old German soldier in the 134th Saxons Regiment, confirmed this. His entry for that Christmas Day describes how he and his fellow soldiers climbed over their trench top to collect and bury some bodies of dead comrades. He recorded:

Soon, we noticed some English soldiers coming towards us. They were friendly and we all spoke together. One of the Englishmen brought a football from their trenches and a lively game ensued. How marvellously wonderful, yet how strange it was. The English officers felt the same way, and after we had got the better of them they challenged us to another match the

next day. We agreed, but our commander was not at all happy
and ordered our unit to move to a different part of the front.

Reports varied, but there seems to have been around forty players
on each side. The soldiers exchanged tobacco, food and alcohol,
sang carols and then returned to their respective trenches to
continue the nonsense of war.

There were several other instances of spontaneous football kick-
abouts between British and German troops. Soldiers in the Bed-
fordshire Regiment reported that their impromptu Christmas Day
game with the Germans ended when the football was punctured
after landing on a tangle of barbed wire. The British commanders
were not amused. The following order was issued to all troops:

The Corps Commander directs Divisional Commanders to
impress on all subordinate commanders the absolute necessity
of encouraging the offensive spirit of the troops, while on the
defensive, by every means in their power.

Friendly intercourse with the enemy, unofficial armistices
(e.g. 'we won't fire if you don't' etc.) and the exchange of
tobacco and other comforts, however tempting and occasion-
ally amusing they may be, are absolutely prohibited.

Football bowed to the inevitable at the end of the 1914–15 season.
League, FA Cup and international matches were suspended and
replaced by low-key regional competitions. In England, players
were banned from being paid and in Scotland wages were restricted
to £2 a week. Footballers who did not enlist were required to take up
jobs that aided the war effort.

A 'temporary' entertainment tax was applied to football match
takings to help with the war expenditure, a draining demand that
lasted until 1957.

The one season that was completed during the war produced one
of the biggest match-fixing scandals in the history of the game. A
bookmaker claimed that the result of the Good Friday First Division
game between Manchester United and Liverpool had been rigged.

United won 2–0 and there had been a flood of bets on that being
the final score at odds of 7 to 1. The bookmaker refused to pay out
on the bets and a Football League committee investigated his
allegations of an attempted betting coup. One of the Liverpool

players caved in under intense questioning and gave full details of the planned sting. It was all plotted in a Manchester pub and former United player Jackie Sheldon was the ringleader. Bets were placed throughout the country on the game finishing 2-0 in United's favour.

Eight players, four from each club, were banned for life. The sentences were lifted on seven of them at the end of the war because they had fought for their country but the pardon came too late for Manchester United inside-forward Sandy Turnbull, who was killed in action.

On the Easter Monday of that same weekend of the fixed match, one game was never finished. Oldham left-back Billy Cook refused to leave the pitch after being ordered off for foul play in a vital First Division match against Middlesbrough at Ayresome Park. The referee, surrounded by protesting players, walked off and abandoned the match with Middlesbrough leading 4-1. After considering the referee's report, the League fined Oldham £350, banned Cook for a year and allowed the result to stand.

In Scotland, Celtic created one of the most astounding records of consistency in football history. They went 62 matches unbeaten from November 1915 to April 1917, when Kilmarnock conquered them 2-0 in the final game of the season.

The Football League rolled back into action nine months after the Armistice, 'bigger and better' than ever. They expanded from 40 clubs to 44, with the First and Second Divisions now made up of 22 clubs each. The shock, particularly for Tottenham, was that the new-look First Division included their north London rivals, Arsenal.

It was naturally assumed that the two teams who finished in the last two places in the 1914-15 season – Chelsea and Tottenham – would retain their First Division status, with Derby and Preston promoted as the top two teams in the Second Division to make up the number to 22. Nobody took into account the Machiavellian manoeuvres of Arsenal chairman Sir Henry Norris. He negotiated behind the scenes and gained the support of powerful Liverpool chairman and league president 'Honest' John McKenna.

Despite finishing fifth in the Second Division in 1914-15, it was Arsenal who were promoted along with Chelsea, Derby and Preston. The team that lost out was Tottenham, and all these years later it still rankles. It gave them the motivation to win a place at the top table through playing rather than politicking. The club that won the FA Cup while still in the Southern League in 1901 ran away with the Second Division title in 1919–20 with an avalanche of 102 goals and a 6 point advantage over runners-up Huddersfield.

Norris, the man who brought Arsenal to Highbury from Woolwich against the wishes of most people in 1913, got the come-uppance wished on him by Tottenham. In 1927, he and another director were suspended by the Football Association and the club was censured for illegally inducing players to join Arsenal. He became involved in a huge libel case, lost and was out of football for the rest of his life. Arsenal, the team he talked into the First Division, has been at the top table ever since.

West Bromwich Albion were the first post-war winners of the league championship, scoring a record 104 goals, but it was Huddersfield who had the most astonishing season on the return of football. They were on the brink of extinction at the end of the war, and were ordered by the League either to go into liquidation or move to Elland Road and amalgamate with the newly formed Leeds United.

There was a huge outcry in Huddersfield and public donations and the wholesale transfer of players cleared much of the debt. The League lifted the axe and what was virtually a Huddersfield reserve team not only won promotion as runners-up to Tottenham but also reached the FA Cup final at Stamford Bridge. They were beaten in extra time by Aston Villa, the goal scored by inside-right Billy Kirton.

Kirton had joined Villa in extraordinary circumstances. He was one of sixteen footballers auctioned at the Hotel Metropole in October 1919 after Leeds City had been expelled from the League for making under-the-counter payments to players throughout the war years. Port Vale took their place in the Second Division, inheriting the 10 points Leeds had collected from the eight games played at the start of that first post-war season.

Four Leeds City directors were kicked out of the game, along with previous managers George Cripps and Sheffield-born Herbert Chapman. They were told they could no longer take any further part in football management or even attend football matches. Chapman appealed and he was, most reluctantly, allowed back into the game after claiming that he knew nothing of the illegal payments.

Chapman was to become one of the most successful managers of the century as the game entered what were, literally, the roaring twenties. Crowds were bigger than ever before and it was about to rain goals.

CHAPTER 6

ALL THAT JAZZ

THE UNSPEAKABLE HORRORS of the First World War were laid to rest beneath a riot of celebration that turned the 1920s into what F. Scott Fitzgerald concisely and colourfully summed up as the Jazz Age. A sense of hopelessness and doom had been replaced by one of euphoria as the young people of the world got up and danced the Charleston, discovered the pleasure of leisure, and played and watched sport like never before. Goodness, they even gave women the vote – provided they were over thirty and of sound mind.

The terraces of football grounds heaved with huge crowds as the game in England rivalled cricket as the national sport. The only time the crowds would be bigger was immediately after the next little global dust-up, but the roaring twenties promised peace and progress – except with our old friends at the Football Association.

They took the game two steps backwards when they walked out on FIFA over the broken-time dispute, just as plans were being made to launch a World Cup. 'It will be nothing without us,' was the dismissive attitude of the home nations, who, having given football to the world, sat back and watched as the rest of the world ran away with the ball.

As the élitist Football Association became more insular, so the northern-dominated Football League flexed its young muscles and started to expand. They added a Third Division, which proved so successful that in 1921 they split it into two – North and South. All the clubs in the Southern League's First Division were elected *en bloc*, and twenty northern clubs were invited to join in the biggest league in the world.

At this time, too many eyes were turned on women's football for the comfort of the amateur gentlemen running – or possibly ruining – the game. A group of ladies carrying out wartime work at the Scottish-owned Dick Kerr tram and railway carriage manufacturing company in Preston, formed a team for fun, and they kept going after the obscenely named 'Great War' finished. They invited a French representative side to play them in the first women's international match in April 1920. A crowd of 25,000 saw them win 2–0 at Preston. Three subsequent matches finished with a win each and a draw. Spectators in France turned out in their thousands to witness the return series, attracted by the novelty of ladies playing football of a high standard.

On Boxing Day 1920, Dick, Kerr Ladies – the comma was an official part of their title – beat St Helen's Ladies 4–0. The gates at Goodison Park were shut with 53,000 spectators shoehorned inside and nearly as many on the outside pushing and shoving their way to nowhere.

Several matches were played against men, who were given the handicap of having to play with their hands behind their backs. The star player of the era was reckoned to be Ada Anscombe, captain of the Pioneer Ladies, who could out-dribble and outrun most defences.

Instead of being excited by the potential of the ladies' game, the sexist Football Association were exasperated by the interest being shown and they decided to cut the grass from under female feet. Women were banned from playing on league and FA amateur club grounds, and any referees offering to officiate at their matches were threatened with suspension. They issued a directive to all clubs:

Complaints have been made as to football being played by women, and the Council feel impelled to express their strong opinion that the game is quite unsuitable for females, and ought not be encouraged.

To prove the case against women playing a 'physically demanding' game, the Football Association paraded doctors who parroted that soccer was 'a potentially fatal' threat to women's health and reproductive powers. However, a neutral doctor said after watching Dick, Kerr Ladies play, 'From what I saw, football is about as likely to cause injuries to women as a heavy day's washing.'

Dick, Kerr Ladies escaped the controversy at home and left for a tour of Canada and the United States but by the time they arrived in Quebec, in September 1922, they found the Canadian Football Association had followed the London lead and banned women's football.

They went ahead with the United States leg of the tour, only to find that all their games were against men! The ladies managed to win three of eight matches, which were played in a friendly, exhibition manner. If anything, the matches put soccer in the United States back several paces. The fact that women were playing the game confirmed what devotees of gridiron – the sport for the well-padded – were always claiming: 'Soccer is for softies.'

Despite all the hurdles and handicaps put in their way by the fuddy-duddy FA, the Dick, Kerr Ladies Football Club remained in existence for 48 years. They played a total of 828 games, won 758, drew 46 and lost just 24. Their goals tally topped 3,500. In their peak year of 1921, they attracted nearly one million spectators, averaging more than 13,500 per game.

The FA attempted to blacken the name of the club by claiming that there were discrepancies in their accounting, and that promised money did not reach charitable causes that were supposed to benefit from their popularity. 'Our accounts,' the ladies icily pointed out, 'are handled by men.' Women had to wait until long after the *next* war for their freedom to play.

Meantime, the men were finding out about another sort of soccer slavery. As well as contracts that bound them hand and foot to their clubs, they were told at the start of the 1922–23 season that the maximum wage was going to be cut from £9 to £8. Once again, strike action was mooted. Once again, it proved to be an empty threat.

The wages chop was forced on the players because of the entertainment tax, despite the game drawing record attendances. In a bid to keep crowd numbers down, and lessen the chances of mass injuries, the FA increased prices for the 1921 FA Cup final between Tottenham and Wolves at Stamford Bridge. The match still drew a capacity crowd of 72,805 and generated record receipts of £15,400.

It was the wettest final on record, with everybody getting soaked by a non-stop downpour. Newly promoted Tottenham, with skipper Arthur Grimsdell, Jimmy Seed and left-wing partners Bert Bliss and Jimmy Dimmock in dominating form, kept their feet better on the quagmire of a pitch.

'Dodger' Dimmock scored the only goal eight minutes into the second half to make Tottenham the first southern winners of the Cup since they first won it twenty years earlier. Spurs manager Peter McWilliam, a winner with Newcastle in 1910, became the first man to play in and then manage an FA Cup winning team.

This 1921 FA Cup final, with thousands locked out, proved there was not a big enough ground in England to cater for all those who wanted to see the daddy of finals. The Football Association were quick to book a new stadium that was being built in Middlesex for the 1924 British Empire Exhibition. It was called, simply, the Empire Stadium, but was soon to be known to everybody in football as Wembley. It would become synonymous with all that was best and, just occasionally, worst about the English game.

Football had the honour of being the first event at the magnificent, twin-towered stadium. On 28 April 1923, Bolton Wanderers played West Ham United in what has gone down in football folklore as the White Horse final.

As the new stadium had been built to hold 127,000 spectators, the Football Association and the ground owners did not even consider making the match all-ticket. Right up until the day of the final, newspaper advertisements and posters were urging football fans to get to Wembley to see history being made – the first match at the Empire Stadium.

It had been erected at a cost of £750,000 in just 300 working days. Contrast that with the Millennium Dome, which took three years to build at a cost of £750 million-plus. Workmen on the Empire Stadium, including former German prisoners of war, used 25,000 tons of concrete, 1,500 tons of steel and half a million rivets, the final work being carried out just three days before the big match. By the time the game was over, a lot more work needed doing – repairing gates that had been smashed down by the milling mob that got in without paying.

The FA had spectacularly underestimated the interest in the first match at the new stadium. It was calculated that more than 200,000 people got in to see the game, a little matter of 73,000 over the ground's capacity. The wonder is that nobody was killed as thousands of fans spilled on to the pitch to the point where not a blade of grass could be seen. Wembley's new turf, the first sod of which was laid by the future George VI, was in danger of being churned up by a human tide.

Slowly and patiently, a policeman on a white horse – PC George Scorey on Billy – nudged and nursed the spectators back behind the touchlines. While all this was going on, desperately concerned officials discussed calling off the match, until it was pointed out that 1) this could enrage the crowd and cause more of a problem, and 2) the king, George V, was on his way by motorcar from Buckingham Palace as the VIP guest.

As the king arrived, the crowd broke spontaneously into the National Anthem and, miraculously, the game kicked off just forty-five minutes late.

West Ham, whose strength lay on the wings, were enormously handicapped by the fact that the crowd were on, and often pitch-side of, the touchline. Police had to drive an avenue through the tightly jammed fans every time a player took a corner, and there were many instances when the ball bounced back into play off spectators without a throw-in being awarded.

When Bolton inside-forward David Jack scored the first goal at Wembley in just two minutes, West Ham skipper Jack Tresarden was battling to get back on to the pitch after venturing into the packed crowd to retrieve the ball.

The players stayed on the pitch at half-time because they feared they might never get back on if they tried to force their way through to the dressing rooms. Tresarden, who had made his England debut two weeks earlier, said, 'We could not see the players' tunnel. If we had gone off we might never have found the pitch again. The best pass I had all afternoon was from a spectator.'

Bolton's victory-clinching goal eight minutes into the second half came from a rifled shot from Scotsman John Smith. It hit the human wall of spectators crammed against the back of the net and rebounded into play, with many people thinking it had hit a post.

The official attendance was given as 126,047, with 90,520 people paying at the turnstiles on the day and another 32,527 buying tickets in advance. The total income was £27,776 of which £4,206 went to the taxman, the stadium got £4,714, and the FA and both teams received £6,365 1s 8d each. The final count would indicate that more than 70,000 fans got in without paying. Not all of the ticket holders managed to see the game, and £2,797 was refunded to people who either could not find their seat or could not get into the ground. Not surprisingly, from then on all FA Cup finals have been ticket-only affairs.

The season ended happily for West Ham. Two days later they won a vital Second Division promotion match at Sheffield Wednesday, and they went up to the First Division for the first time despite a final-match defeat by Notts County.

The real hero of the afternoon at that historic first FA Cup final at Wembley was PC George Scorey. He was interviewed by just about every newspaper in the land, and his thirteen-year-old horse Billy became even more famous than any ridden by popular champion jockey of the time, Steve Donoghue. This was George's story:

I had my wedding coming up and that was the only thing on my mind at the time. When I was told to report for duty at Wembley I didn't think a lot of it because I'm not a keen follower of football. I could not believe it when I saw how many people came spilling on to the pitch. You could not see any of the ground, and there seemed no way the game could be played.

All the credit must go to Billy. I almost reluctantly started to push people back over the touchline, convinced it was a hopeless task. He quickly got the idea and gently but firmly nosed them back. They were a good-natured lot, and moved back out of Billy's way without protest. I kept shouting, 'Clear the pitch, gentlemen . . . make room for the players. If you want to see the game, move back, please.'

It took about forty minutes, I suppose. There were other policemen working hard, too, so don't give me all the praise. I stayed and watched the game, but was not that interested. I just wanted to get Billy home and fed. When my fiancée asked me what sort of day I'd had I replied, 'Nothing out of the ordinary, lass.' It was only when I saw the newspapers with

*dozens of photographs of Billy clearing the pitch that I realised
we must have done something pretty special.*

Had PC Scorey and Billy been at Old Trafford on 7 May 1921 for the last match of the season, they would have brought the official crowd total to fifteen! Stockport County, already relegated and with their ground shut because of crowd disorder, borrowed Old Trafford for their match against Leicester.

The Second Division game kicked off an hour after Manchester United had played Derby County on the same pitch, and there were just thirteen paying customers. Several hundred United fans stayed to watch, but most had drifted off before the end of a drab goalless draw. It was the lowest recorded attendance in league history.

Burnley won their first league championship in that 1920–21 season despite failing to win any of their last six matches. They had the title virtually wrapped up by Easter thanks to a then record run of 30 consecutive league matches without defeat, winning 21 and drawing nine.

Liverpool nearly equalled the record the following season, losing just once in a run of 30 games that took them to their third championship. Their star man was Belfast-born goalkeeper Elisha Scott, who stood just 5ft 9ins tall but was so athletic that he seemed to be able to cover the goal like a giant piece of elastic.

Unluckiest player of the first Wembley FA Cup final season was, without doubt, St Alban's City forward Billy Minter. He scored seven goals in a preliminary round FA Cup tie against Dulwich Hamlet on 22 November 1922. Dulwich won 8–7!

A new craze started in 1923, the forerunner of Fantasy Football. John (later Sir John) Moores founded the Littlewoods Pools company with a start-up capital of just £100. He began with a team of helpers handing out coupons to spectators at Old Trafford. It quickly became a nationwide postal business and inspired a revolution in mail-order enterprises.

Welsh football was enjoying a Golden Age in the 1920s. Wales won the home championship for the second successive year in 1924. In centre-half Fred Keenor and Scottish left-back Jimmy Blair, Cardiff provided both captains in the Wales–Scotland match.

Cardiff would have won the league championship in 1923–24 but for an attack of cold feet by their top marksmen. On the final day of the season, they were a point ahead of Huddersfield. A win at Birmingham would give them the title.

With the score deadlocked at 0–0, Cardiff were awarded a penalty after the ball had been punched off the goalline by a Birmingham defender. Most of the Cardiff players suddenly made themselves invisible, not wanting to take the responsibility, and the penalty was left to Len Davies, who had never taken a spot-kick in his life. His penalty was saved, the game ended goalless and Cardiff lost the title to Huddersfield by 0.241 of a goal in the days when goal averages rather than goal difference decided matters. Huddersfield had scored 60 goals and conceded 33, while Cardiff's record was 61 and 34.

Three years later, Cardiff became the first club to take the FA Cup out of England after they had been unlucky to lose the 1925 final. They beat roasting-hot favourites Arsenal with a freak goal scored by Scottish forward Hugh Ferguson. He mis-hit a shot from twenty yards that should have been comfortably saved by Welshman Dai Lewis in the Arsenal goal. Lewis went down in instalments, the ball hit his chest and screwed away into the net.

Lewis later blamed his handling error on the sheen on his brand-new Arsenal jersey and ever since then it has been a Highbury superstition always to wash the goalkeepers' new jerseys before they are worn.

Herbert Chapman, managing Arsenal in their first appearance in an FA Cup final, was a prominent and inspirational force throughout the 1920s. He guided Huddersfield to two successive league championships and left them on their way to a hat-trick when joining Arsenal in 1925, where he was about to create another championship hat-trick team.

The Sheffield-born former mining engineer was an average player with Northampton, Notts County and Tottenham, remembered more for his yellow boots than anything he achieved while wearing them.

Those yellow boots were a colourful sign that here was a man with an individual outlook, and he brought to football management innovative ideas that were ahead of their time. He was not only a master tactician but also a born public-relations genius. It was his idea, for example, to get London Transport to rename Gilllespie Road tube station Arsenal.

While he was in charge at Highbury, the club experimented with floodlighting, all-weather pitches, rubber studs, white footballs and numbers on players' shirts. They tried the numbers against Sheffield Wednesday at Hillsborough on 25 August 1928, the same day that Chelsea wore numbers against Swansea at Stamford Bridge.

Chapman was never afraid to spend Arsenal's money in the transfer market. In 1925–26, he persuaded chairman Sir Henry Norris to pay Sunderland £2,000 for thirty-four-year-old England international inside-forward Charles Buchan. The little matter of Sunderland receiving an extra £100 for every goal Buchan scored in his first season meant that, 21 goals later, Arsenal had to double their pay-out!

Buchan worked with Chapman on a plan to stop the runaway goalscorers of the 1920s. Between them, they came up with the game-changing 'stopper' centre-half idea. Other clubs, including Newcastle and Rangers, had experimented with a similar plan, but it was Arsenal who established a centre-back system that cramped the movement of centre-forwards.

Following Buchan's announcement that he would be retiring in 1928, Chapman negotiated football's first £10,000 transfer. He asked Bolton to name a price for their 1923 FA Cup final hero David Jack. They suggested what was then the mind-blowing sum of £13,000 but Chapman beat them down to £10,890, which triggered more 'football madness' headlines.

Chapman realised, before anybody else, the publicity potential of the newfangled broadcasting system called the wireless. He encouraged the BBC to come to Highbury and the first broadcast of a football match took place when Arsenal played Sheffield United in a First Division game on 22 January 1927. An 'announcer' gave listeners a running commentary while a colleague alongside him called out numbers. These referred to sections of the playing field that listeners could follow on a 'pitch chart' published in the *Radio Times*. This popularised the phrase 'back to square one'.

The announcer was Captain H.B.T. Wakelam – a rugby union man who had played for Harlequins. He was assisted by Mr C.A. Lewis as the section caller and summariser. The few listeners found it somewhat confusing that Captain Wakelam kept using rugby phrases, and when, three months later, the 1927 FA Cup final was the first to be broadcast live, future Arsenal manager George

Allison, a journalist, was booked as commentator. The 'sections and summaries' were by Derek McCulloch, whom those of a certain age will remember as 'Uncle Mac' of BBC Radio Children's Hour ('Goodbye children, everywhere').

Chapman arrived at Highbury just as the game was being revolutionised by a change in the aggravating offside law. Since 1866, the rule had stated that there should be three opponents between an attacking player and the goal and, as a result, many attacks were suffocated. Now it was decided that a player remained onside if there were two opponents between him and the goal.

The change was largely due to one man, Bill McCracken. The Newcastle United and Ireland full-back had turned the practice of springing the offside trap into a work of art. His method of sprinting forward to catch players offside proved so successful that defenders throughout the League started to copy his tactics. Consequently, many games were becoming frustrating stop-start affairs, and goals started to dry up.

In the last season played under the old offside law, a total of 4,700 goals were scored in the League. With the introduction of the new law in 1925, the total rocketed to 6,373. One team did quickly manage to find tactics to counter the new offside law, and they had one of the best defensive records in the League. The club was Hull City and their manager was one Bill McCracken!

The joyous new game came just at the right time to bring some cheer into the drab lives of millions of working-class men, who were suddenly finding that the promise of a grand life in the aftermath of war was turning out to be an illusion. They were sinking in a sea of disenchantment, and football was proving to be a haven, away from the miseries of mass unemployment and the General Strike.

One player stood out, literally, head and shoulders above all others with the arrival of the new offside law. Take a bow William Ralph Dean, universally known as Dixie, which he detested. Dixie – in those pre-politically correct times – was a reference to the fact that he had thick, black curly hair that would have been perfect for dreadlocks. Once, coming off after a match at Tottenham, a fan called him a black bastard. A policeman went to remonstrate with the spectator, but Billy said, 'I'll handle this.' He jumped into the crowd, thumped the spectator and rejoined the team. The beaming

London policeman gave him the thumbs up and said, 'That was a beauty, Billy, but I never saw it.'

No less a person than Dixie Dean swore the story was true. It was all part and parcel of the folklore that made him one of the best-known and best-loved players in the history of English football.

George Camsell, a powerful centre-forward with Middlesbrough, set what most people thought was an unbeatable record when he scored 59 goals in the Second Division in 1926–27. Amazingly, Dean went one better the following season and his goals came in the top division.

Many years later, when I interviewed him in my role as *Daily Express* football reporter, he recalled the astonishing final league match of the 1927–28 season against Arsenal, when he went into the game at Goodison needing three goals to set the new 60 goal record:

> I can recall every second of the game because I am being continually reminded of it. No matter where I go on Merseyside, there's always somebody who tells me they were there and describes my goals. If they're all telling the truth, there must have been a hundred thousand in Goodison that day!
>
> I was never one for counting goals. I left that to others. I was too busy trying to get the ball into the net to worry about numbers and records. But I went into this game with the world and his brother telling me I needed three goals for the record.
>
> What's not easy to forget is that Arsenal took the lead in about the second minute. I suppose that woke me up, and I banged in an equaliser almost from the re-start.
>
> A couple of minutes later, I was brought down for a penalty, and as I picked myself up the crowd were chanting, 'Give it to Dixie.' You don't forget that sort of thing, y'know. Everybody shouting your name. Makes you feel ten feet tall. I was a cocky kid of just twenty-one, and I suppose I had no nerves. I grabbed the ball and put the spot-kick away for my fifty-ninth goal.
>
> It seemed to take forever before I got the magic sixtieth. There were something like seven minutes left when Alec Troup floated over the perfect corner and I headed it into the net. It was claimed that the crowd sucked the ball over the line.

Somebody told me later that it was the fortieth goal I'd headed in a season in which I got one hundred goals in all competitions. And just think, a year earlier I'd somehow survived a motorcycle crash in which I broke my jaw and fractured my skull. We Birkenhead boys are tough old nuts, y'know.

People ask me if that sixty-goal record will ever be beaten. I think it will but there's only one man who'll do it. That's that feller who walks on the water. I think he's about the only one.

Dixie Dean – they don't make them like that any more. The man who had prowled the pitch like a lion for Everton and England was limping heavily at the time of the interview, a couple of years ahead of having a leg amputated.

'That Tommy Smith kicked me,' he said, the Birkenhead-bred humour still alive and well inside him. This was around the time that Bill Shankly said, 'That Tommy Smith could start a riot in a cemetery' – Tommy, like Dixie, had become a legend in Liverpool.

It was not all smiles and success for Dixie in that 1927–28 season. Just five weeks before his record-breaking sixtieth goal he had been a member of the England team taken apart by a Scottish side that became known evermore as 'The Wembley Wizards'.

The date 31 March 1928 – when the Scots played England off the park on the way to a 5–1 victory – deserves to be engraved in gold lettering in the annals of Scottish football history.

This match marked the second visit of Scotland to Wembley. For the Scots, it was like trying to tumble the walls of Jericho. An estimated 20,000 made the trek south to cheer on the boys in blue.

Earlier in the day, Cambridge had won the Boat Race with ease, leaving the Oxford crew labouring in their wake over the Putney to Mortlake course. Nobody would have guessed that in the afternoon England's footballers would be sunk without trace.

A mixture of despair and derision had greeted the Scottish selectors when they announced their team – despair because the side included eight Anglo-Scots, and derision because the tallest of the five forwards stood just 5ft 7ins.

The Scottish newspapers were unmerciful in their criticism of the selectors. How could they ignore so many home-based footballing masters who had not sold their soul to English clubs for thirty pieces of silver? Who was going to stop the tall, heavily built English defenders from winning everything in the air?

The critics had overlooked the little matter of the Scots being thoroughbreds, brought up on the traditional passing game, rarely playing the ball above knee height. This was, and always has been, the appeal of Scottish football. They play to feet as they follow the old creed – 'It's fitba' not heidba'.

Music-hall comedians in England wondered aloud on stage whether the Scots would be bringing Snow White with them to go with the vertically challenged players in Scotland's team. In those days, they got straight to the point and the Scots were dismissed as a team of dwarfs.

On paper, it was difficult to see how the wee Scots would be able to unhinge an England team that included such exceptional players as Huddersfield skipper and right-back Roy Goodall, West Ham goalkeeper Ted Hufton, then considered as good as any custodian in the world, rocketing Arsenal winger Joe Hulme, Birmingham's barnstorming Joe Bradford and, of course, the king of Goodison, William 'Dixie' Dean. As it turned out, even the Dean of football was forced to take a back seat.

Fast-forward from 1928 to 1963 to a vicious English winter when the country was buried under snow, which virtually wiped out two months of the football season. Since there was no football action to report, the late, lamented *Daily Herald* (which in 1964 became the broadsheet *Sun*, with the tabloid version just a twinkle in Rupert Murdoch's eye) filled the sports pages with tales of great matches of days gone by. Jimmy McMullan was one of the raconteurs. He was living in retirement in Sheffield, close to the Hillsborough ground where he had once been the manager of Sheffield Wednesday. Any self-respecting Scot with a proper knowledge of Scottish football history will know that McMullan captained that team of Wembley Wizards in what was, without doubt, the game of his life.

He was a specialist left-half, an elegant, thoughtful player whose precise passes steered Manchester City to the Second Division championship and two FA Cup finals. By the time of my interview with him for the *Herald* he was sixty-eight and confessed to being more than happy to be reminded of a magical match that was played two days after his thirty-third birthday. He spoke with a

Scottish burr that still carried the echoes of his hometown of Denny in Stirlingshire:

> *It was the nearest thing you will ever see to perfection on a football field. We were a team of wee men but with hearts as big as buckets, and with footballers as skilful as have ever played the game.*

This was not an old man being deceived by a fading memory. The Scottish forward line read: Alec Jackson (Huddersfield), Jimmy Dunn (Hibernian), Hughie Gallacher (Newcastle), Alex James (Preston) and Alan Morton (Rangers).

Jackson at 5ft 7ins was the tallest of them, Morton at 5ft 4ins the smallest, but each of the players carved out careers that made them giants of the game. A quick and quirky right winger, Jackson helped Huddersfield to their third successive league title. Dunn joined Everton to play alongside Dean in the 1933 FA Cup winning team. Gallacher was a sensational goalscoring, drink-imbibing legend with Newcastle and later Chelsea. James became the 'Emperor with the baggy shorts' genius of Arsenal, and Morton was the original 'Wee Blue Devil' about whom Rangers fans wrote ballads to mark his fantastic feats. Stylish right-back Jim Nelson was the 5ft 8ins 'giant' of the side.

Skipper McMullan was himself only 5ft 5ins, and he led out the smallest team ever to play in an international match at Wembley (and that probably includes schoolboy internationals!). He continued:

> *The night before the game I said to the lads, 'When you go to bed, pray for rain.' Our prayers were answered and there was a downpour that made the pitch just that little bit slippery. I knew we had the forwards who would make life hell for the English defenders trying to turn on a wet surface.*

Rain was still falling when Scotland took the lead in the third minute, just seconds after England had gone close to scoring. Huddersfield left-winger Billy Smith cracked a low shot against the base of a Scottish post. McMullan collected the rebound and released the ball to James, who exchanged passes with Dunn before pushing it into the path of Morton out on the left wing. He raced down the touchline and then lofted the ball into the goalmouth.

Alec Jackson came galloping in from the right to head the ball into the net. The vertically challenged men had snatched the lead with a headed goal! It was one of the few times they played the ball above ankle height. McMullan remembered:

> That was just the confidence booster we needed. We started to pass the ball around as if we owned the place, and the England defenders were panicking. Alex James then scored a fantastic solo goal a minute before half-time, shooting from long range when everybody expected him to pass. The timing of the goal could not have been better for us.
>
> It was a marvellous piece of individual brilliance by Alex. I remember that the only time he got ruffled that day was when the skip arrived carrying our new kit. The shorts were too brief for him because his liking for baggy shorts had become an obsession. We had to send an official back to the team hotel to get him the right sort of long shorts.
>
> At half-time we decided we would just keep pushing the ball around to feet. The English were making the mistake of marking our wingers with their wing-halves, and this gave our inside-forwards freedom, on which they thrived.

There was a swagger and cockiness in the way the Scots played in the second half, and just about everything they tried on a soaking-wet surface came off. Their ecstatic supporters made Wembley sound like Hampden as their blue-shirted heroes stitched together multi-pass movements as if embroidering a giant tapestry.

In the sixty-fifth minute Alec Jackson scored a carbon copy of his first goal, and almost immediately Alex James made it 4–0 when he steered the ball home after Hughie Gallacher had powered through the middle of the demoralised England defence.

Jackson completed his hat-trick five minutes from the end with a spectacular mid-air shot after Morton had once again mercilessly gunned past defenders, who were left tackling thin air.

Huddersfield marksman Bob Kelly hammered in a last-minute free kick from fully forty yards to give England some sort of consolation, but it was like arriving at a party after the last drink had been poured. The Scots had helped themselves to the sweet wine of victory.

The match deserves this much prominence in the history of the game. It was *the* outstanding international performance of the 1920s, perhaps of any pre-Second World war decade. Let the modest, unassuming man who led the Wembley Wizards to that glorious victory have the final word:

> *My abiding memory is of seeing Hughie Gallacher sent crashing by an unnecessarily wild tackle early in the game. Hughie had a wild temper and I was worried that he was going to retaliate. But as he pulled himself up he winked at me and said, 'Don't worry, Skip. I'll get my own back with fitba.' That was when I knew this was going to be our day.*

Of all the Scottish footballers featured in this lightning history of the game, nobody was more talented than Hughie Kilpatrick Gallacher and, sadly, nobody was as tragic. He could control just about everything on the football pitch but in his private life he stumbled from one crisis to another. It reached a chilling climax when Gallacher committed suicide by stepping into the path of an Edinburgh express train the day before he was due to appear in court on a charge of ill-treating his son. He was fifty-four years old.

One thing that everybody who witnessed Gallacher in action – spectator, team-mate or opponent – agreed on is that he was the *complete* centre-forward. He was compact, quick, had natural positional instinct, dribbled like a winger, could control the ball and shoot with either foot and, despite standing just 5ft 5ins tall, managed to beat much taller defenders in the air. Hughie led the line like a conductor, pointing to where he wanted the ball delivered and then completing the orchestration by being there when it arrived. God help the team-mate who did not meet his perfectionist standards. He could deliver volleys of abuse, dropping words like hand grenades.

Some startling statistics support Hughie's claim that he deserved the best service from those around him. He scored 387 goals in 543 league games (only Jimmy McGrory, 410, and Arthur Rowley, 434, found the net more times), and in 19 international appearances for Scotland between 1923 and 1935 he scored 22 goals. Few players in the world have bettered a goal a game in the international arena.

If only he could have passed a pub like he passed a football. Throughout much of his career and his later life he was a prisoner of alcohol.

His long-running battle against officialdom hit a new low when he was suspended for two months after an infamous clash with a prominent referee, Arthur Fogg. During a match against Huddersfield on an ice-bound pitch, Gallacher felt the referee had failed to give him at least two blatant penalties after he had been tackled off the ball. He let fly with a torrent of abuse as the final whistle blew and the referee asked for his name.

'If ye don't know who I am ye've no reet being on the pitch,' Hughie told him. 'Anyway, what's YOUR name?'

'Fogg,' the referee replied.

'Aye,' said Hughie, 'and you've been in a fog all afternoon.'

It did not end there. Gallacher followed the referee into his dressing room and attempted to push him into the bath.

Fogg refereed two more matches in which Hughie played and each time Hughie scored five goals as his version of a two-fingered salute to the official. 'He'll know who I am now,' he told teammates.

Rumours that Gallacher had a drink problem gathered strength when he was sent off for 'acting in a drunk and disorderly manner' during a tour match in Budapest. The Football Association disciplinary committee, rather generously, accepted his explanation that because it had been such a hot day, he had washed his mouth out with whisky and water. The saying 'If you believe that, you'll believe anything' comes to mind.

Scotland had an even more prolific goal poacher than Gallacher in these crazy 1920s. Jimmy McGrory scored a remarkable total of 550 goals during his career, including a record eight when Celtic beat Morton 9–0 in a Scottish First Division match on 14 January 1928 – but he could not get into that Wembley Wizards team!

Another exceptional goal-collecting record was set in that purple season of 1927–28 when Millwall scored an all-time record 127 league goals on their way to promotion from the Third Division South.

If there was an award for the Goal of the Decade, I think it would have to go to Celtic's Patsy Gallagher. Playing against Dundee in the 1925 Scottish Cup final at Hampden Park, 'Mighty Atom' Gallagher dribbled past five defenders before being sent crashing with a tackle five yards from the goal. As he fell Gallagher managed to lodge the ball between his two feet, and somersaulted with the ball into the net. That sort of circus-trick goal might break today's action-replay machines.

The 1920s were coming to their close when proof positive arrived that the rest of the world was not just catching up with but overtaking the 'Old Masters'. England were beaten for the first time by a foreign side when Spain stroked and strolled their way to a 4–3 victory in Madrid on 15 May 1929.

It was England's third tour match in a week, and followed on from victories over France (4–1) and Belgium (5–1), with George Camsell – deputising for the absent Dixie Dean – scoring two and four goals respectively.

Spain's British coach, Fred Pentland, a forty-six-year-old former Middlesbrough and England winger, made sure that the match kicked off under a high-noon sun, and the Spanish players got stronger as the English wilted after leading 2–0 and then 3–2. Nobody saw any warning signs. The defeat was put down to the heat.

Five months later, the repercussions of the Wall Street crash were reverberating right around the world. The 1930s were going to be a tough old time for everybody, including footballers.

CHAPTER 7

THE 'WIZARD OF DRIBBLE' LIFTS THE DEPRESSION

THE 1930s were earth-shaking years during which the world again went to the brink of war. Desperate, disgruntled men protested on their feet with hunger marches, Hitler and Nazism took an iron hold on Germany and buddies begged for dimes in the United States, where prosperity had been replaced by punishing poverty in the Great Depression. This was the bleak backdrop for the launch of the greatest football tournament of them all, the World Cup.

Two French visionaries, following in the footsteps of Robert Guérin, stubbornly pushed for a World Cup formula against what had become a rising tide of indifference. They were Henri Delaunay (later, the father of European football) and Jules Rimet, after whom the first World Cup trophy was named as a tribute to his pioneering work.

The British influence on this momentous milestone sounds like a none-too-gently snoring zzz – zilch, zero, zippo. The World Cup express was about to leave and it would be 1950 before the home countries finally climbed on board, by which time the World Cup had developed into the most compelling of all sporting competitions.

When FIFA called for volunteers to stage the first finals in 1930, they were in no danger of being crushed in the rush. Six contenders eventually came forward – Holland, Hungary, Italy, Spain, Sweden and Uruguay, who, as winners of the 1924 and 1928 Olympic titles, were the uncrowned champions of the world. Uruguay were scheduled to celebrate their independence in 1930 and they saw the World Cup as the perfect platform to give them international standing. They pledged to build a special 100,000 capacity stadium and promised to pay the full expenses of all participating teams.

This generosity swung the FIFA vote, much to the disgust of the European bidders. France, Yugoslavia, Belgium and Romania were the only Europeans tempted to make the three-week round sea journey. The rest sulked at home, saying that it was too long for their players to be away from their clubs, even though it was the middle of the summer.

Romania's entry gave a whole new meaning to 'By Royal Appointment'. King Carol II, known as the 'Playboy King', insisted that a representative team be sent to the World Cup finals after the original invitation had been turned down because the players could not get the necessary two months off work. The King selected the team himself and then arranged time off, with full pay, for each of the players. They were eliminated from the tournament after playing just two matches.

When King Carol was overthrown in 1940, he fled to South America where he was warmly remembered as the 'football-mad king'. In Romania he was remembered as just 'mad'.

The four European teams set sail together on 21 June 1930 aboard the famous immigrant-carrying Italian liner *Conte Verde*, departing from Villefrance-Sur-Mer and calling in at Rio de Janeiro to pick up the Brazilian squad. They arrived in Montevideo on 4 July. With five teams on board, other passengers talked of 'whizzing footballs' on all the decks as the players trained for the coming challenge.

The new arrivals joined seven other teams, which, plus the hosts, made a total of thirteen entrants. Uruguay had hoped for at least eleven more. The other countries were Argentina, Bolivia, Chile, Mexico, Paraguay, Peru and the United States. All eighteen games were played in three stadiums in Montevideo and, as expected, the best of the South American countries were too powerful for the European challengers so far from home.

French inside-forward Lucien Laurent went into the record books as the first scorer of a World Cup goal in the 4–1 opening-match victory over Mexico. France were then involved in a bizarre game with Argentina that set the benchmark for World Cup wackiness.

Brazilian referee Almeida Rego caused a near riot by getting his timing wrong. France were pressing for an equaliser when Senor Rego blew the final whistle just as French left-winger Marcel Langiller was shaping to shoot at the end of a fifty-yard run. Hundreds of Argentinian fans came dashing on to the pitch to celebrate their team's victory while referee Rego was surrounded by French officials arguing that he had blown the whistle six minutes too early, and with Langiller poised to score.

Rego's linesmen confirmed the clock-watching complaints and so the embarrassed referee had to order mounted police to clear the pitch. He instructed the teams to come back from the dressing rooms, where several players were already in the bath. Argentinian inside-forward Roberto Ciero fainted when he was told he had to return to the pitch.

It took police and armed guards nearly half an hour to clear the playing area and then the two teams played out the last six minutes without further score.

The French captain who had proudly led his team out for the first match of the first World Cup finals on that Sunday afternoon, 13 July 1930, the day before Bastille Day, was Alex Villaplane. Fifteen years later, the same Alex Villaplane was shot by French resistance fighters for allegedly collaborating with the Nazis during the Second World War.

In the semi-final, the United States faced Argentina. Nicknamed 'the shot-putters' by the French, the heavily built Americans were no match for the more skilful Argentinians, who turned a 1–0 interval lead into a 6–1 walkover.

Six of the United States squad were British-born – Scots Andy Auld, James Brown, Jimmy Gallagher, Bart McGhee, Alexander Wood and Liverpudlian George Moorhouse. Most of them played their football after emigrating to America, so it is wrong to say – as is often reported – that the USA were fielding imported British professionals.

Here's one for the trivia quizzes: who was the first British-born player to score a World Cup finals goal? Answer: Edinburgh-born Bart McGhee, in America's opening match of the tournament against Belgium. Bart was the son of 1886 Scottish international Jimmy McGhee.

There was a wonderful moment of farce in the semi-final when the United States trainer raced on to the pitch to treat a player. He stumbled, dropped his box of medical supplies and smashed a bottle of chloroform. As he bent to pick up the box he took the fumes full in the face and slowly folded to the ground like a puppet that has had its strings cut away. He had to be carried back to the touchline bench to recover.

In the other semi-final, Uruguay went behind to a fourth-minute goal against Yugoslavia, but recovered to beat them 6-1, thus setting up the 'dream final' against Argentina.

Ten chartered boats, spilling over with Argentinian supporters, sailed across the River Plate to Montevideo for the final at the Centenario Stadium but only the first two to sail docked in time. The other eight were delayed by thick fog. Match referee Jan Langenus was on board the first of the boats.

Perhaps the cliché 'a game of two halves' was first uttered when officials were discussing plans for the final, due to be played on 30 July 1930 – 30 July was to become an historic date in English football, England winning the 1966 World Cup on that day. They could not decide whether to play with a ball manufactured in Uruguay or a ball made in Argentina. The compromise was that they played with two balls!

Argentina led 2-1 at the end of the first half, playing with their ball. Belgian referee Langenus, resplendent in knickerbockers, came out for the second half carrying a Uruguayan ball, and the host country went on to win 4-2.

Centre-forward Hector Castro, who clinched victory with a last-minute goal, had only one hand, having lost part of an arm in a childhood accident.

FIFA President Jules Rimet, the man who had done most to get the tournament out of the starting blocks, presented the trophy to winning captain Jose Nasazzi, and the World Cup was up and running.

Bitter disappointment raged in Buenos Aires when the news of

Argentina's defeat was relayed back from Montevideo. The Uruguayan consulate came under attack with bricks and stones, and police opened fire to disperse the angry mob. Several days later, open revolution hit the streets of Buenos Aires and the country's President Irigoyen was overthrown in a military coup. The deep despair over the World Cup defeat had helped fan the flames of revolution.

In Montevideo, the triumphant Uruguayan players – allegedly amateurs – were feted and paraded as national heroes. The government decided to reward them by presenting each player with a plot of land that included a newly built house.

Back in England, the World Cup barely got a mention in the newspapers. Most interest in the summer of 1930 centred on a twenty-two-year-old Australian batsman called Don Bradman, who was on his way to 974 Test runs at the fairly impressive average of 139.14.

At the same time as Bradman was making a world-record 334 Test runs at Headingley in August 1930, a skinny fifteen-year-old with a sallow complexion was reporting to Stoke City Football Club to start work as an office boy. His name was Stanley Matthews and he was about to kick off an astonishing career that would stretch across thirty-three years and make him, arguably, the most famous player ever to kick a football – certainly up there with Pele, Puskas, di Stefano and Maradona.

The Maestro later recalled his early days when I interviewed him for a television programme that I scripted:

I have so much to thank my dad for. His name was Jack Matthews, and he was famous in the Potteries district where I grew up as the Fighting Barber of Hanley. He was a professional featherweight boxer, and also had his own little barbershop business.

Almost as soon as I could walk, I used to go on early morning training runs with Dad and my older brother. That regime became an obsession with me that lasted throughout my career. Dad used to preach that fitness was everything, and every single day of my life I used to run and follow a series of exercises. This is why I lasted so long in the game.

The skill Dad showed in feinting with his fists somehow

came naturally to me with my feet, and I was good enough as a lad at St Luke's school in Hanley to play for England school-boys. I think Stoke City started to show an interest in me the day I scored twelve goals in a match when I was supposed to be playing at centre-half!

My dad not only taught me about the importance of fitness, but also that I should look after my money. When Stoke paid me a £10 signing-on fee in 1932 he took me to open a savings bank account and also arranged for half of my £8 weekly wages to be paid in.

Matthews made his debut for Stoke in 1932, at the age of seventeen, in a Second Division match against Bury. He became known as 'the Wizard of Dribble' but to go with his baffling dribbling tricks, Matthews could swerve and accelerate in such a way that defenders were continually left in his wake. He was probably the greatest liar who ever played the game. His feet would tell an opponent that he was going one way while in his mind he knew he was going in a different direction altogether. He would shuffle up towards a full-back, throw him off balance with a dip of the shoulder, twist and turn him while juggling the ball between his feet and then accel-erate past with a sudden injection of pace.

When later asked how premeditated was the sudden swerve that deceived so many defenders, Matthews – by then Sir Stanley, the first footballer ever to be knighted – shrugged his famous shoulders, almost as if about to sell a dummy, and replied, 'It just came naturally, something I used to produce under pressure. You can't teach it. Either you can do it or you can't. It's an instinctive thing and I could always throw a defender off balance with it.'

Apart from the occasional game at inside-right, Matthews spent his entire career out on the right wing from where his pinpoint centres and crosses created hundreds of goals. Tommy Banks, one of the full-backs he famously hounded, said, 'If there was an Olympic race over ten yards, Stan would win the gold medal. There is nobody quicker over the distance.'

Loved and admired as he was by the public, Matthews was not always the flavour of the month with selectors and, sometimes, his own team-mates. The amateur selectors, most of whom had never kicked a ball in top competitive football in their lives, could rarely make up their minds whether his stop-start, now-you-see-me-now-you-don't style of dribbling helped or hindered the attack. Stifled grumbles came from team-mates that he hogged the ball too much and did nothing at all in the cause of defence, but he climbed above all the criticism to become the greatest and best-known footballer of his generation.

The 1930s started on an ominous note, with the *Graf* zeppelin hovering over Wembley Stadium during the 1930 FA Cup final in which Arsenal beat Huddersfield 2–0. The dark shadow it cast was a portent of things to come for the world.

Six days before the final, Arsenal were involved in an amazing league game. Stand-in centre-forward David Halliday scored four goals as Arsenal came back from 3–1 down at half-time to draw 6–6 with Leicester City. Halliday was not picked for the final.

There was an even more impressive individual scoring performance on 1 February 1930 when Northern Ireland centre-forward Joe Bambrick netted an international record six goals in a 7–0 win against Wales in Belfast. His fans used to chant 'Head, heel or toe, give it to Joe.' His six hit came during a season in which he scored a mind-boggling 94 league goals for Linfield. The following season Fred Roberts beat the record with 96 goals in 47 Irish League games for Glentoran.

West Bromwich Albion made history in 1930–31 when they became the first team to gain promotion from the Second Division and win the FA Cup in the same season.

England restored their pride against Spain at Highbury on 9 December 1931 when they hammered the Spaniards 7–1 to avenge the 4–3 defeat in Madrid. The talk before the game had been of the Spanish goalkeeper Ricardo Zamora, rated the finest custodian in the world and paid £40 a week by Real Madrid, then the highest wage in the game. A great character, he did a lap of honour before the game, waving to the crowd and dancing to a melody of Spanish tunes being played by the band at the mischievous request of Dixie Dean. Zamora, a 6ft 5ins giant with huge hands, never recovered from letting in a soft goal in the third minute and left the pitch in tears after the seven-goal slaughter. 'I threw his ears to the crowd,' joked Dixie.

Has there been a more unforgettable debut than that of Stan Milton in goal for Halifax on 6 January 1934? He had to pick the ball out of his net 13 times in a Third Division North match against Stockport County. His league career lasted just 17 games.

The most tragic story of the 1930s occurred at Ibrox on 5 September 1931. Celtic's brilliant twenty-two-year-old goalkeeper John Thomson died in hospital five hours after a collision with Rangers forward Sam English. They both went for a fifty-fifty ball. Neutral observers said it was an accident and no fault of the Rangers man but bigoted fans took sectarianism to new depths and hounded the Northern Ireland international out of the Scottish game.

Without question, the decade belonged to Arsenal, the team other clubs loved to hate. Veteran supporters could still remember how they had virtually conned their way back into the First Division immediately after the Great War.

Herbert Chapman's team became trailblazers under the baton of their baggy-shorted Scot, Alex James. They were the first southern club to win the league championship, in 1930–31, with a record collection of 66 points (in the days of two points for a win).

The following season they were on the wrong end of a crazy decision in the FA Cup final. In the thirty-eighth minute of the game against Newcastle United at Wembley, Jimmy Nicholson crossed a ball that had clearly gone over the Arsenal dead-ball line before he connected. The Arsenal players stopped playing and waited for a goal kick to be awarded. Newcastle centre-forward Jack Allen nonchalantly headed the ball into the net unchallenged for what, amazingly, was to be an equalising goal.

Everybody in the ground seemed to know the ball had gone out of play with the exception of referee Bill Harper. It is a sign of the discipline of teams in those days that not a single Arsenal player protested when the referee pointed to the centre circle. They just got on with the game in a mood of dumb disbelief.

Referee Harper said after the match, 'Take it from me, it was a goal. As God is my judge, the ball was in play. I don't care what other people may say. I was eight yards away, and I know what I saw.'

Mr Harper became the first referee to be proved wrong by modern technology, although pretty archaic by the standard of today's instant-action replays. Film from British Movietone News proved beyond doubt that the ball had gone out of play before it was crossed, and the camera clearly showed that the referee was twenty-five yards behind the play.

Jack Allen scored a second goal for Newcastle in the seventy-second minute to make them the first team to come from a goal down to win an FA Cup final since they themselves did it in 1910. Nobody said 'Lucky Arsenal' after this match as their dream of a double died, and they eventually finished second in the League to Dixie Dean's Everton.

Arsenal made up for their disappointment in devastating fashion by capturing the next three league championships, a hat-trick overshadowed by the sudden death from pneumonia of their genius of a manager Herbert Chapman in 1934. The last Arsenal FA Cup defeat he witnessed remains possibly the greatest giant-killing of them all. Third Division Walsall, a team that cost just £69 to put together, tumbled mighty Arsenal out of the third round of the Cup in 1933. In the second half, Arsenal full-back Tommy Black conceded a penalty with a violent foul. This angered the fair-minded Chapman more than the defeat, and within a week Black had been sold to Plymouth.

Players wore numbers on their backs in the Cup final for the first time in 1933. Winners Everton were numbered from 1 to 11, and runners-up Manchester City from 12 to 22. A reader's shirty letter in the London *Evening News* fumed, 'I have been following football for thirty years without need of numbers to help me identify the players. They will be using shirts as advertising boards next.' The letter was not signed Mystic Meg.

Manchester City were back at Wembley the following season, this time coming from a goal down to beat Portsmouth 2–1. City's nineteen-year-old goalkeeper Frank Swift, destined to become an all-time great, was so overcome at the final whistle that he fainted on his goalline.

England measured themselves against the best team in Europe at Stamford Bridge on 7 December 1932 when they took on the Austrian 'Wunderteam' coached by former Bolton player Jimmy Hogan and managed by the redoubtable Hugo Meisl. Austria, who played a classic passing game similar to the Wembley Wizards of Scotland, were on an eighteen-match unbeaten run, including recent crushing victories over Scotland (5–0), Germany (6–0), Switzerland (8–1) and Hungary (8–2). England won a seesawing match 4–3 but most neutrals thought the better team came second.

However, the game against Austria was just a precursor to a match that was considered to be the unofficial world championship. Italy came to town and the clash became known as the Battle of Highbury.

The Italians had just staged and won the second World Cup finals. In the final in Rome on 10 June 1934, they beat Czechoslovakia 2–1 after extra time, and after being a goal down in the seventieth minute. Raimundo Orsi, one of three South Americans in the Italian team, equalised with an astonishing curling shot, and Angelo Schiavio snatched the winner in the ninety-seventh minute of an exciting, evenly fought match. Fascist dictator Benito Mussolini presented the trophy to Italian captain and goalkeeper Giampiero Combi.

The day after the final, Orsi tried more than twenty times to repeat his big bender for the benefit of a posse of photographers. He failed each time.

FIFA considered the finals a success despite a boycott by the top South American countries, led by Uruguay, who were still incensed that so many European teams snubbed the 1930 tournament. This time, there were qualifying rounds and, bizarrely, even the host country had to qualify before sixteen nations lined up for the finals.

In England, there was an arrogant assumption that, had they entered, they – the Old Masters – would have won the World Cup. Italy were equally convinced that they would still have been crowned champions even if England *had* taken part. On 14 November the argument was settled in a match that stretched Anglo-Italian relationships to breaking point.

England, with barnstorming Ted Drake one of seven Arsenal players in the team, were presented in the press as Drake's Armada going into battle with the army of Mussolini.

The game was just minutes old when a shuddering challenge by Ted Drake left Italy's famously ruthless centre-half Luisito Monti with a broken bone in his foot. As the Argentinian was carried off, his team-mates lost their tempers and their composure, turning every tackle into an act of retaliation for what they saw as a deliberate plan to injure Monti.

As tempers overruled the talent of the Italians, England rushed into a 3–0 lead inside fifteen minutes. Manchester City left-winger Eric Brook made amends for a missed penalty by heading in a cross from nineteen-year-old Stanley Matthews. Brook then scored with a sweetly struck free kick, and Drake made it 3–0 when hooking in another Matthews cross.

Eight England players had to be treated for injuries at half-time, including skipper Eddie Hapgood whose nose was broken by an Italian forearm.

At least two Italian players deserved to be sent off, but the Swedish referee seemed mystified and confused by all the mayhem around him. Perhaps he was concerned about upsetting the huge contingent of Italian supporters swelling the Highbury crowd.

Vittorio Pozzo, Italy's highly respected manager, calmed his players down at half-time and it was all England could do to contain the World Cup holders as they produced some magnificent football in the second half. Italy pulled back to 3–2 with two goals from stylish centre-forward Giuseppe Meazza, and bruised and battered England were relieved to hear the final whistle signalling a victory that was, to say the least, hard earned.

For the record, the seven Arsenal players in the team were: Frank Moss, George Male, Eddie Hapgood, Wilf Copping, Ray Bowden, Ted Drake and Cliff 'Boy' Bastin.

In 1934, a significant change occurred at the Football Association when Stanley Rous took over as secretary from the long-serving Sir Frederick Wall, who retired. Rous was a visionary, much more outward looking than any of his predecessors, and he eventually led England into the family of FIFA, of which he was to become the powerful president. A former Watford schoolmaster, Rous had refereed the 1934 FA Cup final and had a deep knowledge of international football thanks to officiating at matches around the world.

Rous set about redrafting the laws of the game and created a coaching network that brought new organisation to grassroots football. Among his disciples was a young schoolmaster, Walter Winterbottom, who would eventually become the first England team manager.

One of Rous's initiatives was the introduction of the diagonal system for referees and linesmen, so that the man in the middle always knew where his assistants were. He experimented, in trial matches, with a referee officiating in each half of the pitch. Pitch markings were changed to the ones we know today, with the two arcs added to ensure players were ten yards from the ball when a penalty was being taken (there was no alternative metric system in British football then).

Three extraordinary individual goalscoring performances graced the 1935–36 season. One was by Ted Drake, playing with an injured knee. He had nine shots at goal for Arsenal against Aston Villa in a First Division match at Villa Park on 14 December 1935. One shot was saved, another hit the bar and the other seven finished in the back of the net.

I caddied for golf-fanatic Ted while writing a feature article about him when he was scouting for Fulham after a nine-year reign as Chelsea manager. He recalled that seven-goal barrage, in his pleasant Hampshire burr:

> I should not have been on the pitch because my knee was giving me hell. But we'd already lost Alex James and Joe Hulme with injuries, so I reluctantly told manager George Allison that I would give it a go.
>
> I deliberately adopted a shoot on sight policy because I wanted to get rid of the ball as quickly as possible before any Villa defender tried to tackle me and make my knee worse.
>
> The ball just kept flying into the net. In the very first minute of the match I went tumbling and landed flat on my face off the pitch. The Villa fans howled with laughter, but I think it fair to say I had the last laugh.
>
> The Villa players were very sporting about it. They applauded me off, and all autographed the match ball. But I paid a heavy price for that game. I was out for much of the rest of the season, and had to have an operation.

The way Arsenal are dominating this chapter is a fair reflection of the way they monopolised much of the 1930s. Their football was physical – Wilf Copping was the Norman Hunter of his day, in spades! – but they had a mix of skill (Alex James), speed (Joe Hulme and 'Boy' Bastin) and raw power (Ted Drake and Ray Bowden).

Twelve days after the seven-goal Drake deluge, Robert 'Bunny' Bell came up with a nine-goal barrage for Tranmere in their 13–4 demolition of Oldham Athletic on Boxing Day. Twenty-four hours earlier, Oldham had won the Christmas Day meeting between the same two sides, 4–1.

Bell's nine goals were a league record until Joe Payne took over on Easter Monday, 13 April 1936. He was the first, and remains the only, league player to reach double figures when he crashed in ten goals for Luton in their 12–0 battering of Bristol Rovers in a Third Division South match at Kenilworth Road.

Payne was Luton's third-choice centre-forward and had been playing at wing-half in the reserves. The twenty-year-old former coal miner from Bolsover was called into the team at the last minute because of an injury crisis.

For the first twenty minutes he grew accustomed to the pace of the match and then started the most remarkable goalscoring streak in league history. He had helped himself to a hat-trick by half-time, and found the net consistently throughout the second half when he scored virtually every time he was in possession. His record-making tenth goal came in the eighty-sixth minute. He was lying on the ground outside the penalty area with his back to goal when the ball landed alongside him. He swivelled while still on the ground, connected with the ball and sent it arrowing into the net. It was one of those days for the man who forever more was known as 'Ten Goal' Payne.

Attendances were huge as men turned to football as a temporary release from the miseries of unemployment. Scotland's match against England at Hampden Park in 1937 drew a then world-record crowd of 149,547. Scotland won 3–1 in the first international match in which shirt numbers were worn.

In 1938, a new broadcasting medium that was one day to revolutionise the game took its first look at football. After experiments at Highbury, featuring Arsenal against their reserve side, television made its football debut at Wembley for the 1938 FA Cup final between Preston and Huddersfield.

Only a few hundred people in the Home Counties could tune in to the broadcast, but those who did watch the flickering black and white pictures saw one of the most dramatic of all Cup final finishes.

Referee A.J. Jewell was consulting his watch as the goalless game drifted into the last minute of extra time. BBC television commentator, Commander Tom Woodrofe, told his handful of viewers, 'Well, only seconds left. If anybody scores now I will eat my hat.'

No sooner were the words out of his mouth than Huddersfield's England centre-half Alf Young mistimed a tackle on Preston's Scottish international inside-right George Mutch. Penalty!

As Mutch picked himself up and prepared to take the kick – no doubt with Commander Woodrofe busy eating his words, if not his hat – his Preston team-mate, one Bill Shankly, told him, 'Ye'd best not miss it, George.'

Mutch hammered the ball with all his might and the last kick of the match crashed into the net off the underside of the crossbar. Commander Woodrofe was probably not the type of man to have said, 'Some people think it's all over . . . it is now.'

Huddersfield were one of six clubs involved in a nail-gnawing finish to the First Division season in 1937–38. They were all pinned together at the bottom of the table with 36 points on the final Saturday. Stoke, Birmingham, Portsmouth and Grimsby all won, leaving the result of the match between Huddersfield and Manchester City to decide which of them would join West Bromwich Albion and go down.

Manchester City were the reigning league champions, and the top scorers in the division, but they lost 1–0 and were relegated. Only 4 points separated the 11 bottom clubs.

It was hailed as a victory for Fascism when England's footballers gave the Nazi salute before their match against Germany in the Berlin Olympic Stadium on 14 May 1938. Stanley Matthews, one of the players who raised his hand in the direction of the main stand where Goering and Goebbels were among the 110,000 crowd, told me many years later:

> *When we were told we should give the salute, we were very unhappy about it. At first, our captain Eddie Hapgood insisted we would not do it. But the British ambassador assured us that it would be the right thing to do in the political atmosphere of the time.*
>
> *In hindsight, it's easy to say it was wrong, but you have to remember that around about then Prime Minister Neville Chamberlain was involved in delicate negotiations with Hitler, and we didn't want to do anything to upset the applecart.*

People got mad about it after the war, but there had been no atrocities at the time. Obviously, I wish we hadn't done it. But it's easy to be wise after the event.

Eddie Hapgood, who was a darn good skipper, said, 'OK lads, we'll do it and then play out of our skins to beat them.'

England did exactly that, romping to a 6–3 victory. They led 4–2 at half-time and in the second half there was little sign of the swastika banners that had been waving all around the ground in the first half. The sixth and final goal showed Matthews at his dazzling best. He turned the German defence inside out before pushing the ball back into the path of West Ham's Len Goulden, who made the net bulge with a thumping shot from twenty-five yards.

A month later in France, Italy retained the World Cup, again with no British participation. England were offered a late place after war-torn Spain and Anschlussed Austria had withdrawn, but they refused.

There were some bizarre moments in the finals. Leonidas da Silva, flamboyant star of the Brazilian attack, was unhappy playing against Poland on the muddy pitch at Strasbourg. He decided he would have better stability if he went back to his boyhood days when he played barefooted. However, the moment he removed his boots and tossed them nonchalantly over the touchline, the referee ordered him to put them back on because it was in contravention of the laws of the game to play without boots. Leonidas, the 'Black Diamond', was sure-footed enough to score four of the goals in Brazil's 6–5 victory. Ernest Willimowski scored four goals for Poland and finished on the losing side.

Italian skipper Giuseppe Meazza must have had that sinking feeling when he scored the semi-final penalty against Brazil that clinched a place in the final for the Cup holders. As he steered the spot-kick into the net, his shorts, torn earlier in the game, slipped down to leave him exposed. His celebrating team-mates hid his blushes until a new pair were produced.

Hungarian goalkeeper Antal Szabo startled visitors to the dressing room after Hungary's 4–2 defeat by Italy in the final in Paris on 19 June 1938. He told them, 'I have never felt so proud in my life.' As his audience looked on dumbstruck, he explained, 'We may have lost the match but we have saved eleven lives. The Italian players received a telegram from Mussolini before the game that read, "Win or die!" Now they can go home as heroes.'

England accepted an invitation to take on Italy in Milan on 13 May 1939 in a game billed as 'The Old Masters versus the World Cup holders'. England came away with a 2–2 draw but most observers felt it should have been a 2–1 victory. It seemed that everybody but the German referee saw centre-forward Silvio Piola fist the ball into the net for Italy's second goal. Everton wing-half Joe Mercer said, 'He gave the ball a punch of which Joe Louis would have been proud.' England's goalscorers were Willie Hall and Tommy Lawton.

Tottenham inside-right Hall notched nine goals in his ten England appearances, five of them against Northern Ireland on 16 November 1938 at Maine Road. Three of those goals came in a three-and-a-half minute spell, then the fastest international hat-trick on record.

Stanley Matthews scored the only England hat-trick of his career against Czechoslovakia at White Hart Lane on 1 December 1937. He had been stung by criticism that he could not finish and did not have a left foot. His three goals were all scored with his left foot, including the winner in a 5–4 thriller. England had been reduced to ten men by injury and Matthews switched to inside-right.

Wolves started the 1938–39 season by selling Welsh international inside-forward Bryn Jones to Arsenal in a world-record £14,500 deal, and they finished it at Wembley in the FA Cup final against Portsmouth as one of the hottest favourites in history.

Major Frank Buckley, their eccentric but wise manager, had got acres of publicity by telling the press his players were on a course of monkey gland treatment that would improve their stamina and strength. It was a load of codswallop, of course. The medication was just a new form of immunisation against the common cold, but it made great copy for headline-hungry journalists. Major Buckley was not so much a spin doctor as a spin surgeon.

Portsmouth manager Jack Tinn countered by getting the press to believe that the white spats he wore at every match were lucky. He had Pompey winger Freddie Worrall do them up before each game, and always the left one first. Again, it was a load of nonsense but the press lapped it up. That final was one of the most heavily publicised ever, attracting a crowd of 99,370, the biggest Wembley attendance since the White Horse final.

Wolves had narrowly missed out on the championship, while Portsmouth had struggled all season long in the lower reaches of the First Division. On paper it was no contest, but on the pitch it was a completely different story. The Wolves players, for once not responding to their driving captain Stan Cullis, froze and Pompey purred to a comfortable 4–1 victory. Jack 'Spats' Tinn said later:

When, before the match, the traditional autograph book arrived from the Wolves dressing room, I showed the signatures to our players. Their names were scrawled and unintelligible. 'Look,' I said, 'their hands are shaking so much with nerves they cannot even sign their names properly.'

This was the last FA Cup final for seven years, which explains why Portsmouth pop up in quizzes as 'the team that has held the FA Cup for most successive years'.

With war clouds gathering over Europe, Jules Rimet reclaimed the trophy that bore his name from the Italian FA. He thought long and hard about where it would be safest and – with French logic – finally decided that the only place was the bedroom. So for the duration of the Second World War, the Jules Rimet trophy nestled under his bed as football was once again interrupted by shooting of the unacceptable kind.

CHAPTER 8

THE FOOTBALL WORLD AT WAR, TWO

N O LIVES were untouched when Prime Minister Neville Chamberlain made his chillingly historic broadcast on Sunday, 3 September 1939 – '. . . this country is now at war with Germany.' Football was allowed no chance to repeat the folly of the First World War, when the game continued through the first year despite a storm of protests. It was shut down immediately.

The third week of the Football League programme had been completed the day before the broadcast. Blackpool were on top of the First Division, already the only side still with maximum points. Just below them were Arsenal, fresh from a 5–2 victory over Sunderland, four of their goals coming from Ted Drake. Tommy Lawton scored two for Everton in their draw with Blackburn. It was a mouth-watering start to the season, quickly followed by a mouth-smothering end. It would be seven years before nationwide league football resumed.

All sport throughout the country was called off. Emergency regulations banned the assembly of large crowds because the Government did not want to give the imminently expected German bombers easy targets.

As the 'phoney war' – when Britain and the Germans sparred without throwing any explosive punches – stretched from weeks into months and from autumn into winter, it was announced that sport could be played on a restricted basis.

At a joint emergency meeting, the League and the FA decided to suspend the contracts of all professional players, but they were later given permission to continue their careers with any club where it was convenient for them to play. Their match fees were restricted to 30 shillings (£1.50), and ten regional leagues and wartime cup competitions were organised. Away matches were restricted to those with return journeys that could be comfortably completed in daylight.

'Guest players' became common, with professional footballers playing alongside amateurs in any game they could find close to where they were stationed. Aldershot, with its huge Army base, had one of the strongest teams in the land.

Spectators would turn up to regional matches not knowing whom they were likely to see play. Somebody as illustrious as Tommy Lawton could be leading the attack, or it could be Bill the local butcher.

Lawton, who had followed Dixie Dean in the No. 9 Everton and England shirts, was arguably the biggest box-office draw at the time. He epitomised the have-boots-will-travel attitude the players were forced to adopt. During the five years of the war, he played for Everton, Tranmere, Aldershot and Chelsea. He also turned out for Morton while honeymooning in Scotland, and appeared twice in one Christmas Day programme. He played for Everton in the morning, helping them to a 3–1 victory over Liverpool, and then scored twice for Tranmere in their 2–2 draw at Crewe in the afternoon.

In all, during his wartime service with the physical training corps, Lawton scored 212 goals, which put him third on the top marksman list behind Albert Stubbins (Newcastle, 226) and Jock Dodds (Blackpool, 221). This prolific scoring never finds its way into the official records, and Lawton is credited with 'only' 231 career league goals. Like so many of that generation, the peak years of his playing days were lost to the war. He represented England in 23 unofficial international matches, with only Joe Mercer (27) and Stanley Matthews (29) making more appearances. It's sad – offensive, even – that the players of that era have not been given more recognition for their international footballing feats. They were never awarded caps, and even after the war, earned very little for each appearance and had to travel third class. FA officials, including Stanley Rous, rarely travelled anything but first class.

My old friend Billy Wright, for whom I was a long-time ghost-writer and eventually biographer, once showed me a letter from Stanley Rous informing him that he had been selected for his England debut. It began, 'Dear Wright' – no mister, and certainly no Billy. This neatly summed up the master-servant attitude of the times.

Many people assumed that footballers were given a soft ride during the war, which caused undisguised and widespread resentment, but the fact that more than ninety professional players lost their lives in action is evidence that this was a myth.

Winston Churchill encouraged the continuation of international football when he took over as Prime Minister in 1940. He did not know one end of a football from the other (unlike Field Marshal Montgomery, who was a fanatical Portsmouth supporter) but the PM *did* understand the value and impact of the game on the nation's morale. Huge crowds were attracted to a series of matches between England and Scotland – as many as 130,000 turned up at Hampden, and there were always more than 70,000 at Wembley. Proceeds mostly went to the Red Cross and other wartime charities.

England and Scotland played against each other in sixteen wartime matches, the English winning eleven with two drawn. A typical England team read: Swift; Scott, Hardwick; Britton, Cullis, Mercer; Matthews, Carter, Lawton, Hagan, Compton. The most celebrated players gathered together by the Scots read: Dawson; Carabine, Beattie; Shankly, Dykes, Busby; Waddell, Walker, Gillick, Black, Liddell. All of them were exceptional footballers and they did not have a thing to show that they had represented their country. They brought pleasure to thousands in those bitterly bleak times and deserve official recognition even now, more than sixty years later. The fact that there was a war on did not mean they gave anything less on the pitch in terms of effort and skill. Try telling any of the thousands who flocked to those matches that they were not watching 'proper' international football.

From an English point of view, the most memorable of those wartime games was the October 1943 encounter at Maine Road. England won 8–0 with what witnesses among the 60,000 crowd described as the greatest team performance they had ever seen. Tommy Lawton scored four goals inside ten minutes. One of his goals was hooked into the roof of the Scottish net while he sat on the ground with his back to the target.

Stanley Matthews rivalled Lawton for the man-of-the-match rating. He ran the Scottish defenders into dizzy disarray, having a hand – or, rather, a golden right boot – in five of the goals. He scored the eighth himself, dribbling around a queue of defenders in a run from the halfway line before rounding the goalkeeper and steering the ball into the empty net. Even the Scottish players and fans applauded that moment of sheer magic.

Many funny and peculiar events made the wartime league programme memorable. On Christmas Day morning 1940, Brighton travelled to Norwich City having mustered just five players for the match. Their goalkeeper followed on later, arriving at the ground five minutes after the kick-off on board a fire-engine that he had thumbed down while running to the stadium. Brighton's team was completed by Norwich City reserves and volunteers from the crowd. Result: Norwich 18, Brighton 0.

The Notts County records for 1940–41 show that they called on 132 players during the season, and a Bradford City player revealed that he had appeared for eight different clubs in nine weeks.

The Compton brothers, Leslie and Denis, played alongside each other in Arsenal's attack against Clapton Orient on 8 February 1941. Leslie, usually a centre-half, scored ten goals and Denis two in a 15–2 victory.

Stan Mortensen, who was one of England's finest forwards in the immediate post-war years, made his international debut in 1943 – for Wales. He was on the England bench as twelfth man for the wartime international against Wales at Wembley. Ivor Powell was injured in the second half and England agreed that Mortensen could replace him. England won 8–3.

Morty, a bomber pilot, was carried unconscious from his crashed plane in the last year of the war and had a metal plate inserted in his head. He went on to become one of the immortals of the game. They were a different breed in those days.

The football pools companies were in danger of going out of business when the Royal Mail refused to deliver the coupons because they were not considered essential mail. The companies formed a Unity Pool, with a share of the stakes going to charity. By 1943, football-linked charities had raised more than £70,000 for the Red Cross.

Before the 1940 retreat from Dunkirk, an Army XI captained by Stan Cullis and including players of the calibre of Wilf Copping, Tommy Lawton and Joe Mercer, played three matches against a French international team. These games were more official than the kick-abouts that took place on the beaches during the D-Day landings of 1944, and less remarkable than the spontaneous game involving a squad that parachuted into Holland and a local Dutch team. The parachutists, in full battle dress, won 5–2.

In Egypt, there was such a huge concentration of troops during the North African campaign that a League was set up with teams adopting the names of English clubs.

Even more extraordinary were the football competitions organised in prisoner of war camps. The Geneva Convention stressed that PoWs should be allowed sporting facilities, and their parcels often included footballs. In Stalag Luft I, sixty teams, one for each hut, organised themselves into five leagues. Stalag Luft VIIB had fifty teams competing in a cup competition, with the prize of a barrel of beer for the winners.

Escape tunnels were often dug while football matches acted as a distraction to German guards hooked on watching the games, and the 1970s film *Escape to Victory*, starring Sylvester Stallone with Pele and Bobby Moore in cameo roles, was not too far from fact. One true story could not have been dreamt up by a Hollywood scriptwriter with an over-active imagination, or even by a Westminster spin doctor. This is a potted version.

It is the winter of 1945 and British troops are launching an offensive in the last months of the war. They capture a German soldier in Belgium who, just days earlier, had escaped from a Russian prisoner of war camp. The ragged-uniformed soldier tells his new captors in good English, 'I would much rather be with you than the Soviets.'

He identifies himself as Private First Class Bernhard Trautmann of the Bremen regiment. His name is written down as Bert. He looks the stereotypical German, just over 6ft tall and with corn-coloured hair and light blue eyes.

Shipped back to a relaxed British prisoner-of-war camp in

Lancashire, twenty-two-year-old Trautmann starts to play football with his fellow prisoners. He had been an outstanding all-round athlete in his hometown of Bremen, and was a specialist centre-half. When nobody will volunteer to go in goal, Bert fills the position and is soon diving around making saves like a real natural goalkeeper.

At the end of the war, he is still held prisoner to help rebuild bomb-shattered Britain. He starts playing in local matches and is spotted by the semi-professional club St Helens Town. Bert falls in love and marries an English girl.

There is huge controversy when Manchester City sign him from St Helens in 1949 to take over from the legendary Frank Swift, and complaints flood in from Manchester's large Jewish community. Rabbi Altman meets Trautmann and announces, 'He is a decent fellow, unconnected with any German crimes. I give him my blessing to play for Manchester City.'

Many City fans of a certain age will tell you that Trautmann became as reliable a last line of defence as the worshipped Swift over the next 554 league and FA Cup games.

He will always be remembered for the 1956 final at Wembley when he played on despite a shooting pain in his neck after a late dive at the feet of Birmingham City forward Peter Murphy. After collecting his winner's medal, Bert went to hospital where an X-ray revealed he had broken his neck. He was in plaster for several months but returned to play for another seven years before becoming a successful businessman.

Trautmann retired to Spain, warmed by memories of an astonishing life and a playing career with Manchester City that lifted him into the land of legend alongside the fabulous Frank Swift.

There are those who believe he was even better than that other foreign goalkeeping idol of Manchester, Peter Schmeichel. Now there's a sentence that will launch a thousand arguments.

When the FA Cup resumed in 1946, Raich Carter inspired Derby County to a 4–1 win in extra time against Charlton, despite the ball bursting during the game. Home and away ties were played on the way to the final and collectors of trivia can ask: 'Which team was beaten in a round of the FA Cup but still went on to reach the final at Wembley?' Answer: Charlton Athletic, who lost the second leg of their third-round tie to Fulham but went through 4–3 on aggregate.

Derby got to Wembley from a 4–0 semi-final replay victory over Birmingham City that drew a midweek record crowd of 80,407 to Maine Road.

In the final, Charlton's Bert Turner became the first player to score for both sides in an FA Cup final. He turned the ball into his own net to give Derby a second-half lead, and cancelled it out sixty seconds later with a pile-driver of a free kick. Not for the last time, football reporters reached for the 'hero-and-villain' cliché. Derby, with inside-forward masters Carter and Peter Doherty running the show, were clearly the better side, but they did not translate their superiority into goals until extra time when Jackie Stamps, who had been wounded at Dunkirk, scored twice and Doherty once.

Charlton were back at Wembley the following year and this time they won although history did repeat itself when the ball burst again. Scottish winger Chris Duffy scored the only goal against Burnley with a right boot that he rarely used except to stand on. Duffy set some sort of record by virtually running a lap of the pitch in celebration. Sam Bartram, a red-headed, larger-than-life character who was the greatest of the uncapped goalkeepers, could be considered football's first sweeper because of the way he used to run out of his penalty area to control the ball with his feet before passing to a Charlton team-mate. He was ill with food poisoning in the week leading up to the semi-final, and played with a hot poultice strapped to his stomach.

Sam, who later became a respected football reporter with the *Sunday People* after trying his hand at management with Luton, said of the burst-ball incident in the 1946 final:

The score was 1–1 when Jackie Stamps, who had the kick of a mule, took a shot that I had covered. As it left his foot there was a hissing sound that we could hear despite the roar of the crowd. When the ball reached me it was a triangular shape and it was all I could do to catch it. I later asked the ref if it would have counted as a goal if the ball had gone into the net, and he said it would have because he could only change it once it was dead. 'Dead?' I said. 'The ball was mortally wounded!' The odds of it bursting were calculated at one million to one. The fact that it happened again the following year was beyond belief.

In one of the oddest interludes in English football, Moscow Dynamo came to Britain for what was something of a magical mystery tour. They came, they saw, but did not concur with very much about the game in Britain. Little was known about them when they arrived in November 1945, and little more was known when they suddenly disappeared home without warning just over two weeks later.

They would not allow anybody to watch them train, would eat only meals prepared at the Russian embassy, insisted on bringing their own referee and demanded the use of substitutes, which was then pretty near unheard of in British football.

Such was the interest in the 'Mystery Men of Moscow' that 82,000 spectators crammed into Stamford Bridge for their first match, against Chelsea. The Dynamo team presented embarrassed Chelsea players with bouquets of flowers before the kick-off, and then with a precise passing game came back to draw 3–3 after trailing 2–0 against the London club. Most neutral witnesses agreed that Dynamo were the better team.

Next they went to Wales and destroyed Cardiff 10–1 before returning to London for a prestige match against an Arsenal side including guest players Stanley Matthews and Stan Mortensen. The game was played at White Hart Lane because Highbury was still being used as an Air Raid Precaution centre.

Nobody, including the 55,000 crowd, saw much of the game. A thick fog shrouded the ground, and few reporters were quite sure how Dynamo managed to come from 3–1 down to win 4–3. Visibility was down to five yards and the Russian referee patrolled one side of the pitch with his two linesmen on the far touchline.

The Russians then travelled to Glasgow, where they continued in a fog of their own making. They drew 2–2 with Rangers in front of a 90,000 crowd at Ibrox Park in a game threaded with ill temper. After that, and without warning, the Dynamo team flew home to Moscow, shunning a scheduled final match against an FA XI at Villa Park. It was later reported that as they had gone through the tour unbeaten, each of the players was made a Hero of the Soviet Union.

The joy of that early post-war football period was scarred on 9 March 1946 when thirty-three spectators were crushed to death and another 500 injured as two terrace barriers collapsed during Bolton's sixth-round FA Cup tie against Stoke City at Burnden

Park. The gates had been closed behind a capacity 65,000 crowd but it was estimated that many thousands more managed to force their way in.

The accident happened at the start of the game and, first of all, the referee led the teams off but the police recommended that the match continue because of fears of a crowd panic. The game was played without a half-time break and without any goals. Most of the crowd were unaware of the disaster.

There has never been a club debut quite like the one Len Shackleton made for Newcastle United against Newport County when league football resumed at the start of the 1946–47 season. But then, there has never been another footballer quite like Shackleton. For him, the football field was a stage and he cast himself in the role of entertainer extraordinary. He was Gazza without the hang-ups.

'Shack' – as he was known and idolised throughout the north east – believed football should be fun and he had a vast repertoire of tantalising tricks that bemused the opposition, amused the fans and often confused his own team-mates. When he took his football seriously there were few more explosive exponents of the game, as he proved in his first match for Newcastle after a £13,000 transfer from Bradford Park Avenue. His presence in the side lured a crowd of 52,137 to Tyneside for the Second Division game as witnesses of what was not so much a match as a massacre.

Shack scored six goals as Newcastle romped to a record 13–0 victory. Amazingly, the match had started with Magpies' centre-forward Charlie Wayman missing a second-minute penalty.

In the last match of the season, Newcastle went to Newport needing a win to clinch promotion and were beaten 4–2 by a County side already doomed to relegation. Yes, it's a funny old game.

Shackleton later moved to Sunderland, where he developed a prolific but often prickly partnership with highly skilled Welsh international centre-forward Trevor Ford. It was no secret that they didn't always get on with each other. In one famous incident, after Trevor complained that Shack never passed to him, Shack dribbled the ball around four defenders and the goalkeeper and then stopped the ball dead on the goalline before pushing it back into the path of Trevor twenty yards behind him. 'Now don't say I never [blankety blank] pass to you,' shouted Shack as Trevor steered the ball into an empty net. The linesman flagged Shack offside and the goal did not count!

Following his retirement, Shack wrote a controversial autobiography, *The Clown Prince of Soccer*, in which, under the chapter heading 'What the average director knows about football', he left the page blank. He became a respected football writer and, reminiscing in the press box one day, he regaled those of us present with this story, which captures the times in which he played:

> *After scoring what I considered one of my finest ever goals to help England beat world champions Germany at Wembley in 1954, I was handed a third-class rail ticket for the overnight sleeper back to Sunderland. I said to the Bowler Hat handing me the ticket, 'Couldn't you raise enough money for a first-class ticket?' The FA official said that all the first-class tickets had been sold.*
>
> *When I got to King's Cross I had no trouble transferring to first-class because there was plenty of space, and I was happy to pay the five pounds difference out of my own pocket. By the time I'd paid tax and expenses, I was left with just £20 out of my £50 match fee. The Wembley receipts for the match were over £50,000, but we footballers, who had drawn the crowd and the money, were considered third-class citizens by those blinkered fools who ran the Football Association.*

Shack's goal against the Germans – an impudent chip as the goalkeeper came charging towards him – was his last act for England. He was axed after collecting a paltry five caps. He would have won dozens more but for being a rebel – without a pause!

From 1946, England had a full-time manager in Walter Winterbottom. Educated at Oldham Grammar School and then Chester College, Winterbottom combined a teaching job with playing amateur football for Royston and Mossley. In 1934, he signed on as a professional for Manchester United but his playing career was cut short by a spinal injury.

Walter became a college lecturer and, on the outbreak of the war, joined the RAF. He was made a wing commander and seconded to the Air Ministry where he was appointed Head of Physical Training. He resumed his playing career as a guest for Chelsea and was twice called up as an England reserve for wartime international matches, understudying master centre-half Stan Cullis.

Walter had already arranged to return to teaching after the war when he got a call from Football Association secretary Stanley Rous, who invited him to take over as the supremo of English football, responsible for the development of the game at all levels. He was just thirty-three. Rous had been impressed by Walter when they met on an experimental coaching course that Sir Stanley had set up in 1937. They formed a strong alliance that had a wide-ranging impact on post-war English football.

In the first half of his sixteen-year tenure as England's first full-time manager, Walter was given access to arguably the greatest English footballers of all time. The names of the prominent players of that era echo like a roll call of footballing gods – Stanley Matthews, Tom Finney, Tommy Lawton, Raich Carter, Len Shackleton, Wilf Mannion, Nat Lofthouse, Stan Mortensen, Jackie Milburn, Frank Swift, Billy Wright, Neil Franklin and a poised, purposeful right-back called Alf Ramsey.

With players of that quality to call upon, England should have cemented their traditionally held reputation as the masters of world football. It is an indictment of the overall system rather than Winterbottom's management that even with all this talent on tap, English international football went into a decline.

Despite the stature of his job, the bespectacled, scholarly looking Winterbottom managed to keep a low public profile. The only time he used to make it into the headlines was when the football writers lined up like a firing squad following any defeat. It was a standing joke in Fleet Street that the sports desks of the national newspapers had 'Winterbottom Must Go' headlines set up for every match. He would shrug off the searing criticism and get on with his job as if nothing had been said, and he would greet the journalists who had been sniping at him with friendly courtesy. He was a true gentleman.

His influence on post-war English football is greater than almost anybody else's, yet to the man in the street – and on the terraces – he was a little-known figure. It was as a coach that he made his most telling contribution, combining the role of England manager with what he saw as the more important job of the Football Association's Director of Coaching. In fact, it was made clear to him right from the off that he was the FA coach first and England manager second. According to Rous, 'Most of the FA councillors did not want a national team manager, but I persuaded them to appoint one, rather reluctantly. They gave Walter the responsibility but saw to it that they retained the power. Anybody assessing what Walter achieved for English football must think of him first and foremost as a coach and an organiser *extraordinaire.*'

Winterbottom was the father of English coaching. He set up a nationwide network of FA coaching schools, and among his many disciples you will find such outstanding proponents of the art as Ron Greenwood, Bill Nicholson, Bobby Robson, Dave Sexton, Malcolm Allison, Don Howe and a young bearded Fulham forward called Jimmy Hill.

He was handcuffed throughout his time as England manager by having to defer to amateur selectors, most of whom had vested interests in their choices because of their allegiance to various league clubs and local associations. He painted this disturbing picture of an England team selection meeting, which could come straight out of the pages of a Monty Python script:

> *When I first took the job, each selector would arrive at our meetings with his personal list of who should play. We used to discuss and discuss until we were down to, say, two goal-keepers and then a straight vote would decide. Then on to the next position, and so on through the team. Before they made their final decision I would be asked to leave the room while they deliberated. I would be called back in and told the line-up. It was asking almost the impossible to get the right blend with this way of selecting a team. At least in the later years I was able to present my team and then let them try to argue me out of it. The trick of it was to stick to the men who were most important, and to make concessions to the committee where it didn't matter so much.*

Typical of the dithering that went on was whether to play Stanley Matthews or Tom Finney on the right wing, which had the entire nation debating 'Matthews or Finney?' They would select Matthews for one match and then Finney would be the flavour of the month. One day, after a defeat in Switzerland, they panicked and boldly picked both Matthews *and* Finney together in the same attack. The match was against Portugal in Lisbon on 25 May 1947. England won 10–0!

England paralysed the Portuguese with two goals inside the first two minutes through debutant Stan Mortensen and Tommy Lawton. Matthews and Finney ran down the wings as if they owned them, and Portugal's defence just caved in under the non-stop pressure. England were 5–0 up at half-time and then repeated the dose in the second half after Portugal had substituted their goalkeeper, who went off in tears. Both Morty and Lawton scored four goals each, and Matthews and Finney got on the scoresheet. Wilf Mannion was the only forward who did not score but his passes were important ingredients in the goals banquet. This was how Billy Wright, playing at right-half, remembered it:

> I can honestly say that this was the closest thing I ever saw to perfection on the football field. Everything we tried came off, and Portugal just didn't know what had hit them. There was a dispute before the game over which ball should be used. Walter demanded the usual full-size ball that was common to most international matches, but the Portuguese coach wanted a size-four ball, the type used in our schoolboy football.
>
> The referee ordered that we should play with the full-size ball and Stan Mortensen had it in the back of their net within twenty seconds of the kick-off.
>
> It seemed to take the goalkeeper an age to retrieve the ball and he was fiddling around on his knees appearing to be trying to disentangle it from the corner of the netting. We were in possession within seconds of the restart and realised the goalkeeper had switched the ball for the smaller one, and a minute later he was also fishing that out of the back of the net!
>
> It seemed so obvious that we should be playing both Stanley Matthews and Tom Finney. But in those days you dare not poke your nose in and make a suggestion to the selectors. They knew it all.
>
> This was the match in which Tommy Lawton jokingly complained to Stanley Matthews that the lace was facing the wrong way when he centred it.

Stanley Rous was a master politician and it was he who talked the home countries into joining the FIFA fold. To celebrate, a combined

Great Britain side played the Rest of Europe at Hampden Park in front of 135,000 spectators in May 1947. The Great Britain team powered to a 6–1 victory against a side composed of players from ten different countries and playing like the passing strangers that they were. For the record, the Great Britain team was: Frank Swift (E); George Hardwick (E), Billy Hughes (W); Archie Macaulay (S), Jack Vernon (NI), Ronnie Burgess (W); Stanley Matthews (E), Wilf Mannion (E), Tommy Lawton (E), Billy Steel (S), Billy Liddell (S).

The Rest of Europe were skippered by Irishman Johnny Carey, who was playing a leading role in helping Matt Busby reconstruct Manchester United. Busby had taken over as manager of the debt-ridden club in 1945, and was, literally, rebuilding from the ruins left behind by Hitler's *Luftwaffe*. There was a deep bomb crater at the heart of the Old Trafford pitch and the stands had been blitzed. Fortunately for United, Busby, toughened by his former life down the pits, found the challenge appealing rather than appalling. In his first public statement of intent when he became £15-a-week manager, Busby said, 'I am determined that United will provide the footballing public with the best in the game. We will develop the finest young players, and they will grow up playing the Manchester United way.'

Busby provided dynamic action to go with his words. Making full use of his innate Scottish organisational sense, he moulded and managed three majestic teams during his glorious twenty-five-year reign at Old Trafford.

Many old pros in the game consider the first Busby-built team of the 1940s and early 1950s to have been his best. That side's impressive impact on the immediate post-war years gives powerful weight to the argument. In the six years following the war, United captured the league championship once (1951–52), were runners-up four times and won a classic FA Cup final against Blackpool at Wembley in 1948. This was the team skippered by Gentleman Johnny Carey and featuring the fabulous forward line of Jimmy 'Old Bones' Delaney, Johnny Morris, Jack Rowley, Stan Pearson and Charlie Mitten. Delaney was a battle-hardened Scot whom Busby considered, at £4,000, one of his greatest ever buys.

Stan Mortensen scored for Blackpool in every round of their 1947–48 FA Cup run, and he completed the full house with a goal against United at Wembley as the Seasiders took a 2–1 half-time

...he cobbles (*above*) or over fields (*below*) 'mass football' was popular with everybody
...he establishment. It was said you had to be possessed to play it. We now call it the
...ession game.

An artist's impression of the 1895 England-Scotland match at the Kennington Oval.
crossbars and Beckham haircuts were things for the future.

Aston Villa won the FA Cup for the second time in three years in 1897 at the peak o
their Golden Age. This time they managed to keep hold of the FA Cup, having had it
stolen in 1895.

British Ladies' Football Club was formed in 1895, drawing huge crowds but also
e criticism from the sexist Football Association. It was the start of a 75 year fight for
gnition.

not two Father Christmases. On the far right is William McGregor, founder of the
tball League, and alongside him Lord Kinnaird, who played in a record nine FA Cup
ls and served the FA for more than 50 years. Both were Scots, showing the English
r to get themselves organised.

Above left Billy Meredith, the Welsh 'Wizard of Dribble' who was as skinny as a pipe cleaner. He played in the red *and* blue of Manchester – and made the establishment see red with his pioneering union activities.

Above centre What's a cricketer doing in *Football and All That*? This is the unique R.E. 'Tip' Foster, the only man to captain England at football and cricket.

Above right Alf Common, football's first £1,000 player, was said to be built like a brick outhouse, or words to that effect.

Left Steve Bloomer, a ghostly looking man who haunted defences for Derby and England.

was the Cecil B. De Mille-style crowd scene (*above*) that threatened to have the Wembley FA Cup final in 1923 abandoned before a ball had been kicked. It gave a ⟨??⟩e new meaning to a crowded goalmouth. Then along came PC George Scorey on his ⟨??⟩e horse Billy, slowly and patiently, to clear the pitch (*below*). It is estimated that ⟨??⟩e than 200,000 got in to see the match between Bolton and West Ham, although the ⟨??⟩ial attendance was 126,047. Hardly surprisingly, from then on the FA Cup final ⟨??⟩me all-ticket.

Two of the legends of game who bridged the 1920s and 1930s with their gallery of goals - Dixie 'the Headmaster Dean (*far left*), and th mixed-up genius Hugl Gallacher, who tragica ended his life under tl wheels of the London Edinburgh express.

Arsenal, under the guidance of manager Herbert Chapman (*bel left*) were THE team o 1930s, with the goals Ted Drake (*below righ* helping them dominat the domestic scene. It almost made people outside Tottenham for that Arsenal had 'con their way into the Firs Division.

stiff at the top before the
-off to the 1938 World Cup
l between Italy and
gary. *Right*: England
lkeeper Bert Williams looks
k in anger as he is beaten by
USA goal in the 1950 World
finals.

mous sign of the times – England's players give their controversial Nazi salute in
in in 1938.

It is only fitting that Stanley Matthews (*left*) and Tom Finney should appear together, even though the selectors were reluctant to play them in the same forward line. When they did finally play on either wing, England beat Portugal 10–0, and Matthews was jokingly criticised by four-goal Tommy Lawton for crossing the ball with the lace facing the wrong way.

Garrincha, in action here (*left*) in a 1962 World Cup finals match against Mexico, could be mentioned in the same breath as Matthews and Finney. The gifted Brazilian winger was born with deformed legs that meant he had virtually two left feet. He left defenders not knowing what foot to stand on.

lead. The BBC reported that for the first time one million viewers watched a football match – a sign of things to come. Those million people saw one of the greatest of all finals on their nine-inch TV screens. It is enshrined in United folklore how Busby and Carey took turns during the half-time interval in imploring, 'Just keep playing football.' United did exactly that in the second half to emerge 4–2 winners. That was always the Busby creed – *just keep playing football.*

Mind you, Matt would have pronounced it fitba'. He liked to recount the true story of how, when he was playing for Liverpool before the war, a census official came to the door and asked him what he did for a living. He told her in his thick West of Scotland accent, and she wrote on the census form 'Fruitboiler'.

With Delaney performing baffling tricks out on either wing, that 1940s Busby team rattled in goals with Gatling-gun regularity and lured massive crowds to Maine Road, the ground they shared with Manchester City for three years while Old Trafford was being repaired. They pulled in a league record attendance of 82,950 for a First Division match against Arsenal on 17 January 1948. That first Busby team have retained a special place in the hearts of all followers of what was an exciting and adventurous footballing period, when scoring goals took priority over trying to stop them.

In those immediate post-war years, British menfolk – women were in a small minority – flocked to football as their escape from the Age of Austerity, just as they had done in earlier decades when hardship and deprivation were the lot of most working people. Food, clothes and petrol were still rationed and the nation was aching from the painfully personal recollections of thousands of dead and missing countrymen. Clement Attlee's Labour government had been voted into power on the back of the refurbished Lloyd-George slogan, 'A home fit for heroes'. All the heroes were on the sports fields – Denis Compton, for instance, scored 18 centuries off his own bat in the summer of '47 and the football gods drew spectators by the millions.

The total attendance for the 1947–48 season topped 40 million for the first time. In Scotland, 143,470 spectators saw Rangers beat Hibs in a Scottish Cup semi-final, and 133,570 attended the Scottish Cup final replay, an all-time record for a midweek afternoon match. The Government became so concerned about the effects of absenteeism on plans to rebuild bankrupt and blitzed Britain that it soon banned midweek afternoon kick-offs.

Just as it seemed crowds had reached their peak, the records were shattered again in 1948–49 when aggregate attendances for league matches exceeded 41.2 million. On Saturday, 16 October 1948, the record for a single day reached just under 1.2 million.

While the clubs were coining it, little of the extra revenue was getting into the pockets of the 'slave' players. They had to threaten strike action yet again before they got a meagre £1 rise, making the maximum wage £9.00 during the season and £7.00 in the summer.

Minimum prices to stand on the terraces at First Division games had been raised to 1s 6d ($7\frac{1}{2}$ p), and you could get the best seat in the house for 5s (25p). The weekly wage for footballers was gradually – and grudgingly – increased season by season until in 1958–59 it was capped at £20 per week and £17 in the summer. Only at the back end of their careers did such players as Stanley Matthews, Tom Finney, Tommy Lawton and Billy Wright earn a princely £20 a week, of which £8 went straight to the taxman. These were the days when players were handed their wages in brown envelopes. Imagine that today. Many Premiership players would need a sack!

Billy Wright once worked out that, including average £4 win bonuses (£2 for a draw), he earned around £15,000 in thirteen years of post-war league football with Wolves. Added to this, he received three loyalty benefit cheques, two for £750 and a final one of £1,000, plus an estimated £2,000 in trophy-winning bonuses and a £1,500 Provident Fund pay out on his retirement in 1959.

It was no secret that some clubs rewarded star players with backhanders to keep them sweet but there was none of that pocketlining at Wolves. The chances of 'Honest Stan' Cullis giving under-the-counter payments was as likely as Roy Rogers having his white stetson knocked off in a fight.

The most Billy earned playing for England was £50 a match, and his total income from all 105 internationals was less than £4,000. Yet Billy was better off than most of his colleagues, and during the course of his career collected around £10,000 from various sponsorship contracts and another £6,000 from publishing deals. His total earnings while skippering one of the most successful clubs in the land and captaining his country in 90 out of 105 matches amounted to just over £40,000, and that includes the commercial extras. Several Premiership footballers today earn more than that in a week. It is, of course, hard to compare and Billy didn't do badly, but let's remember it came from a thirteen-year post-war slog.

In this era of innocence, you could count football agents on the fingers of a one-armed bandit. Bagenal Harvey was a respected forerunner of what has now become a rash of 'players' representatives', and he started off with Denis Compton. He negotiated the famous 'Brylcreem Boy' advertisement, for which Compton received £1,000 a year – hardly a king's ransom but very tasty at a time when Billy Wright was lending his name to commercial ventures for small one-off payments.

Douglas Cox, managing director of Purity Soft Drinks for more than fifty years, revealed that he arranged for Billy to endorse his products in the 1950s when he was captain of both Wolves and England. His name and image were printed on thousands of table coasters. Douglas recalled, 'Billy brought his landlady Mrs Colley along to negotiate with me. We shook hands on a fee of twenty pounds, of which I know Billy gave half to Mrs Colley.'

Many people would have felt bitter at such poor returns but there was not a bitter bone in Billy's body. 'I was never ever motivated by money,' he told me. 'It sounds corny, but I would honestly have played for England for nothing. You could not beat the moment of pulling on the England shirt and leading the team out. For me, it was all about pride. I loved every second of it.'

That summed up the attitude of many players of that generation. They were content to play for pride as much as profit.

Tommy Lawton was not one of them. He was always bitter that he was underpaid throughout his career. Arguably Britain's greatest ever centre-forward – well, head to head with his old Everton teammate Dixie Dean – Tommy was once overheard by a selector grumbling about the pathetic money he received for playing for his country. He was dropped without explanation for the next two matches.

In 1947, Tommy became locked in an acrimonious contract dispute with Chelsea after just one season at Stamford Bridge. In the November he was sold to Third Division Notts County for what was then a British record £20,000. A lot of eyebrows were raised over the deal, with whispers about how much of the money had found its way into Tommy's pocket to persuade him to give up First Division football. As far as Tommy was concerned, he was worth every penny he could get his hands on. Like so many of his contemporaries, he had been cruelly robbed of his peak years by the war. Now he was trying to make up for lost time.

Another ex-Evertonian, Joe 'Bow Legs Banana Smile' Mercer, had no complaints about his 1946 move to Arsenal. In 1947–48, he led the Gunners to the league championship when they headed the table from start to finish, and two years later he lifted the FA Cup at Wembley – not bad for a thirty-six-year-old who had been told by Goodison clubmate Dixie Dean eighteen years earlier, 'Your legs wouldn't last a postman a round.'

Joe was a baby compared with Neil McBain, the oldest man ever to play league football, a record that stands to this day. McBain was the manager of New Brighton when he was forced to select himself for a Third Division North match on 15 March 1947 after his only goalkeeper had pulled out with an injury. Scotsman Neil, a pre-war half-back, played in goal for the one and only time in his life in a 3–0 defeat at Hartlepool. He was 51 years 120 days old.

On the international front, England's stock went up overseas when they followed their 10–0 pulverisation of Portugal with a 5–2 victory over Belgium in Brussels and then a magnificent 4–0 win against Italy in Milan. Goalkeeper Frank Swift was captain and before the kick-off against Italy, Stan Mortensen promised him a goal. Morty kept his word in the fourth minute when he finished a forty-yard sprint down the right wing with a shot on the run as he cut in. The ball crashed into the far corner of the Italian net from the tightest of angles. Morty then made a goal for Tommy Lawton, and two individual efforts from Tom Finney in the second half finished off the opposition.

In an unhappy coincidence, both captains in the match, Valentino Mazzola and Swift, were later to die in air crashes. The Italian team included six of the gifted Torino side, all of whom were tragically killed in an air crash a year later. Mazzola, whose two sons later played for Italy, was among the victims. Swift, travelling as a journalist with Manchester United, was killed in the 1958 Munich disaster.

FA Cup romance was in the air in 1948–49 when, in the fourth round, Southern League Yeovil Town put out 'Bank of England'

Sunderland in extra time. In those days, if the scores were level, FA Cup ties went into extra time in the first match, in order to save petrol.

Yeovil were led by player-manager Alec Stock, a former Army major, who was to become one of the great characters among managers. Alec was a master propagandist who played mind games with the opposition long before Alex Ferguson got stuck into the psyche of Kevin Keegan and Arsene Wenger. When Yeovil drew all-star Sunderland, Alec – at twenty-nine, the youngest player-manager in the game – got to work with some psychological warfare.

Yeovil's Huish Park pitch had a slope on it that ran ten feet from corner to opposite corner. Years later, he spoke of that game, in his staccato short sentences, so brilliantly impersonated by Paul White-house when playing his 'Ron Manager' character:

We were not fit to be in the same county as them, let alone on the same pitch. Knew I needed to do something to cut them down to our size. Couldn't do it by talking about our players. The fact that I could get into the team with a dodgy ankle showed how bad we were. So I decided to make the pitch our secret weapon.

In truth, the slope was not that pronounced. I set about making it sound like the bloody North face of the Eiger. To every reporter who came within hearing distance, I said, 'Wonder if Sunderland's players have the calves to stand up to our hill?'

I knew I must be getting through to them because their chairman rang our chairman to ask if the Sunderland players could train on the pitch. I flatly refused. Told our groundsman in the hearing of a journalist, 'If you see a single Sunderland player step foot on that pitch before the match take a shotgun to him.'

By the time it came to the kick-off, they were convinced they needed climbing boots. We were a team of part-timers, but it was they who ran out of steam when the game went into extra time. All in the mind, y'see.'

It is part of football legend how Stock shot Yeovil into the lead in the twenty-sixth minute. Sunderland, including the great Clown

Prince Len Shackleton in their expensive side, snatched an equaliser through Jackie Robinson. Fourteen minutes into extra time Shack, of all people, mis-hit a pass to let Eric Bryant in for the goal of a lifetime. Alec recalled:

> In the last couple of minutes, Sunderland were awarded a free kick just outside the box. Fog was swirling about the place and we could hardly see the man taking the kick. As we stood in the wall, I announced to the players standing with me, 'Anybody ducks, they're sacked.' Every man did his duty and we cleared the danger.

The reward for Yeovil was a fifth-round match away to Manchester United at Maine Road. The result was an 8–0 victory to the Cup holders. The crowd was, wait for it, 81,565.

'Kept us going,' said Alec. 'We were up to our necks in debt and that Cup run saved us.'

Wolves put Manchester United out in a semi-final replay and went on to win the Cup with two goals from Jesse Pye in a 3–1 victory over Leicester City. Billy Wright proudly climbed the thirty-nine Wembley steps to collect the Cup from the then Princess Elizabeth. Before that month of May was out, he was skippering England for the first time, starting a run of ninety games as captain, a record later equalled by Bobby Moore.

Portsmouth, strengthened by being able to call on the finest footballing sailors based in the town, won the first of back-to-back league championships in 1948–49. In a moving ceremony at Fratton Park, their number-one supporter, Field Marshal Montgomery, handed over the trophy.

In Scotland, Rangers made history in 1948–49 by becoming the first team to win a treble. Even more extraordinary, their Old Firm rivals Celtic did not run them close for any of the trophies. Rangers won the League by one point from Dundee, beat Clyde 4–1 in the Scottish Cup final and scored a 2–0 victory over Raith in the League Cup final.

Ask anybody from across the Irish Sea which was the first foreign side to beat England at home and they will tell you, 'Ireland.' England were beaten 2–0 by a Republic of Ireland side at Goodison Park on 21 September 1949. Nine of the Irish players, including magnificent captain Johnny Carey, were playing for Football

League teams. The other two were with Shamrock Rovers but all of them were born in the Republic, and they will always insist that they were the first overseas side to beat the Old Masters on their own territory.

However, far more painful blows were waiting just around the corner for England in the revolutionary 1950s.

CHAPTER 9

THE MORTIFYING FIFTIES

T HE FIFTIES promised to be the best of times for English football – they turned out to be the worst. England's World Cup debut ended in humiliation and the proud record of being unbeaten at Wembley tumbled to Hungary in a match that exposed English football as embarrassingly outdated. Towards the end of the decade came the heartbreak of the Munich air disaster, which virtually wiped out a brilliant young Manchester United team.

England had the players with the ability to win the World Cup when they entered the tournament in 1950 but the Football Association made a complete hash of it. The evidence speaks for itself.

The FA saw fit to organise a goodwill tour of Canada at the same time as the World Cup finals were being held in Brazil. Then they ummed and ahhed when Manchester United requested that none of their players should be considered for either tournament because they had arranged a trip to the United States.

Walter Winterbottom, battling against this blinkered club-before-country attitude, almost had to get on his knees to have first choice for the World Cup. As it was, he had to go to Brazil without England's most famous player, Stanley Matthews, who was sent on the totally meaningless Canadian trip as a footballing ambassador.

Special arrangements had to be made to fly him down to Rio for the finals and he arrived after England had won their opening match 2–0 against Chile. Stanley had crossed through so many time zones that he quite literally did not know what day it was.

Winterbottom wanted to play Matthews in the second game, against the United States at Belo Horizonte, and Stanley Rous argued the case for him with the chairman of the selectors, a Grimsby fish merchant by the name of Arthur Drewry. In fact, Drewry had been appointed the lone selector for the World Cup and he was not to be persuaded. 'My policy is never to change a winning team,' he said dismissively.

On one of the blackest days in English football history, the United States beat England 1–0 with Stanley Matthews among the spectators. It was like leaving Wellington on the bench at Waterloo.

Skipper Billy Wright told a story from that 1950 World Cup tournament that captures the amateurish way in which England approached international football. Nobody had bothered to check what food the hotel would serve in Brazil and the players complained that they could not eat it because it was too spicy. Winterbottom decided the only way round the problem was to go into the hotel kitchen and do the cooking himself. Talk about head cook and bottle washer! Can you imagine Sven in a chef's hat? 'Svedish meatballs, anybody?'

England's utter shame against the United States could not be mitigated by assuming the Americans were not really Americans, as reported at the time. The football writers had failed to do their homework and stories that England had been beaten by a team that had arrived via Ellis Island, with only a couple of true Americans among them, were not true. All but three of the team were born in the United States. The immigrants were Joe Maca from Belgium, Ed McIllveney from Scotland and the goalscorer, Larry Gaetjens from Haiti.

A deflected shot from centre-forward Gaetjens eight minutes before half-time gave the United States a victory that caused a shock that could have been measured on the Richter scale. England hit the woodwork three times and what seemed a certain face-saving goal from an Alf Ramsey free kick in the closing minutes was miraculously saved by the diving goalkeeper, Borghi, a professional baseball catcher. Another Ramsey free kick had earlier found the back of the net but the referee whistled for an infringement. England spent 85 per cent of the game in the American half but finished up the losers.

Nobody could have felt more frustrated than Stanley Matthews, who sat watching impassively from the sidelines. Had he been on the pitch, just his name and reputation alone would have frightened the life out of the Americans.

The goalscoring hero Gaetjens was later reported to have died in a Haitian jail after helping to organise a guerrilla movement against the island's dictator, 'Papa' Doc Duvalier. His name will live on in football history.

England needed to beat Spain in their third match to go through to the next phase but even with Matthews and Finney operating on the wings they could not make the breakthrough and their feeble World Cup challenge finished with a 1–0 defeat. Finney was tripped twice in the penalty area against Spain but each time the referee waved play on. It was one of those games, one of those tournaments.

The seeds of England's World Cup humiliation had been sown two months earlier when centre-half Neil Franklin, arguably the finest player ever to wear the No. 5 England shirt, literally walked out on his country.

Franklin was the best known and most talented of a cluster of league footballers who joined the outlawed Colombian league in Bogota. Sick to death of his slave-labour wages in Britain, Franklin went to seek his fortune on foreign fields only to find frustration. The disillusioned Stoke City captain soon returned home with empty pockets to find he had been banned from international football. It was four years before England found an adequate replacement for the cultured Franklin in the shape of Billy Wright. He had been playing his heart out at right-half while the selectors tried no fewer than eleven players in their fruitless search for the man who could command the centre of the defence.

Franklin's last match for England was against Scotland in the 1950 Home International Championship, which had been nominated as a World Cup qualifying group. The top two teams were guaranteed a place in the finals.

The Scottish FA decreed that they would send a team only if they won the domestic title, putting enormous pressure on their players before the deciding match against England at Hampden Park. With Franklin masterful in defence, England beat them 1–0 thanks to a second-half Roy Bentley goal that suddenly silenced a crowd of 133,250 spectators trying to roar Scotland to Rio.

So England went to Brazil, and the Scots stayed behind, even though a place had been booked for them as runners-up. It is difficult to fathom who was the more blinkered in those days, the Scottish or English football rulers.

While England took the long haul home after their defeats by the United States and Spain – it probably never occurred to those in charge that staying to watch the remainder of the tournament could have taught them so much – Uruguay went on to win the World Cup. The tournament was organised on a league basis and Uruguay beat hosts Brazil in front of a world-record crowd of 199,854 in the deciding match at the Maracana Stadium in Rio. The game was refereed by England's George Reader, who later became chairman of Southampton. Brazil needed a draw to take the trophy, but the Uruguayans came from a goal down to win 2–1 and so lifted the Cup for a second time. Sweden beat Spain 3–1 to clinch third place.

Fortunately, some memorable club football compensated for the miserable England performances during the fifties. Tottenham's elegant push-and-run side, masterminded by manager Arthur Rowe, purred to the Second and First Division titles in successive years, 1949–50 and 1950–51. Alf Ramsey, Bill Nicholson, Ronnie Burgess and Eddie Baily were the key players. Joe Mercer's Arsenal refused to be overshadowed by their north London rivals, winning the FA Cup in 1950. That was Denis Compton's last match and his brother Leslie also collected a winner's medal. In the same year, Leslie became the oldest ever England debutant, aged thirty-eight. Arsenal were league champions in 1953.

The undisputed FA Cup kings of the fifties were Newcastle United. They completed the first of back-to-back FA Cup final victories in 1951, beating Blackpool and then Mercer-motivated Arsenal the following year. Among their heroes were the Chilean-born Robledo brothers, George and Ted, whose parents ran a restaurant in Barnsley, where the brothers kicked off their careers.

Victory over Manchester City gave Newcastle a third triumph in their favourite competition in 1955 but City battled their way back to Wembley the following year and this time had the satisfaction of

winning. Don Revie was the tactical genius who inspired Manchester City's 3–1 win over Birmingham City, the game in which
goalkeeper Bert Trautmann famously played through the last
minutes with a broken neck. Revie perfected a deep-lying
centre-forward role in the style of famous Hungarian Nandor
Hidegkuti, which became known in England as 'the Revie Plan'.

For the record, just three players appeared for Newcastle in all
three of those Cup final wins in the fifties – right-back Bobby
Cowell, dribbling winger Bobby Mitchell and 'Wor' Jackie Milburn,
who was idolised on Tyneside. As a lightning-fast centre-forward,
he lived up to his 'JET' initials.

For a nation now watching the FA Cup final each year on tiny
nine-inch black and white television screens, it seemed that all
roads led to Wembley. The competition with its mix of heroism and
heartbreak really caught the collective public imagination.

One player made four appearances at Wembley in the 1950s, and
every game was the talk of the football world. Step forward Ernie
'The Imp' Taylor. Those of a certain age will dip into the further
reaches of their minds to come up with a vintage memory of the wee
Wearsider, and all are bound to smile as they conjure up his image
because he was such a wonderfully entertaining player.

Sunderland-born Ernie was a shrimp of a footballer, barely 5ft
4ins tall and less than 9 stone wet through. He was a submariner
during the war, claiming that he was the only person on board the
same size as the torpedoes. Small he may have been, but Ernie was
big on talent, an inside-forward who could both scheme and score.

Long after he had hung up his size four boots he excavated these
memories of his first two Wembley appearances, in the FA Cup
finals of 1951 and 1953:

> I played for Newcastle against Blackpool in 1951 when 'Wor'
> Jackie scored two goals, the second from my back-heeled pass.
> When they later agreed to sell me to Blackpool for twenty-five
> thousand quid, skipper Joe Harvey went to the board and
> pleaded with them not to let me go. He said I made the team
> tick. 'Yes,' I said to Joe, 'I am like a ticking bomb and that's
> why they want me out!'
>
> They always call the 1953 final the Matthews final after we
> had come back from 3–1 down against Bolton to win 4–3,

when it should be the Stanleys final. Just before Stan Mortensen took his free kick to complete his hat-trick, I said to him, 'Bet you a tanner you miss.' As the ball hit the back of the net, he said, 'Sixpence you owe me, Ernest!'

Morty scored three of the goals against Bolton but it was the 'Wizard of Dribble' Matthews who conjured the victory with a series of knot-tying runs. The nation cried and sighed as he collected his first FA Cup medal at the age of thirty-eight after years of trying. Now he could retire in peace. The fact that he was still playing more than a dozen years later is one of the great footballing fairy stories.

Ernie Taylor played another game at Wembley in 1953. He got his one and only England cap for the November game against a bunch of alleged amateurs parading as Hungary. The Magical Magyars, driven by Ferenc Puskas, murdered England. Nandor Hidegkuti scored a hat-trick and Ernie's international career was over almost before it had started. That game also marked final England appearances for Alf Ramsey, Bill Eckersley, Harry Johnston, Stan Mortensen and George Robb.

The Hungarians trounced England 6–3 at Wembley and 7–1 in Budapest six months later. The defeat at Wembley was the first inflicted on home territory by a foreign team (not counting the 2–0 setback against the Republic of Ireland at Goodison in 1949), and the seven-goal tanking in Budapest remains the heaviest hiding ever suffered by an England team.

For the rest of his life, skipper Billy Wright remained haunted by a wondrous goal scored by the one and only Puskas during the first match. This is how Billy, shortly before his passing in 1994, recalled the moment that was burned into his memory:

It was as if the Hungarians had stepped off another planet. I will never be allowed to forget how Puskas controlled the ball with the sole of his left boot on the right side of the penalty area. As I made a challenge he pulled the ball back like a man loading a rifle and fired it into the net all in one sweet movement while I was tackling thin air. It was their third of four goals scored in the first half. Geoffrey Green, one of the finest of all football writers, described it beautifully in The Times. *He wrote that I went flying into the tackle like a fire engine going in the wrong direction for the blaze.*

I doubt if there has ever been a better executed goal at Wembley. I became good friends with Ferenc over the years, and we always laugh when discussing that goal. He said it was the most memorable of his career because it was at Wembley where he had always dreamed of playing. His dream was my nightmare. To this day I have never seen football to match that played by Hungary. They were a phenomenal side, and the result had enormous repercussions for our game.

It was the moment of truth. England could no longer claim to be the masters of world football. Walter Winterbottom led the inquests into the defeats, and the reality that England had fallen behind the times with their tactics and their technique had to be accepted. They were still playing the old-fashioned WM formation, with two full-backs, three half-backs and five forwards. The Hungarians played their No. 9 Nandor Hidegkuti as a deep-lying centre-forward and Blackpool skipper and centre-half Harry Johnston had no idea how to mark him. Hidegkuti played hide-and-seek, nipping in unseen for his hat-trick. Even the old men running football were forced to pull their heads out of the sand, and leading club managers were called together to be asked their opinions.

Winterbottom took careful note of their views and gradually training methods, playing tactics and style of kit were all changed. Out went the heavy boots, bulky shinpads, baggy shorts and shirts and the thick socks. Running around football pitches as the main part of training sessions was dropped in favour of more concentrated work with the ball. Appearance money for international players was increased from £30 to £50, which was the equivalent of more than three weeks' wages. Most importantly, the FA selectors accepted at last that they had to start listening to professional opinions, although they were not willing to go so far as to give up the job of picking the team.

The 1953–54 FA Cup tournament produced two major shocks. The first was that Third Division North team Port Vale battled all the way through to the semi-finals before going down to eventual Wembley winners West Bromwich Albion. The second was that Tom Finney did not manage to 'do a Matthews' and collect an FA Cup winner's medal with Preston. It would have been his first major medal but skipper Tom and his team-mates froze on their big day and were beaten 3–2. Ronnie Allen was the West Brom match hero with two goals, one from the penalty spot after Preston wing-half Tommy Docherty was adjudged to have fouled Ray Barlow. To this day, the Doc vehemently disputes the decision!

Most neutrals wanted to see Finney on the winning side as reward for a magnificent career. He was on a par with Matthews but never quite managed to gain the same place in the hearts of the general public outside Preston, where he was – and remains – the king. Ask professional players from that era to rate them and you will find the majority pick Finney as the superior all-round footballer. He did not have as many tricks in his locker as Stanley but he could play in any forward position and was capped in four of the five forward roles.

Finney scored what was then a record 30 goals for England in 76 matches, and another 187 league goals for Preston during a career in which he was never booked. A modest, gentle man, he was as great a sportsman as he was a footballer. It was a disgrace that he had to wait until 1998 to get a long overdue tap on the shoulder. Talk about a long day's journey into knighthood.

Throughout his career, Sir Tom ran a plumbing business – hence his nickname 'The Preston Plumber' – but even he could not plug the leaking holes in the England defence against the Hungarians in their 7–1 blitz in Budapest during the build-up to the 1954 World Cup finals. Perhaps the biggest shock of the whole decade was that the Hungarian side failed to win the World Cup in Switzerland. They went into the finals as the warmest favourites of all time. Olympic champions, they were shamateurs rather than amateurs because many of them were serving in the Hungarian Army and playing for the services side Honved. Ferenc Puskas was known as the Galloping Major, reflecting his rank, although he never ever galloped on a football pitch. He was always smooth and almost glided over the turf.

The Hungarians had gone four years without a single defeat, including crushing victories over both England and Scotland in home and away matches on their way to Switzerland. In their opening matches of the finals, they beat Korea 9–0 and an under-strength West Germany 8–3. Puskas was wickedly fouled in the match against the Germans and was limping heavily with an ankle injury by the end of the game. He later claimed that the tackle that damaged him had been a deliberate attempt to put him out of the tournament.

The Hungarians' concentration was interrupted more than somewhat by an ugly dressing-room brawl with the Brazilians after an ill-tempered quarter-final, which they won 4–2. The game became known as the Battle of Berne, with players from both sides trying to kick each other rather than the ball. English referee Arthur Ellis had to call the police to try to restore order after he had sent off two players for having a full-scale fist fight. It got even worse after the final whistle, with the Brazilians attacking the Hungarians in their dressing room. Players from both sides were cut and gashed by broken bottles in the most violent incident in World Cup history.

Minus the injured Puskas, Hungary had a scare in a classic semi-final against Cup-holders Uruguay. They led 2–0 at half-time but the Uruguayans pulled level in the second half to force extra time. Juan Hohberg was a coat of paint away from completing a hat-trick for Uruguay before Sandor 'Golden Head' Kocsis scored two of his typical headers to clinch a place for Hungary in the final against a now full-strength West Germany.

Hungary's long unbeaten record finally crashed, heartbreakingly for them, at the hurdle of the World Cup final. Puskas, less than 100 per cent fit, scored one goal and had another perfectly good-looking one ruled offside by English referee Bill Ling but the unheralded West Germans, splendidly marshalled by Fritz Walter, became the new champions with a 3–2 victory. Despite that defeat, the Hungarian team of the early 1950s will always be remembered as one of the greatest combinations ever to operate on a football pitch.

Both England and Scotland, qualifiers from the Home International Championship, were sent packing by Uruguay. The Scots, beaten 1–0 by Austria in their World Cup finals debut, were destroyed 7–0 by Uruguay. The match was played in a heatwave. 'We were given such a chasing that we came off at the final whistle with sunburned tongues,' was how Scottish right-half Tommy Docherty summed it up. Manager Andy Beattie, standing in for Matt Busby, resigned as Scotland manager during the tournament, following an argument over interference by the amateur selectors.

England, with Billy Wright switching to centre-half after winning 60 of his 105 caps at wing-half, battled through to the quarter-finals before Uruguay eliminated them with a comfortable 4–2 victory.

The quarter-final between Austria and host nation Switzerland produced one of the most remarkable of all World Cup matches. The Austrians were 3–0 down after 23 minutes. Ten minutes later they were leading 5–3. By half-time the score was 5–4 and Austria had missed a penalty. They finally won 7–5, all 12 goals coming in the space of just 49 minutes of playing time.

Two teams dominated the domestic scene in the 1950s, Manchester United and Wolves – Matt Busby against Stan Cullis, continuing a rivalry that had often featured on the pitch. Wolves' decade of achievement under Cullis deserves a prominent place in this history of the great game of football.

All that glistered on the English soccer scene during the 1950s were the old gold shirts of Wolves as they powered through a startling sequence of success.

After two team-building seasons when they flirted with life in the bottom half of the table, Wolves made a spirited challenge for the 1952–53 championship. They finally finished third behind Joe Mercer's Arsenal and Tom Finney's Preston, a race won on goal average by the north London giants. For Wolves, it was just a beginning. The next seven seasons were truly golden years.

Billy Wright was the chief motivator on the pitch for all but the final year of the decade, by which time he had voluntarily climbed off at the top of the mountain. While he was the heart of the team, master tactician Stan Cullis was the brains. Billy provided the drive, Cullis the direction.

Cullis famously put a heavy emphasis on fitness and strength, and the team gave the overall impression of muscularity and raw power. Yet there was also a thread of artistry running through the side, and they provided a procession of players for the England team.

The Wolves method of pumping long balls out of defence for their forwards to chase might appear to be a crude tactic on paper but on the pitch it was mightily effective. With sneering criticism of the method, so-called purists in the game dismissed it as 'kick-and-rush' but it was a goal rush. In their peak years, Wolves scored 878 goals and, astonishingly, topped the century mark in the First Division in four consecutive seasons.

The Cullis theory was a simple one. He argued that one long ball, accurately placed in the path of fast-moving attacking players, could do the work of three or four short passes and in half the time. The modern name for it would be route one. It was not particularly pretty, but it was extremely potent.

Cullis had been schooled by Major Frank Buckley, his famous predecessor as Wolves manager, who was a tough disciplinarian and a firm believer in the doctrine of quick and simple attacking football; also of discovering and developing young talent rather than raiding the transfer market. Cullis did not *buy* his teams – he *built* them, and many outstanding Wolves players came off the conveyor belt at Wath Wanderers, the Wolves nursery club in South Yorkshire, which was run for them on professional lines by former Molineux winger Mark Crook. Every Wolves team – from the 'cubs' through to the first team – was fashioned around the controversial but successful long-ball game.

With blond hero Wright as their shining role model, the Wolves youngsters were encouraged to battle for every ball as if their lives depended on it, and then to move it into the opposition penalty area as quickly as possible. The biggest sin any Wolves player could commit was to shirk a challenge – and to dwell on the ball instead of releasing it was rated nearly as serious. A player pulling out of a tackle knew he faced the even more unnerving experience of having to explain his action to the awesome Cullis, who considered football to be first and foremost a physical game. He was, remember, out of the 1930s school where barging and charging were a vital and integral part of the game.

To support his long-ball theories, Cullis made use of the computer-like mind of statistician Charles Reep, a football-loving wing commander who was stationed at RAF Bridgnorth, close to Wolverhampton. Reep had a system of plotting and recording in detail every move of a football match, and he fed Cullis with facts and figures to strengthen his argument that long, direct passes provided the most efficient and successful method of breaking down a defence. Cullis claimed that if too much time was spent in building up an attack with a series of short passes, it gave the opposition time to cover and allowed fewer opportunities for his forwards to shoot at goal.

For all the criticism of the Wolves style – or, rather, the alleged lack of it – nobody could dispute that the Cullis system brought startling results. Under the Cullis-Wright axis, Wolves were FA Cup winners in 1949, league champions in 1953–54, 1957–58 and 1958–59 and FA Cup winners again in 1960, the season after Billy Wright's retirement. They finished out of the top three in the First Division just three times between 1950 and 1961. In the same period, the reserves won the Central League title seven times and the youth team reached three FA Youth Cup finals. They narrowly missed a hat-trick of championships in 1959–60 when Burnley won their final match of the season. By beating Wolves to the title by a point, Burnley stopped them becoming the first team in the twentieth century to pull off the league and FA Cup double after they had beaten Blackburn 3–0 in the 1960 Wembley final.

In the first fifteen post-war seasons, Wolves' final positions in the First Division were 3, 5, 6, 2, 14, 16, 3, 1, 2, 3, 6, 1, 1, 2 and 3, and in each of the last four seasons they scored over a hundred league goals, a feat that remains unsurpassed. Wolves put together one of the most successful seasons ever achieved by an English club in 1957–58. They won the championship with a near-record 64 points, the reserves topped the Central League, the third team won the Birmingham and District League, the fourths carried off the Worcester Combination League and Cup, and the youth team won the FA Youth Cup.

From this golden era, Wolves will be best remembered for pioneering European club football under floodlights. They mastered the mightiest teams in Europe in a series of unofficial club championship matches at Molineux. Honved of Budapest – virtually the Hungarian national side that had ripped the heart out of the England team – Moscow Spartak, Moscow Dynamo and Real Madrid were all conquered in so-called 'friendlies'. The games were played at full throttle because of the enormous international prestige and pride involved.

These midweek evening games were screened live on television – a rarity in those days – and the exciting exploits of Wolves captured the nation's interest and imagination. The series proved to be a trailblazer for European inter-club competitions. The influential French sports newspaper *L'Equipe* noticed that English newspapers were calling Wolves the kings of Europe, and they proposed a proper competition to decide just who were the champions of

Europe. Typical of our insular football hierarchy, the European Cup kicked off in 1955–56 without English involvement, just as the World Cup had been allowed to start with British teams on the sidelines. The Football League and FA Cup competitions were seen as the be-all and end-all, and European football was considered a bridge too far.

After all Wolves' visionary groundwork, English clubs were virtually forbidden to compete in Europe – commencing with 1954–55 league champions Chelsea – in the 'Euro' controversy of the fifties. When Real Madrid, masterminded by the arrogant and artistic Argentinian Alfredo di Stefano, won the first of five successive European Cup finals, it hardly merited a mention in the English media. England had been left behind yet again. The Scots saw the potential of the tournament and allowed Hibs to enter. They reached the semi-final before being eliminated by Reims.

Meanwhile, Wolves – the club that did most to engineer interest in European club football – concentrated on domestic competition and battled with Manchester United for the unofficial mantle of England's greatest club side – the Cullis Cubs v. the Busby Babes.

Sir Matt Busby went on record near the close of his career with this assessment of the team that provided his greatest opposition:

> *Wolves in those days stood for everything that was good about British football. They played with great power, spirit and style. Their performances against top-class continental teams gave everybody in the game over here a lift. Stan Cullis moulded his teams in his own image. They were honest, straightforward, uncomplicated, and full of zest and determination.*

Matt Busby built his first great team when the nation was still living in the shadow of war. By the mid 1950s, he had laid the foundations of a second team that brought joy to the hearts of everybody lucky enough to see them in action. They were the incomparable, the almost unconquerable and, ultimately, the tragic Busby Babes.

Playing with staggering skill and panache, they won the league championship in 1955–56 by an overwhelming margin of 11 points (this, of course, still in the days of two points for a win). Never had the title been captured so conclusively and never by a younger team – their average age was under twenty-three. The Busby Babes scored 83 goals on the way to the title, going through the season without a single home defeat. Tommy Taylor (25 goals) and Dennis Viollet (20) netted more than half the goals between them. The following season, United scored 103 goals, beating Tottenham to the championship by 8 points. Liam Whelan (26 goals), Taylor (20), Viollet (16) and eighteen-year-old Bobby Charlton (10) were the leading marksmen.

While their main rivals, Wolves, were having equal success with the controversial long-ball game, United were performing with more style and sophistication. There was latitude as well as longitude to their lines of attack and their players were actively encouraged to make progress with the ball at their feet, rather than rush it forward in the Wolves way.

Busby Babes Roger Byrne, Duncan Edwards and Tommy Taylor were key men in the England team that took on and beat Brazil in a memorable international showdown at Wembley on 9 May 1956. It was billed as the 'Old World meets the New' and Brazil arrived with many of the players who, two years later, would win the World Cup in such dazzling fashion.

England got off to a flying start, with Tommy Taylor and Sheffield United inside-forward Colin Grainger scoring inside the first five minutes. The Brazilians pulled smoothly back to 2–2, and then John Atyeo and Roger Byrne each had a penalty saved by goalkeeper Gylmar. The penalty misses sandwiched a second goal by Taylor, laid on for him by Stanley Matthews, at his magical best against one of the all-time great left-backs, Nilton Santos.

There was a farcical hold-up following a dispute over a free kick quickly taken by Johnny Haynes. The ball was caught by Santos and the Brazilians staged a walk-off protest when the referee awarded a penalty. By the time peace was restored, it was no wonder that Bristol schoolteacher Atyeo failed with the spot-kick.

Grainger, who combined playing football with singing in a nightclub, crowned a memorable debut with a second goal five minutes from the end of one of the most exciting and dramatic games ever witnessed at Wembley – 4–2 to England.

Haynes asked forty-one-year-old Matthews for his autograph before the match. The old maestro's hands were shaking so much with nerves that he was unable to sign. By the end of the match it was Nilton Santos who was shaking at the knees after being given the run-around for one of the few times in his career. At the end of the game, he told Stanley, 'Mr Matthews, you are the king.'

In 1957, Aston Villa prevented United from pulling off the league and Cup double. Goalkeeper Ray Wood was carried off with a fractured cheekbone in the FA Cup final after a sickening collision with Irish international winger Peter McParland. Underdogs Villa won 2–1.

By 1958, the Busby Babes had developed into one of the most exciting and explosive combinations in world football, yet they were still not at the peak of their full power and potential when cruelly decimated by the horrific Munich air disaster.

United players Geoff Bent, Roger Byrne, Eddie Colman, Duncan Edwards, Mark Jones, David Pegg, Tommy Taylor and Liam Whelan were among those killed in Munich on 6 February 1958 on their way home from a successful European Cup quarter-final match against Red Star Belgrade.

Also among the dead were football journalists Alf Clarke, Don Davies, George Follows, Tom Jackson, Archie Ledbrooke, Henry Rose, Eric Thompson and former England goalkeeping hero Frank Swift, travelling as a *News of the World* reporter.

The heart had been ripped out of the Manchester United team but the legend of the Busby Babes lives on in the minds and the memories of all those privileged to have seen these young Saturday giants in action. Also, the mass loss of writing talent left national newspaper sports departments with vacancies and hurried forward many careers – a heartbreaking way for me to make an early entry into Fleet Street from the springboard of a local newspaper.

Just a few days before the Munich tragedy, on 1 February, the Babes played Arsenal at Highbury in what was to prove their final league match. There has never been a game quite like it. A crowd of 63,578 gathered to watch as United continued their bid to become the first post-war team to complete a hat-trick of league championships.

They also, of course, had their sights set on the European Cup, and four days after this Saturday showdown with the Gunners they were scheduled to play Red Star in the second-leg quarter-final tie in Belgrade.

Arsenal and the Busby Babes produced a game of football that deserves to be captured in oils rather than words. It looked as though it was all over bar the shouting, and the shooting, at half-time. United were leading 3–0 with goals from midfield giant Duncan Edwards, young blond inside-forward Bobby Charlton and England centre-forward Tommy Taylor. Remarkably, Arsenal pulled level early in the second half with three goals in three minutes. David Herd – soon to be a United player – scored the first, and Jimmy Bloomfield netted twice in sixty seconds.

The Babes took a deep breath and came straight back at Arsenal. Dennis Viollet headed in a Charlton cross and, with twenty minutes to go, Tommy Taylor scored an exquisite solo goal from the tightest of angles to make it 5–3.

Arsenal were down but not out. They clawed back another goal through Derek Tapscott before the final whistle signalled the end of an unforgettable encounter that was cheered and applauded non-stop for ten minutes by the lucky thousands who had witnessed it. Both sets of players knew they had taken part in something special, and they left the field arm in arm. The teams that day were:

Arsenal: Kelsey; Stan Charlton, Evans; Ward, Fotheringham, Bowen; Groves, Tapscott, Herd, Bloomfield, Nutt.

Manchester United: Gregg; Foulkes, Byrne; Colman, Jones, Edwards; Morgans, Bobby Charlton, Taylor, Viollet, Scanlon.

Five days later the Busby Babes were no more. Just twenty-four hours after a 3–3 draw in Belgrade had taken them into the European Cup semi-finals, the team's BEA Elizabethan airliner stopped off in Munich for refuelling. The plane crashed on take-off on the snow-bound runway at the horrendous cost of twenty-three lives.

That extraordinary match at Highbury took on extra significance. It serves as an epitaph for a great young team and the spirit in which they played their football. Would the Busby Babes have beaten Fergie's Fliers? There's another subject for endless argument.

Matt Busby miraculously survived the Munich air crash, fighting back from death's door to return to football. He had the courage, vision and character to build a new squad to carry on the standards set by the team that died at Munich. His efforts were justly rewarded when Bobby Charlton, another Munich survivor, led United to the European Cup in 1968. This achievement had seemed within the compass of the Busby Babes and it was fitting that their successors became the first English winners of that esteemed trophy. They could never have done it without the inspirational leadership of Busby, who well earned his unofficial title, 'Father of Football'.

Busby was a fiercely proud Scot, brought up close to poverty. His father and uncles had all been victims of the appalling First World War. Toughened by the environment in which he grew up, Busby could be stubborn and independent to the point of bloody-mindedness in the all-consuming cause of United.

In 1956, he went against the wishes of the Football League management committee and accepted an invitation for United to take part in the European Cup, a competition that the chiefs blindly believed should remain beneath the consideration of their clubs. All-conquering Real Madrid beat them 5–3 on aggregate in the semi-final, and they had again reached this stage of the competition at the time of the Munich crash. United became pioneers in Europe, and the terrible irony was that their boldness was to cost the lives of so many young flowers of English football.

With Busby's right-hand man Jimmy Murphy doing a splendid job as stand-in manager, United battled through to the 1958 FA Cup final just three months after the disaster. This was the irrepressible Ernie Taylor's fourth game at Wembley. He recalled:

> *You could wash your face in the tears of Manchester United fans that day. Jimmy Murphy got special dispensation to buy me from Blackpool just days after the Munich air crash. Bolton beat us 2–0 in the final after Nat Lofthouse had committed grievous bodily harm on our goalkeeper Harry Gregg. But no complaints. That was the way the game was played then. We had wanted so badly to win the game for Matt Busby, who had been allowed out of hospital to watch the final. But it wasn't to be. Lofty saw to that with his two goals. It couldn't have happened to a nicer bloke than the old Lion.*

Nat Lofthouse would forever be known as the 'Lion of Vienna' after scoring a sensational goal for England in the Austrian capital on 25 May 1952. Eight minutes from the end, with the game deadlocked at 2–2, Tom Finney collected a long throw from goalkeeper Gil Merrick, and quickly made a pass that sent Lofty clear just inside the Austrian half. He galloped forty-five yards with a pack of defenders snapping at his heels, and collided with oncoming goal-keeper Musil as he released a low shot. Flat out, unconscious, he was the only person in the packed Prater Stadium who did not see the ball roll over the line for the winning goal. The Bolton hero was carried off on a stretcher but, still dazed, returned for the final five minutes. He struck a shot against a post in the closing moments.

Here's a fact about the Bolton team that Nat led to victory over Manchester United in the 1958 FA Cup final that illustrates how times – and fortunes – have changed. The Bolton team cost exactly £110 to put together, their £10 signing-on fees. Six of the team were Lancashire lads, true local heroes. Each of them was on £20 a week, and their individual bonus for winning the Cup was £50. The entire team picked up between them less than today's players would spend on champagne on a night out.

The Munich disaster had serious ramifications beyond Old Trafford. England had lost three key players in left-back Roger Byrne, centre-forward Tommy Taylor and the young wonder Duncan Edwards, who every professional from that era will say was one of the greatest all-rounders ever to set foot on a football pitch.

They always say you can remember where you were and what you were doing the day John F. Kennedy died. The same can be said for any English football followers who were around in 1958. This was how England skipper Billy Wright remembered it:

How could I ever forget that terrible day! It was a Thursday and it coincided with my thirty-fourth birthday. I was feeling nice and chirpy as I made my way back from training on the bus. I had a little Ford by then, but used to lend it to my landlady's son, Arthur Colley, so that he could drive to work. Arthur and I shared the same birthday – February 6. So that morning we had had our usual routine of singing 'Happy Birthday' to each other and I left the Colley house with a smile on my face.

I was sitting day-dreaming on the bus after our training session when I spotted a billboard outside a newsagent's that screamed, 'Man United Air Crash!' I could not believe what I was seeing. We were due to play them on the Saturday and had been discussing how to try to counter their wonderful football.

I jumped off at the next stop and bought the Wolverhampton

Express & Star. *The stop press story was a first report that the Manchester United plane had crashed on take-off. It said that many were feared dead, but at that stage there were no names.*

Over the course of the next couple of hours we slowly learned the horrible facts. As well as the players, many of my good friends among the football writers had perished.

Along with everybody else, I spent the next twenty-four hours almost permanently weeping over the cruel loss of so many friends and colleagues.

If there could be such a thing as good news from an incident like this, we heard that young Bobby Charlton had escaped unhurt and that Matt Busby and Duncan Edwards were injured but likely to live. So it was more tears two weeks later when that young giant Duncan finally lost his battle for life. That hurt more than anything because he represented the future of our game. Big Dunc, as we called him, was at least three years short of his peak, and he could already be rated in the 'genius' bracket.

It was all so tragic, and away from the personal sadness there were the wider repercussions that our national football team had been dealt a mortal blow. Yes, you could say that was a birthday I would rather forget.

A measure of the effect the crash had on the England football team can be found in the statistics. From beating world champions West Germany at Wembley in 1954 with that Len Shackleton chipped goal, England had won 16 and drawn eight of 25 internationals, losing just one. After Munich and up to Billy Wright's 105th and final game in 1959, England won six and drew six of 20 international matches, losing eight.

You do not need to be a football expert to realise that this record would have been greatly improved had Roger Byrne, Duncan Edwards and Tommy Taylor been available for selection. Their loss meant that England had been weakened in every department – defence, midfield and attack.

No team in the world could have afforded to lose players of this calibre and still have hoped to make an impressive impact in the World Cup finals in Sweden in the summer of 1958. The tournament was to be dominated by a magnificent team from Brazil, and they introduced a new player who was to become a force in world football. Enter Pele!

Since the first World Cup finals in 1930, Brazil had been exhibitionists extraordinary, continually tripped up by their suspect temperament whenever the major prize was within shooting distance. Critics sniffed that they were jugglers who became clowns when the pressure was at its peak. In the 1958 World Cup they set out with steely determination to prove they could win as well as entertain, and they beat Sweden 5–2 in a memorable final in Stockholm.

The Swedes took a 1–0 lead in the fourth minute through Nils Liedholm, later to become one of the world's finest coaches. It was the first time Brazil had been behind in the tournament. They hit back with purpose, giving full rein to their 'samba soccer' on a rain-sodden surface. Vava equalised in the ninth minute and scored again in the thirtieth, both goals created by the ball-playing Garrincha.

Ten minutes into the second half, the young prodigy Pele produced a moment of magic, signalling that here was a glittering talent for all to enjoy for years to come. Positioned in the heart of the Swedish penalty area, with his back to the goal, he caught a high, dropping ball on his thigh, hooked it over his head, whirled round close-marking centre-half Gustavsson in time to meet the ball on the volley and sent it powering into the net. It was pure poetry.

Mario Zagalo, who went on to manage Brazil's 1970 World Cup winning team, beat two defenders before shooting their fourth goal in the seventy-seventh minute. In the hectic closing stages, Agne Simonsson reduced the lead before Pele applied the finishing touch with a deftly headed goal from Zagalo's centre.

Brazil had unveiled a new formation to international football – 4-2-4, a variation on the system the Hungarians had introduced in the immediate post-war years. They illuminated a tournament in which Wales and Northern Ireland did the United Kingdom proud by reaching the quarter-finals. Scotland went out as bottom club in their pool, while England lost a play-off to Russia.

Wales may have fared even better but for an injury to the magnificent John Charles. Equally brilliant whether at centre-half or centre-forward, the former Leeds United star was arguably the greatest of all British footballers. He is rarely included in 'Top 10' lists because he spent his peak years with Juventus, where he was hero-worshipped as *Il Buono Gigante*, the Gentle Giant. John had cost a then record £65,000 when joining Juventus from Leeds in April 1957. If he were playing at his peak today, his transfer fee would have gone some way towards clearing the huge debts accumulated by Leeds. It was only after his death in February 2004 that John was given the domestic acclaim he deserved as a true master of the game.

Pele made a World Cup scoring debut against Wales – minus Charles – and that goal put Wales out of the tournament. Pele had been summoned into the side, along with Garrincha, after England had become the only team to hold the Brazilians to a goalless draw. Clever defensive tactics worked out by future Spurs manager Bill Nicholson, Walter Winterbottom's right-hand man in Sweden, were the main reason for that.

The England selectors came in for unmerciful media criticism for a series of blunders. They took a squad of twenty players when twenty-two were allowed, leaving behind Stanley Matthews, Nat Lofthouse and two young goalscoring machines called Jimmy Greaves and Brian Clough. They included Bobby Charlton in the squad after he had scored spectacular goals against Scotland and Portugal in his first two international appearances within just a few weeks of the Munich air disaster. Then, for some unfathomable reason, they did not select him for any of the games.

While it was Pele who got most of the headlines after his hat-trick against France in the semi-final and his two goals in the final, Brazil had an even more fascinating character in Garrincha.

There has never been another footballer in the same mould as Garrincha, a nickname meaning 'Little Bird'. Manoel Francisco dos Santos was born a cripple in the mountain village of Pau Grande in 1933. An operation left one leg shorter than the other and both legs were so bowed you could have run a pig through them without him knowing. After the operation he had what were virtually two left feet, and he used to wear two left boots when playing. This helped him confuse defenders, and when there was a ball at his feet he could be the most bewildering, bewitching and stunning winger on the planet, like a speeded-up version of Stanley Matthews.

He was such an individualist that even Brazilian coaches, with their preaching of freedom of expression, were petrified of his independent spirit. It was only after a deputation of his team-mates had pleaded on his behalf that he was selected for his World Cup debut after being left on the sidelines for the first two games.

Garrincha's contribution to the World Cup victories of 1958 and 1962 was greater than anybody else's. He tried to motivate the Brazilians again in 1966 but a cartilage operation and injuries sustained in a car smash had robbed him of much of his magic. He won 68 caps while playing for Botafogo, Corinthians and Flamengo, and got as much publicity for his wild off the pitch lifestyle as his extraordinary performances with the ball at his odd feet.

Along with Wales, Northern Ireland were the surprise team of the tournament. Inspired by manager Peter Doherty, and with Danny Blanchflower and Jimmy McIlroy pulling the strings in midfield, they battled through to the quarter-finals. They were handicapped by injuries to key players, and were finally eliminated by a French team that had two of the tournament's major stars in Raymond Kopa and Just Fontaine. With Real Madrid maestro Kopa providing the passes, Fontaine scored a World Cup record thirteen goals. He now lives in a house in France called *Treize*.

The fifties were a busy decade for football and the major events often distract attention from some other extraordinary happenings. For instance, Pegasus, the 'new Corinthians' made up of graduates from Oxford and Cambridge, drew a crowd of 100,000 to Wembley for the 1951 FA Amateur Cup final against Bishop Auckland. Without a ground of their own, Pegasus won seven away games on the way to the final, which, much to the delight of neutrals, they won 2–1.

On 28 November 1951, in the 2–2 draw with Austria at Wembley, Arsenal right-winger and Gloucestershire opening bat Arthur Milton made it into the record books when he became the last player to be capped by England at both cricket and football.

Irish international Charlie Tully scored a goal direct from an inswinging corner. He was playing for Celtic against Falkirk in a Scottish Cup tie on 20 February 1953. Ordered to take it again, he promptly repeated the trick.

Leicester City's Arthur Rowley, signed from Fulham, scored a hat-trick in both home and away league matches against his old club in 1952–53. They went towards his all-time scoring record of

434 league goals. His brother Jack Rowley, who played for Manchester United, was reckoned by many to have the hardest shot in the League. He once scored four goals for England in a 1949 international match against Northern Ireland.

Derek Dooley, barnstorming Sheffield Wednesday centre-forward, had to have his right leg amputated after a collision with the Preston goalkeeper in a league match on 14 February 1953. He had scored a remarkable 46 goals in 30 league games the previous season.

The Charles brothers – John and Mel – and the Allchurch brothers – Ivor and Len – all played for Wales against Northern Ireland in Belfast on 20 April 1955. John scored a hat-trick in a 3–2 victory.

Floodlights were switched on for the first time in an FA Cup tie on 28 November 1955 when Carlisle played Darlington in a second-round replay at Newcastle. The first league match played under lights was Portsmouth against Newcastle on 22 February 1956, and the first in Scotland was when Rangers beat Queen of the South 8–0 at Ibrox on 7 March 1956.

Stanley Matthews played his final match for England in Copenhagen on 15 May 1957 – a World Cup qualifier in which England beat Denmark 4–1. He was forty-two and this fifty-fourth cap came twenty-two years after his first one.

The first Scottish championship won by Hearts was achieved in extraordinary fashion in 1957–58. They lost only one of their 34 league matches, and scored a record 132 goals, conceding just 29. Rangers trailed in second 13 points behind.

And now for something completely different – fasten your safety belts for an action replay of one of the most extraordinary matches in the history of the Beautiful Game. The venue – the Valley. The date – 21 December 1957. The teams – Charlton Athletic at home to Huddersfield Town, managed by Bill Shankly, two years away from starting to build his legend at Liverpool.

Charlton were reduced to ten men early in the first half when their skipper and England international centre-half Derek Ufton was carried off with a broken collar bone. Huddersfield were 2–0 up at half-time, and cantering.

Within seven minutes of the second half, Huddersfield had rocketed 5–1 ahead, the one Charlton goal coming from the right boot of veteran left-winger Johnny Summers.

Huddersfield started to stroll around with the confident air of a team that, understandably, considered they had the game won. After all, they were easily dismantling a defence missing its best player and that had conceded 120 goals when being relegated from the First Division the previous season. With just thirty minutes to go, it would need one of the comebacks of the century for Charlton to save the game.

Cue Summers. He scored a second goal with a right-foot shot, and a minute later set up team-mate John Ryan for another. Charlton 3, Huddersfield 5. During the next ten minutes, Summers added three more goals – all with his right foot – taking his tally to five. Charlton 6, Huddersfield 5.

Amazing? You ain't seen nuttin' yet.

In the eighty-eighth minute, shell-shocked Huddersfield gathered themselves for one more charge and snatched an equaliser. Enough's enough. The Valley crowd was dizzy with the excitement of it all, many of them no longer sure what the score was, but Johnny Summers had one more trick up his sleeve. He dashed down the left wing and sent a last-minute pass into the path of Ryan, who hammered it into the net. Charlton 7, Huddersfield 6.

No pressman had the courage to tell Shankly that this was the first time in Football League history that a team had scored six goals and finished on the losing side. For once in his life, Shankly was speechless.

Summers, a chirpy Cockney who had travelled the football roundabout with Fulham, Norwich and Millwall, commented, 'I wore these boots for the first time today, and I have never scored a goal with my right foot before. Today I got all five with my right. Amazing, ain't it?'

At the age of just thirty-three, lovely Johnny Summers was cut down by cancer. Suddenly, it was winter – but those lucky enough to have been at the Valley on that astonishing afternoon in December 1957 will always be warmed by the memory of that Summers day.

Another goal-gorged game was set in London nearly a year later, on 11 October 1958. Tottenham beat Everton 10–4 at White Hart Lane in Bill Nicholson's first match in charge. Tiny schemer Tommy 'The Charmer' Harmer laid on six goals and said after the match, 'Don't expect us to do this every week, Boss.'

Billy Wright became the first player in the world to win 100 international caps when he led England out against Scotland at Wembley on 11 April 1959. Watched by his singer wife Joy, of the Beverley Sisters, six days after the arrival of their first child, Billy was chaired off at the end of the game, which England won 1–0 with a Bobby Charlton header.

Billy had started that season with a wake-up call when he played in a Wolves defence destroyed by Chelsea wonderkid Jimmy Greaves at Stamford Bridge. At eighteen, Greavsie was the youngest player to score five league goals in a match, a feat he achieved three times. It was after this game that thirty-five-year-old Billy decided he would be hanging up his boots at the end of the season.

One player was keeping pace with Greavise. At Middlesbrough, Brian Clough led the Second Division marksmen, for the second successive season, with 42 goals.

Wembley FA Cup finals were continually being ruined by injuries in the days before substitutes were allowed, and one of the worst was the 1959 final in which Nottingham Forest beat Luton 2–1. Roy Dwight, scorer of the first Forest goal, was carried off with a broken leg after thirty-two minutes. His tearful young cousin Reg was watching from the stands. Reg Dwight would shed tears again at Wembley when, as Watford chairman – and by then better known as Elton John – he sat in the royal box watching Everton beat his team 2–0 in the 1984 final.

In the last major transfer of the decade, Matt Busby broke the British record by buying Albert Quixall from Sheffield Wednesday for £45,000. It was worked out that our Albert was worth his weight in gold.

Now a golden decade beckoned – the sixties, when the players at last broke the shackles of soccer slavery and England – yes, England – ruled the world.

CHAPTER 10

1966 AND ALL THAT

E NGLAND'S 1966 World Cup triumph deserves a chapter to itself! English fans had waited an eternity, suffered the slings and arrows of outrageous fortune and had often witnessed the powers that be shooting themselves in both feet, unable to do anything about it. Now, at long last, the country that gave football to the world were the true masters. OK, it was a brief reign that possibly took the game back a couple of paces, but for a short spell in the mid sixties, England were on top of the world.

The man who made it all possible was Alf Ramsey, who had earned the nickname 'The General' when playing at right-back for the famous 'push-and-run' Tottenham team of the early 1950s. He took his tactical ideas to the football outpost of Ipswich, and in his first job in management turned a bunch of has-beens, no-hopers and misfits into the 1962 league champions.

Ramsey won the title against all the odds by introducing a system that completely foxed opposition defences. He played Scottish left-winger Jimmy Leadbetter in a withdrawn position to make a line of three players across the midfield. He had replaced the favoured 4–2–4 formation with 4–3–3. Little did anybody realise that a World Cup-winning plan had been hatched on the playing fields of sleepy Suffolk.

The championship triumph so impressed the Football Association that they turned to Ramsey to succeed Walter Winterbottom as

England manager in 1962, after Burnley's Jimmy Adamson had turned down what he saw as a poisoned chalice. Alf took the job only on the understanding that *he* would pick the team, putting the amateur selectors out of work and their noses out of joint. They would get their own back one day.

Ramsey was a man who, with his Romany ancestry, literally had gypsy in his soul. When – metaphorically speaking – he looked into his crystal ball six months before the 1966 finals and predicted that 'England will win the World Cup', more people should have taken notice instead of smirking.

Usually as mean with his quotes as a miser is with his money, Ramsey stepped out of character when he made that public statement. He tossed aside his customary cloak of caution and went against history – it was thirty-two years since the host country had won the tournament.

There was a grand bit of fun before the World Cup shooting started. The Football Association managed to lose the precious Jules Rimet trophy, which was stolen while on show at a stamp exhibition in Westminster just weeks before the kick-off to the greatest football show on earth.

A massive police and public hunt was launched and just when it looked as if football's greatest trophy had disappeared into the smelter's pot, it was unearthed by a dog called Pickles, who sniffed it out from its hiding place under a bush in Norwood, south London. Pickles and his owner, Dave Corbett, collected a £6,000 reward and a man who had demanded a £15,000 ransom for the return of the Cup was jailed for two years.

The FA learned their lesson and chairman Joe Mears – owner of Chelsea long before the Ken Bates and Roman Abramovich dynasties – secretly arranged to have a copy made. All those films and photographs you see of England players parading the trophy in the weeks after the triumph have one thing in common – it is not the real Jules Rimet trophy but a replica, which is now on show at the National Football Museum in Preston.

What happened to the original Jules Rimet trophy? It was won outright by Brazil and they managed to lose it, too, when it was stolen in 1983. This time there was no Pickles around to sniff it out and it has never been seen since.

Major trophies are now used for presentation ceremonies only, and are quickly replaced by replicas. Nobody will confirm it but you can be sure that the Rugby World Cup that was paraded through London following England's triumph in 2003 was not the real thing.

Back in 1966, outsiders found it difficult to understand Alf Ramsey's pre-tournament confidence during the group matches. England made heavy work of a goalless draw with Uruguay, and hardly set the Wembley grass alight with victories over Mexico and France.

In a bitterly fought quarter-final, England accounted for a talented but temperamental Argentinian side 1–0 after their wonderfully skilled skipper Antonio Rattin had been ordered off because of his contemptuous attitude towards the West German referee, Rudolf Kreitlin. He later explained, 'I sent him off because of a look in his eyes. I did not need to speak his language. The look on his face was enough to show that he thought that he was in charge of things. Only one of us could referee the game, and it was not going to be him. His arrogance and defiance caused great disruption.'

It took the English head of the referees' panel, Ken Aston, working with interpreters on the touchline, ten minutes to restore order as the entire Argentinian team threatened to walk off. Rattin, one of the most talented players in the tournament, took five minutes to saunter around the perimeter of the pitch and in to the dressing rooms, leaving chaos and confusion in his wake. There had never been such a commotion in a game of this importance. The Argentinians saw it as a European plot and, back in Buenos Aires, embassies were attacked.

The winning goal against Argentina was scored by West Ham striker Geoff Hurst, who was making his World Cup debut because of an injury to Jimmy Greaves. Even greater things were to come from a player who just five years earlier had been a nondescript wing-half on the fringe of the West Ham first-team.

For the first time in the tournament, England had played without a recognised winger as Alf went to the source of his success at Ipswich. England's 'Wingless Wonders' were born in that quarter-final, and their 4–3–3 formation was to change the face of football. There would be many imitators and almost overnight touchline-hugging wingers started to disappear from sight.

While everything started to go to plan for England, the tournament turned into a sorry shambles for defending champions Brazil, who were bidding for a hat-trick, following their successes in Sweden in 1958 and in Chile in 1962. Pele was literally kicked out of the tournament in a rough-house group in which they beat Bulgaria 2–0 before going down 3–1 to Hungary and then by the same result to Portugal.

The Portuguese had one of the major stars of the finals in Eusebio, their 'Black Panther' from Benfica via Mozambique. He was the top scorer with an aggregate of nine goals, four of them coming in an amazing quarter-final match against North Korea. The Koreans, a totally unknown entity who had been training together for four years in the guise of being an army side, managed to beat Italy in their group match, and the Italians went home early to a barrage of rotten tomatoes from their traumatised supporters.

North Korea rushed into a 3–0 lead against Portugal at Goodison, and another stunning result seemed inevitable. Then Eusebio took over with one of the greatest one-man shows ever witnessed on a football field. Almost single-handedly, he hauled Portugal back into the game with four goals in thirty-two minutes, propelling his side to a breathtaking 5–3 victory.

Ramsey's 'we will win' prediction gathered a bandwagon of support when England sparkled to a 2–1 win over Eusebio-engineered Portugal in a high-quality semi-final that revealed Bobby Charlton in all his splendour and erased the memory of much of the tedium and tantrums of the early matches. This was the performance that convinced Ramsey he should select the same side for the final, which meant there was no place for fit-again Jimmy Greaves who was, without question, the greatest goal striker of modern times.

That statement can easily be substantiated – Greaves scored an all-time record 357 First Division goals, 44 goals in 57 England games, and 491 goals in all competitions. There was nobody to touch him for knowing how to put the ball in the net. My close friend Jimmy and I once worked it out that 90 per cent of his goals came from inside the penalty area. Of those, 60 per cent were scored with his left foot, 38 per cent with his right and 2 per cent with his head ('I wanted an aspirin if ever I headed those old leather footballs,' joked Jimmy). He played all his football when tackling from behind was allowed, and defenders such as Norman 'Bites Yer Legs' Hunter, Peter 'Cold Eyes' Storey, Ron 'Chopper' Harris, Nobby 'The Toothless Tiger' Stiles and Tommy 'The Iron' Smith were prowling the pitch, all of whom are now bruises on the memory. Goodness knows how many goals Jimmy would have scored in today's game in which hard physical contact has all but disappeared.

It was a calculated gamble by Ramsey to leave Greaves on the sidelines against a powerful West German team that had reached the final with a quarter-final elimination of Uruguay and a semi-final win over the USSR.

In Uwe Seeler, Sigi Held and Helmut Haller the Germans had a striking force that could devastate any defence if given freedom of movement, and lurking out on the left was the tricky but unpredictable Lothar Emmerich, who possessed one of the fiercest left-foot shots in the game.

Motivating the team from midfield were the composed, twenty-year-old Franz Beckenbauer and the elegant, left-footed pass master Wolfgang Overath. They had strength in depth in defence, with Horst Höttges and Karl-Heinz Schnellinger giving them flair at full-back, while Willie Schulz and Wolfgang Weber were solid and reliable partners at the heart of the defence. The one big question mark was against goalkeeper Hans Tilkowski, whom the England players had nicknamed Dracula because he seemed so frightened of crosses.

The teams for this most important game in the history of English football were:

England (in 4–3–3 formation): Banks; Cohen, Jack Charlton, Moore, Wilson; Stiles, Bobby Charlton, Peters; Ball, Hunt, Hurst.

West Germany (in 4–2–4 formation): Tilkowski; Höttges, Schulz, Weber, Schnellinger; Beckenbauer, Overath; Haller, Seeler, Held, Emmerich.

Two sharp showers just before the kick-off made the surface of the Wembley pitch quick and treacherous. Players on both sides showed nerves that were as exposed as barbed wire on a wall, and there was so much tension around that it was inevitable a goal was going to be born out of an error. What nobody expected was that the mistake would be made by the most reliable of all England's players – the cool, commanding Ray Wilson, who had not put a foot wrong at left-back throughout the tournament.

The game was into its thirteenth minute when Wilson seemed to have time and room in which to clear a Sigi Held cross. But instead of his usual pinpoint accuracy, he pushed the ball to the feet of Helmut Haller, a deadly enough marksman without need of such charitable assistance. Haller turned and squeezed a low shot just inside the left post from twelve yards. England 0, West Germany 1.

The home fans tried to console themselves with the fact that the World Cup had not been won by the side that scored first in any of the four post-war finals.

After this sloppy goal, England revealed the discipline and determination that Alf Ramsey had drilled into them during the build-up to the finals. There was no hint of panic or loss of composure. The unflappable Wilson carried on in his usual immaculate style with a poker-face manner that was to serve him well in his later profession as a funeral director.

If anything, the goal acted as an inspiration to England and they began to settle into their stride. They were rewarded for their professional attitude with an equaliser just six minutes later. Overath tripped Bobby Moore and the England skipper took an instant free kick while the German defenders were still regrouping. He floated the ball in from the left and his West Ham team-mate Geoff Hurst drifted behind the German defence to glide a header wide of Tilkowski, who was still feeling the effects of an early collision with Hurst in which he was briefly knocked out.

The action was fast and fluctuating with neither side able to claim domination. West German team manager Helmut Schöen had watched England's victory against Portugal in the semi-final, and he had been so impressed by a phenomenal display from Bobby Charlton that he delegated Beckenbauer to do a man-for-man marking job on the Manchester United schemer. This meant that the two most creative players on the pitch were cancelling each other out.

Roger Hunt squandered a good chance to give England the lead and thoughts briefly arose that Ramsey had been wrong to leave Greaves on the sidelines in these pre-substitute days. However,

England were gradually getting on top, particularly down the right side of the pitch where Alan Ball, the twenty-one-year-old 'baby' of the England team, was providing action to go with his words. He had told room-mate Nobby Stiles before the match, in that Clitheroe Kid voice of his, 'That Schnellinger's made for me. I'll give him such a chasing that he won't know what day it is.'

It was fitting that the red-shirted, red-haired Ball – covering every inch of the right side of the Wembley pitch like the fire from a flamethrower – should set up what most people thought was the match-winning goal twelve minutes from the end. His shot was pushed out by Tilkowski for a corner that the Blackpool marathon runner took himself. The ball dropped at the feet of Hurst, whose shot was deflected by Höttges into the path of West Ham man-of-all-parts Martin Peters. He almost had enough time to pick his spot as he clinically buried the ball in the back of the net from six yards.

The Germans looked out on their feet and a growing victory roar rolled around Wembley. The cheers died in thousands of throats when, with less than a minute to go, Swiss referee Gottfried Dienst harshly ruled that Jack Charlton had fouled Germany's spring-heeled skipper Uwe Seeler.

Emmerich, who had hardly been allowed a kick by his marker George Cohen, crashed the free kick towards goal with his feared left foot. The ball was deflected – Bobby Moore argued that it was by a German hand – to Held, who half hit the ball across the face of the goal. Gordon Banks, the outstanding goalkeeper of the tournament, was wrong-footed because he had reacted for a clean shot from Held. The ball bobbled loose to defender Wolfgang Weber, who bundled it into the England net with the last kick of ordinary time.

Players of both sides tumbled to the ground with sheer fatigue as the referee's whistle signalled extra time. Alf Ramsey came striding purposefully on to the pitch and did a quick walkie-talkie tour of his players, offering them encouragement and advice. He pointed to the drained West German players. 'Look at them,' he said. 'They're finished. You've beaten them once. Now go and do it again.'

The fiercely competitive Nobby Stiles, socks rolled down to his ankles and teeth removed, flourished a fist at his team-mates. He knew he owed Ramsey extra effort. The England manager had threatened to resign earlier in the tournament after Football

Association officials had suggested he drop the Manchester United warrior following a bone-shaking tackle during the match against France.

'Come on, lads,' Stiles said in his thick Mancunian accent. 'Let's stoof the boogers.' Battling Alan Ball responded with a run and a shot in the second minute of extra time that brought a fine save from Tilkowski, who had shaken off his early indecision.

Eight minutes later, after a Bobby Charlton shot from a pass by brother Jack had been turned on to a post, Ball tore past the shattered Schnellinger yet again. This time his centre found Geoff Hurst who spun round and crashed a shot against the underside of the bar. As the ball bounced down, Roger Hunt – the England player closest to the net – immediately whirled round in celebration of a goal. His opinion was supported by Russian linesman Tofik Bakhramov, who signalled with a vigorous nod of the head that the ball had crossed the line, a decision disputed to this day by the Germans.

Skipper Seeler called for one more effort from team-mates who had run themselves to the edge of exhaustion. Beckenbauer, at last released from his negative containment of Bobby Charlton, pushed forward from midfield and was shaping to shoot when he was dispossessed by a tigerish tackle from the resolute Stiles, who was displaying the brand of courage and willpower for which medals are awarded in the field of battle.

Then Haller powered his way through the middle only to be foiled by the long legs of Jack Charlton. The Germans were so committed to all-out attack that they were leaving inviting gaps in their own penalty area.

Celebrating England fans – actually, they were match stewards – were trespassing over the touchline in anticipation of the final whistle when hero-of-the-hour Hurst ended all arguments in the closing seconds of the match. He chased a measured forty-yard pass from the majestic Moore and hammered in a left-foot shot that left Tilkowski rooted in front of his goal like a man facing a firing squad.

BBC commentator Kenneth Wolstenholme roared the memorable words, 'There are people on the pitch . . . they think it's all over . . . *it is now.*'

With virtually the last kick of the match, Hurst had become the first man to score a World Cup final hat-trick, and for the first time the World Cup had come to the birthplace of organised football.

Excuse me for painting myself into this picture of England's finest footballing hour, but not only was I there, collecting quotes for the *Daily Express*, I was also the only journalist to set foot inside the England dressing room as they celebrated their victory.

Len Went, the public relations officer at Wembley and an old friend of mine, nodded and winked me past the security men who had dropped their guard in what were euphoric moments. I managed to hug Bobby Moore, who had been starting out as an apprentice at West Ham at the same time as I was serving my writing apprenticeship on the local newspaper.

Then I felt Alf Ramsey's withering gaze, letting me know I was not welcome. He allowed me a perfunctory shake of his hand, and said, 'You know the rules.'

Even during this greatest victory of his life, Alf was a stickler for discipline. His contention was always that the dressing room – and anything said and done in there – was sacrosanct.

As I backed out into the corridor, I at least had the satisfaction of having tasted a privileged moment of the glory. Ever since, I have boasted 'I was there,' leaving out the minor fact that I was ushered out of the dressing room after just a couple of minutes. What is it about football that it can have the same effect on a man as alcohol? I was drunk with the exhilaration of England's success, and later wrote a personal letter of apology to Alf for breaking his golden rule.

Ramsey, knighted for his glorious deeds of '66, spoke later, away from the frenzy of the dressing room:

Every player did England proud. They showed tremendous character in extra time and thoroughly deserved their victory. It was not an easy decision to leave out Jimmy Greaves, but I felt that this was the right team for the job we faced.

Yes, of course, it was difficult having to omit Jimmy – just as it was tough having to leave out ten other players in the squad. They have all played their part simply by being here.

Our team spirit on and off the pitch – I would call it a club spirit – has been a key factor in our success. It has been suggested that I seemed less than happy at the final whistle but the reason I could not leap to my feet was simply because I was pinned down by trainer Harold Shepherdson and team doctor

*Alan Bass, who were so busy congratulating me that I was
unable to get off the bench.*

Helmut Schöen, the dignified West German manager, said:

*We could argue that Geoff Hurst's second goal did not cross
the line, but why waste breath? The referee and linesman said
it was a goal so that is all there is to it. It would be a pity to
have controversy spoil an occasion in which the game of
football was a winner. It was a splendid match and I concede
that England on the day were just that little bit better than us.
But only a little bit. Allowing for the fact that the game was
played on their home ground of Wembley, I thought we did
very well. On another day and on another pitch, I think we
could have beaten them.*

Alan Ball, who rivalled Geoff Hurst as man of the match, said:

*I died several times out on that pitch. It was really exhausting,
but I kept telling myself that this was the most important
match of my life and that we* had *to win it.*

Martin Peters, the player Ramsey was to describe as ten years ahead
of his time, commented:

*I will never forget the goal I scored. I had time to place my shot
and knew it was going into the net from the moment I made
contact. It was the greatest moment of my career, and I
thought it was going to be the winner until that last-minute
equaliser. Geoff went on to complete his hat-trick and few
people were able to recall who scored our other goal. But for me
it will always be a treasured memory. The only thing that
surprised us all was that Jimmy Greaves didn't get to play, and
we all felt choked for him.*

Four years later, Martin moved from West Ham when he became
football's first £200,000 player. Moving in the opposite direction as
a makeweight part of the deal – Jimmy Greaves.

West Ham manager Ron Greenwood transformed Geoff Hurst's
career – and his life – when he switched him from the role of 'just
another' half-back to a striker who could demolish defences with
his pace and power. The son of a non-league professional, Hurst

was born in Ashton-under-Lyne, Lancashire, on 8 December 1941. He was selected for the England squad for the first time in the 1965–66 season, making his debut in a 1–0 victory over West Germany in a friendly international at Wembley on 23 February 1966. He scored 24 goals in 49 matches for England. His league goals haul for West Ham was 180. He added 30 league goals for Stoke before moving on to West Bromwich Albion.

After that, he became player-manager of Telford United, assisted Ron Greenwood with the coaching of the England team and managed Chelsea until 1981. Then the world of insurance beckoned, where he joined his old West Ham and England team-mate Martin Peters. He was knighted shortly before joining England's bidding team for the 2006 World Cup finals, won by the German team headed by Franz Beckenbauer!

As thrilled as he was by his World Cup final hat-trick, Sir Geoff selects as his most memorable goal his winner against Argentina in the quarter-final game:

> *That goal against Argentina gave me more satisfaction than any other goal I ever scored. It was in my World Cup debut, and it was a carbon copy of a dozen goals I scored for West Ham from a measured pass from Martin Peters.*
>
> *The three goals I scored in the final changed my life, and I find I continue to be the centre of attraction every four years when the World Cup finals come round. I was not sure whether my third goal counted until I saw it go up on the scoreboard. I noticed some fans running on the pitch as I shot and I wondered if the final whistle had gone.*
>
> *I was completely overwhelmed by it all. Just a few days earlier I didn't think I was even going to get a game in the World Cup.*

Spare a thought for Jimmy Greaves, who has never complained about the way he was left out of the team:

> *I knew in my heart that England were going to win the World Cup, and was saying so before Alf made his prediction. The only thing that did not occur to me is that they would be doing it with me looking on as a spectator. I never get involved in all that business about whether Alf should have picked me. He*

*was the manager and selected what he thought was the right
team. Geoff Hurst three goals, England winners of the World
Cup. End of story.*

Not quite the end. Seven years later, after Sir Alf had been
mercilessly sacked by the FA officials he had often held in contempt, he invited my then promotions agency partner, the late Peter
Lorenzo, and I to his Ipswich home for the exclusive story of his
dismissal. When I asked how difficult it was to leave out Jimmy
Greaves for the 1966 final, he said:

*That was the hardest decision of my life. He was quite easily
the finest goalscorer of his generation. I knew that if I got it
wrong, the nation would crucify me. The irony is that substitutes were allowed for the next finals. Had they been allowed
in 1966 there is no question at all that Jimmy would have
played a part in the final.*

Sir Alf left the FA, for whom he had made millions of pounds, with
a paltry £6,500 pay-off. Later that year, a British Trade Salutes Alf
Ramsey testimonial dinner – which I organised with Peter Lorenzo
– raised more than that for him. At London's Café Royal, Prime
Minister Harold Wilson, who was the chief speaker, admitted that
the World Cup had saved his bacon. The economy was in such a bad
state that during the summer of '66 the pound was devalued but the
great British public hardly noticed it because their minds were
concentrated on England's run to the final.

An extraordinary thing happened while the Prime Minister was
paying his tribute to Sir Alf. A mouse ran the length of the top table
until Henry Cooper put out his famous left hand and caught it. He
handed it to a member of the staff who stamped on it. All of this
brought roars from the audience, first of laughter and then of
anguish as the mouse came to its unfortunate end. The Prime
Minister thought it was reaction to his speech!

Mr Wilson was followed by football writer *par excellence*
Geoffrey Green, of *The Times*, who was peerless as an after-dinner
speaker. He took out a mouth organ and started to play 'Moon
River'.

'Alf, old boy,' he said, 'this is to get you in the mood for your new
career. Let's go out busking. Over the moon, baby.'

The twenty-two players in the England squad each received a £1,000 bonus and skipper Bobby Moore was reduced to the humiliating experience of having to threaten to go to court to stop the taxman from taking a bite. What a way to treat heroes.

As the curtain falls on this story of England's finest hour on a football field, let's be clear that Sir Alf Ramsey – sometimes cantankerous, hopeless at media and public relations, but an absolute tactical master – was by some distance the best football manager England have ever had. No crystal ball is necessary to predict that there will never be another quite like him.

CHAPTER 11

THE SWINGING AND SWINGEING SIXTIES

THE 1960s involved much more than England's long-awaited triumph in the World Cup. The first success of British clubs in Europe, the long overdue introduction of substitutes and the ee-aye-adio revolution on Merseyside were all ushered in, and the maximum wage was kicked out, paving the way for today's professionals to swim in money. The sixties had the Beatles, rock 'n' roll, Mini cars, mini-skirts, psychedelia, Ali-psyche and, of course, George Best.

It was a swinging time for everybody apart from those footballers who found themselves redundant as clubs made swingeing cuts to help pay suddenly inflated wage bills.

Fulham's bearded wonder Jimmy Hill led the PFA (Professional Footballers' Association) campaign to kick out the £20 maximum wage as the eloquent union chairman, and it was his Craven Cottage team-mate Johnny Haynes who made the quickest profit. Comedian Tommy Trinder, chairman of Fulham, announced to the press in 1961 that he was making England skipper Haynes British football's first £100-a-week player. 'It was,' according to Johnny, 'the funniest thing Tommy ever said.'

The players owed a big vote of thanks and a few bottles of bubbly to England inside-forward George Eastham, who stood alone against the football barons. He battled in the High Court against what was described as 'a slave contract' and the restraint of trade. Eastham started his one-man war while at Newcastle and finally won it after moving to Arsenal in November 1960. He was the Bosman of his time and does not get enough credit for his courage in taking on, and beating, the establishment.

The Football League caved in after the players once again threatened strike action, and this time they really did mean it. In the space of one week in January 1961, the maximum wage was abandoned and restrictive contracts scrapped. Suddenly, Denis Law, Jimmy Greaves, Joe Baker and Gerry Hitchens found they could earn in England the same sort of money that had tempted them to Italy.

Player power was demonstrated on as well as off the pitch. The decade started with possibly the greatest performance by a club side ever, certainly the finest ever witnessed on a British ground.

The purveyors of this perfection were the footballing aristocrats of Real Madrid, who had dominated the European Cup since its inception in 1955. They were bidding to win the trophy for a fifth successive year when they journeyed to Glasgow for the 1960 final against Eintracht Frankfurt. Hampden Park was heaving with 127,621 spectators, many of them Rangers fans who believed they were gathering to see the end of Real Madrid's reign. They were still flabbergasted by the way Eintracht had blasted Rangers to defeat on an aggregate of 12–4 in the semi-finals, and they were convinced that any team capable of twice scoring six goals against their Ibrox idols could topple the old masters of Madrid.

Real were a team of soccer mercenaries, drawn from all points of the compass to give them punch and panache. It is commonplace now to have multi-national teams but back then it was a rarity. Their formidable defence was shaped around the intimidating Uruguayan centre-half Santamaria and Argentinian goalkeeper Dominguez, but it was for their attacking prowess that they were acclaimed. The forward line was under the intoxicating influence of Alfredo di Stefano, who had come from Colombia via his native Argentina and, at thirty-four, was still one of the world's premier exponents of the footballing arts. He pulled the strings for an attack that included the whiplash left-footed shooting of the incomparable Hungarian Ferenc Puskas, the pace and dribbling skills of home-grown heroes Luis Del Sol and Paco Gento and the invention of Brazilian winger Canario. An indication of Real's riches is that they were able to leave another brilliant Brazilian, 1958 World Cup star Didi, on the bench.

Eurovision was a new enterprise that brought the game 'live' to an armchair audience of millions, and across Europe viewers watched in awe as Real and Eintracht fashioned one of the greatest footballing classics of all time. For nineteen minutes the two teams sparred like stylish boxers looking for an opening for the knockout punch, and then Richard Kress scored for Eintracht to open the floodgates – and it was goals from Real that came pouring through.

Di Stefano, gliding across the Hampden turf like a Nureyev on grass, equalised eight minutes later at the end of a five-man passing movement that had the crowd purring. Scottish teams had pioneered the measured, 'along-the-carpet' passing game, and the spectators were treated to a perfect exhibition of this sophisticated style of play. By half-time di Stefano and Puskas had made it 3–1 to Real, the Puskas goal being a thing of wonder when he somehow managed to fire a rising shot into the net from what seemed an impossible angle.

For thirty minutes in the second half Real produced football so majestic and so artistic that it could have been set to music. By the seventieth minute, it was Real 6, Eintracht 1 – and the peerless Puskas had lifted his personal tally to four goals, including a penalty. Eintracht were playing much more than a walk-on part and after hitting the woodwork twice got the goal they deserved when centre-forward Erwin Stein scored with a stinging shot in the seventy-second minute.

Almost from the restart, di Stefano scored Real's seventh goal, and what a goal. He moved imperiously from a deep-lying position, exchanging passes with colleagues, always demanding the return of the ball, until he ended his advance with a deadly accurate shot that beat goalkeeper Loy all ends up.

Stein had the final word in the ten-goal extravaganza when he intercepted a rare mis-hit pass by Real defender Vidal and rounded goalkeeper Dominguez before scoring.

The breathless crowd gave both teams an ovation that lasted a full fifteen minutes after a marvellous match. Fortunately, it has been preserved on film as evidence of how the game of football can be played at the highest level.

Capped by his native Argentina, Colombia and Spain, legendary centre-forward di Stefano scored more than 500 goals in eleven years with Real Madrid, including 49 in 58 European Cup ties. Surprisingly, he never played in a World Cup final series. He travelled with Spain to the 1962 finals in Chile but was injured in a pre-tournament match.

The son of a bus conductor, Alfredo was born in Buenos Aires on 4 July 1926. He was a worshipped member of the River Plate team in Argentina when he shocked his home fans by signing for the then outlawed Colombian club Los Millonarios in 1949. Three years later, he was involved in a transfer tug of war between Barcelona and Real Madrid.

Real's victory in the battle for his signature coincided with the start of the greatest period in their history, and there was no doubt that it was Alfredo the Great who generated the success.

As moody off the pitch as he was magnificent on it, father-of-six di Stefano wound down his playing career with Espanol before becoming a successful manager with Boca Juniors in his homeland. He returned to Spain as manager-coach of Valencia and later had a spell in charge at Real.

Di Stefano was a man of few words for the media, but later, when he spoke of the game against Eintracht, he said, 'I played in many fine matches, but none greater than the 1960 European Cup final. Everything we tried worked to perfection. It was an honour and a privilege to be part of it.'

Real Madrid scored 112 goals and conceded 42 in 37 European Cup matches from 1955 to 1960 during which they won all five finals. They were finalists in 1962 (losing to Benfica) and 1964 (to Inter Milan) and won the Cup for a sixth time in 1966, beating Partizan Belgrade 2–1 in Brussels.

On the domestic front, Tottenham were playing football in the Real Madrid mould and came swinging into the sixties as the first team of the twentieth century to complete the league and FA Cup double.

Managed by deep-thinking Yorkshireman Bill Nicholson, Tottenham – the 'Super Spurs' – scored a record 115 goals on their way to winning the 1960–61 First Division title by a margin of 8 points from Sheffield Wednesday. They opened the season with eleven successive victories, and remained unbeaten for five more games. Their 66 points equalled the First Division record set by Herbert Chapman's Arsenal in 1930–31.

All five of their first-choice forwards reached double figures with league goals – Bobby Smith (28), Les Allen (23), Cliff Jones (15), John White (13) and Terry Dyson (12). However, it was in midfield that they won most matches, thanks to the combination of skill and strength emanating from skipper Danny Blanchflower, schemer John White and thunder-tackler Dave Mackay. Blanchflower was the poet of the side, Mackay the buccaneering pirate and White the prince of passers.

Spurs won the FA Cup final, completing the double, by beating Leicester City 2–0 at Wembley. They retained the Cup the following season, with Jimmy Greaves – signed from AC Milan for £99,999 – scoring an exquisite goal in the third minute to send them on the way to a 3–1 victory over Burnley. That goal rates with the finest scored at old Wembley. Greavsie was fifteen yards out and he *passed* the ball along the ground through a forest of players' legs and into the net with the unerring accuracy of a Jack Nicklaus putt. Jimmy, never one to boast in his playing days, said just before the players left the dressing room, 'I'm going to get an early one today boys.' If it had been a fluke, it would have been an outstanding goal. The fact that Greavsie meant it puts it up into the classic category.

In the same season, Tottenham were desperately unlucky to lose a two-leg European Cup semi-final against eventual champions Benfica. To this day, Greavsie insists that a 'goal' he scored, which would have put Spurs into the final, was wrongly flagged offside.

It was Tottenham who started the British habit of winning in Europe when they captured the Cup Winners' Cup in 1963, hammering Atletico Madrid 5–1 in the final in Rotterdam. Skipper Danny Blanchflower called on all his famous blarney to talk them into a winning performance after the players had been pitched into a mood of doom and gloom when the motivational Mackay failed a late fitness test.

One of the greatest of all British club teams started to break up almost overnight in 1964. Blanchflower was forced into retirement by a knee injury, Dave Mackay twice broke a leg and John White was tragically killed by lightning when playing a lone game of golf.

Iron man Mackay battled back to lead Tottenham to a 1967 FA Cup final victory over Tommy Docherty's Chelsea, but the team never again scaled the fantastic heights of the early sixties. Bill Nicholson, who had been a key player in the famous Tottenham 'push-and-run' championship side of 1950, said of the history-making double team:

Everything was right. The balance of the side, the attitude of the players, the team spirit. We managed to find the perfect blend and everybody gave one hundred per cent in effort and enthusiasm. We tried to keep our football as simple as possible – imaginative but simple. I kept pushing an old theory: 'When you're not in possession get into position.' The man without *the ball was important because he could make things happen by getting into the right place at the right time. Football is a simple game played properly.*

I could not have had a better captain than Danny to convey my ideas to the players, and when I signed Jimmy Greaves I knew I had the final piece of the jigsaw. I deliberately paid £99,999 for him because I did not want to burden him with being English football's first £100,000 player. He was worth every penny.

Just three weeks before helping Tottenham complete the double, Dave Mackay had what he described as his worst nightmare. He was in the Scotland team massacred 9–3 at Wembley on 15 April 1961.

At the start of the season, England manager Walter Winterbottom pledged, after consultation with the all-powerful selectors, that he would make only injury-forced changes to his side leading up to the 1962 World Cup finals in Chile. He wanted to see what could be achieved by fielding a settled side of players not burdened with the worry that a mistake or brief loss of form could cost them their international place.

Overwhelming evidence that the plan worked is that England won their next five matches, scoring 32 goals and conceding eight. It was one of the best-balanced sides to represent England, and their newly introduced 4–2–4 formation allowed for boldness and adventure in attack from a springboard of disciplined and defiant defence.

The new system revolved around the precise passing skill in

midfield of skipper Johnny Haynes and his versatile side-kick Bobby Robson, who had recently dropped back from inside-forward. Their dual role was to provide the ball for a four-man firing squad that featured the dribbling talent of Bryan Douglas on the right wing and the pace and power of Bobby Charlton on the left wing. In the middle, bulldozing centre-forward Bobby Smith was striking up an understanding with Chelsea's twenty-year-old cheeky chappie Jimmy Greaves, a partnership that was later to prove stunningly productive for Tottenham.

Ron Springett was a safe last line of defence and in front of him the back line of Jimmy Armfield, Peter Swan, Ron Flowers and Mick McNeill was strong and decisive.

In their first four matches together, the new-look England hammered Northern Ireland 5–2, Luxembourg 9–0, a star-spangled Spanish team (with Real Madrid stamped all the way through it) 4–2, and Wales 5–1. But according to many people in the game – particularly north of the border – the real test would come at Wembley from a Scottish side studded with players of the calibre of Denis Law, Ian St John and wing wizards John McLeod and Davie Wilson. It was claimed that England would not find goals easy to come by against a defence that included three of the finest defenders in British football – Eric Caldow, Billy McNeill and the indomitable Dave Mackay.

For Celtic goalkeeper Frank Haffey, it was a match made in hell. His positioning was questionable for the three goals that England scored in the first half, Bobby Robson (nine minutes) and Jimmy Greaves (twenty and twenty-nine minutes) putting the finishing touches to moves masterminded by the supreme Haynes.

Scotland were filled with the false optimism that they could still salvage the game when Mackay and Wilson pulled it back to 3–2 early in the second half. They pushed forward in a suicidal manner and left themselves wide open to counter-attacks.

Haynes probed these gaps with a procession of paralysing passes, and England sank the Scots without trace under a storm of five goals in eleven minutes. Douglas, Greaves, Bobby Smith and Haynes, with two, did the damage. Motherwell inside-left Pat Quinn interrupted the torture before Smith hammered in goal number nine.

Johnny Haynes was carried off shoulder high by the celebrating

England players, while the inconsolable Frank Haffey – cruelly dubbed 'Slap-Haffey' by the headline writers – slumped off the Wembley pitch in tears.

Sir Bobby Robson, now the doyen of football, still remembers the match well:

This was Walter Winterbottom's reward for keeping a settled England side together. We had a tremendous team under-standing, while the Scots were totally disorganised. They blamed their goalkeeper, but we would have given any team a tanking that day. We were just sad at the end that we had not managed to reach double figures. That would have looked great in the record books. Greavsie and Johnny Haynes were un-believable. They were poetry in motion and I felt privileged to be on the same pitch.

England stretched their unbeaten run to eight matches with an 8–0 victory against Mexico, a 1–1 draw in Portugal and a magnificient 3–2 win in Italy before going down 3–1 against Austria in Vienna. They had scored 45 goals and conceded 14 in nine games.

Unfortunately, they had peaked too early and by the time of the 1962 World Cup finals in Chile they had lost much of their rhythm and confidence. With a young Bobby Moore taking over from Bobby Robson, England battled through to the quarter-finals before going down 3–1 to eventual champions Brazil.

Even without the injured Pele, the Brazilians were too good for Czechoslovakia in the final and won 3–1 in a match brightened by the invention of Garrincha and the style of Amarildo, who was hailed as the 'White Pele'. After one of the World Cup victories, Pele was so excited by the performance of Amarildo, his stand-in, that he jumped fully clothed into the team bath to congratulate him.

In 1961, political upheaval caused in-fighting at the Football Association when long-serving secretary Sir Stanley Rous was appointed to the prestigious post of president of FIFA. Sir Stanley fought hard to make Walter Winterbottom his successor at the FA, which would have been a perfect role for the omniscient England manager, but the old-boy network was too strong and the job went to the low-key, civil-service style Denis Follows. A disillusioned Winterbottom moved on to become chairman of the Sports Council, where his expertise earned him a knighthood. As England team-manager, all he got was kicks.

The Big Freeze hit on Boxing Day 1962 and the country was buried under snow and ice until the following March. Where was global warming when you needed it? With nearly 500 matches postponed, it took sixty-six days just to decide the third-round matches in the FA Cup.

Enter the Pools Panel. Faced with bankruptcy, the football pools companies set up a panel of experts to forecast the results. The original panel consisted of former playing heroes Ted Drake, Tom Finney, Tommy Lawton and Rangers legend George Young, along with referee Arthur Ellis, under the chairmanship of Lord Brabazon. Their 'guesstimates' were read out on radio and television as if the matches had actually been played. The entire country was playing what now passes as fantasy football.

In the event, the 1963 FA Cup final was well worth waiting for. The 'king', Denis Law, was at his magical best for Manchester United. Matt Busby had brought him home from Torino for a British record £116,000, and he started to pay back the fee with his virtuoso performance against Leicester City at Wembley. Denis the Menace scored the first goal in a 3–1 victory after half an hour, and his constant probing unsettled Leicester's defence to such an extent that David Herd was able to score two goals against the goalkeeping goliath Gordon Banks.

Law was also the outstanding player for an all-star Rest of the World XI that played England at Wembley on 23 October 1963 to celebrate the centenary of the Football Association. Jinking Jimmy Greaves was the only player who stood out even more than Law. He might have had a first-half hat-trick but for the incredible goalkeeping of Russian 'Man in Black' Lev Yashin. Southampton winger Terry Paine gave England a first-half lead that was cancelled out by the jet-heeled Law, and Greavsie produced a sublime winning goal with just three minutes left of a memorable match.

These were the teams – just take a moment to drool over the names in the World XI:

England: Banks, Armfield, Wilson, Milne, Norman, Moore, Paine, Greaves, Smith, Eastham, Bobby Charlton.

Rest of the World: Yashin, Djalma Santos, Schnellinger, Pluskal, Popluhar, Masopust, Kopa, Law, di Stefano, Eusebio, Gento (subs: Soskic, Eyzaguirre, Baxter, Seeler, Puskas).

The following December, football broke with tradition when players were given Christmas day off. Normal service was resumed next day but the BBC newsreader wondered if it was a joke when he was handed the First Division results to announce to the nation:

Blackpool 1, Chelsea 5
Burnley 6, Manchester United 1
Fulham 10, Ipswich 1
Leicester City 2, Everton 0
Liverpool 6, Stoke City 1
Nottingham Forest 3, Sheffield United 3
Sheffield Wednesday 3, Bolton Wanderers 0
West Bromwich Albion 4, Tottenham Hotspur 4
West Ham United 2, Blackburn Rovers 8
Wolves 3, Aston Villa 3

Sixty-six goals in ten matches – no wonder it's remembered as the day football went Christmas crackers. Three players – Graham Leggat (Fulham), Andy Lochhead (Burnley) and Roger Hunt (Liverpool) – scored four goals each.

The craziest game was at Craven Cottage where Ipswich took a ten-goal hammering. England internationals Johnny Haynes, Alan Mullery, George Cohen and Bobby Robson were in no mood to show Christmas charity but it was a Scot – international utility forward Graham Leggat – who did most to make the Ipswich defenders look like repentant Scrooges determined to give everything away. He could easily have doubled his total of four goals, three of which came in three first-half minutes.

Ipswich, league champions the previous year, managed to laugh off the biggest defeat in their history. John Cobbold, their loveably eccentric Old Etonian chairman, said, 'Our problem was that our goalkeeper was sober. The rest of us, myself included, were still nursing Christmas Day hangovers. Like me, our players were seeing two balls and they kept kicking the wrong one.'

In the return fixture at Portman Road just two days later, Ipswich beat Fulham 4–2. Yes, a funny old game.

In Scotland, the stage was being illuminated by Jock Stein's all-conquering Celtic side, but Rangers were not completely overshadowed. They became the first British team to reach a major European final in 1961, going down 4–1 on aggregate to Fiorentina in the Cup Winners' Cup, which was played over two legs in its inaugural season.

Rangers were well worth watching for the performances of the one and only Jim Baxter, a perfectionist of a player and a prince of playboys. He had his greatest moments at Wembley in the blue shirt of Scotland. In 1963, he helped ease some of the pain of that 9–3 drubbing by steering the Scots to a 2–1 victory in what was Alf Ramsey's second game in charge. Two months earlier, Alf had lost his first game 5–2 in France, and this was the man who would lead England to the 1966 World Cup!

Both England and Scotland were down to ten men within five minutes of the 1963 international, following a collision between England centre-forward Bobby Smith and Scotland defender Eric Caldow. The Scottish skipper was carried off with a triple fracture of the leg. By the time Smith limped back on with a bandaged knee, 'Slim Jim' Baxter had twice beaten England's new goalkeeper Gordon Banks, first after a misplaced pass by Jimmy Armfield and then from the penalty spot. Bryan Douglas scored ten minutes from the end, but the Scots deserved their victory, masterminded by the arrogant, strutting Baxter. He swaggered off at the end with the ball tucked up inside his jersey. Even diehard England fans conceded that he deserved the ball because he had just owned the pitch.

Four years later, Scotland cheekily claimed they were the new world champions after Baxter had guided them to another victory over England – a first defeat in twenty matches, including the World Cup. You will not find a Scot willing to admit it, but their victory was a hollow one against a team reduced to eight fit players. Jack Charlton hobbled at centre-forward for much of the match with a broken toe, Ray Wilson was a limping passenger after getting a kick on the ankle, and Jimmy Greaves was reduced to half pace by a knock in his comeback match, playing in place of Roger Hunt.

Denis Law, feeding on the precision passes of Baxter, was at his tormenting best and gave Scotland the lead after twenty-eight minutes, and it remained at 1–0 until a four-goal rush in twelve minutes. Bobby Lennox made it 2–0 before the injured hero Jack

Charlton bravely pulled one back. Gordon Banks was beaten at the near post by Jim McCalliog for Scotland's third goal, and then Hurst headed home a Bobby Charlton cross for a final score of 3–2. The Scottish players and supporters celebrated as if they had just won the World Cup!

In 1964, Bobby Moore collected the first of his historic hat-trick of trophies by picking up the FA Cup as captain of an all-English, Ron Greenwood-managed West Ham team. A last-minute Ronnie Boyce goal had given them a thrilling 3–2 victory over Second Division Preston. Moore climbed the Wembley steps again in 1965 to collect the European Cup Winners' Cup following a stunning triumph over Munich 1860, and of course he reached his Everest in 1966 when accepting the World Cup (the *real* Jules Rimet trophy) from the Queen.

When lists of the all-time greatest players to grace a football field are drawn up, Bobby is one of the few English players almost guaranteed a place in the World XI. He was a true giant of the game whose reputation as a defensive master will never be diminished by the passing of time. Perhaps the only other English player to be shortlisted for the Greatest World Team of All Time would be Stanley Matthews, who held his passing out parade in 1965, three years after being elected the first European Footballer of the Year. He played his final First Division game for Stoke City at the age of fifty years and five days. But even Sir Stanley might struggle to wrest the No. 7 shirt from, for instance, Garrincha!

Bowing out of the game at almost the same time as Matthews was another great England servant, Jimmy Dickinson. As well as his 48 international caps at left-half, Dickinson played a then club record 764 league games for Portsmouth. He was thirty-nine when he hung up his boots, a mere baby alongside Sir Stanley.

Matthews left the soccer stage just as the football authorities at long last allowed substitutes, first of all only for injury but later accepting that tactical changes could be made. Keith Peacock, father of Gavin, was the first player to come on as a substitute in a Football League game – for Charlton against Bolton at the Valley on 21 August 1965.

The ugly, unacceptable face of football showed itself in 1964–65 when ten professional players were jailed for their part in a match-fixing scandal exposed by the *Sunday People* newspaper. Jimmy

Gauld, a moderate Mansfield Town player, was sentenced to four years as the ringleader. Among the others jailed and banned from football for life were England centre-half Peter Swan and his Sheffield Wednesday team-mate David 'Bronco' Layne, along with former Wednesday player Tony Kay, who had moved to Everton and was on Alf Ramsey's shortlist for the World Cup squad. As Kay's counsel told the Nottingham court where the conspiracy case was heard, 'He has given up for £100 what has been one of the greatest careers of any footballer. He was tempted once, and fell.'

On a much brighter note, the sixties were given a new sight and sound as the Kop choir accompanied the 'Red Revolution' at Anfield with a singing and chanting style of support that was quickly copied by fans around the world.

They had a lot to sing about at Liverpool from the day Bill Shankly took over as boss. He had served his managerial apprenticeship with Carlisle, Grimsby, Workington and Huddersfield, where he introduced Denis Law to the English football scene. The hour and the man came together when he arrived at Anfield on 1 December 1959. Shankly, a fiercely proud Scot from Ayrshire, provided the spark to ignite a Liverpool fire that continues to blaze to this day.

Shankly and Liverpool were made for each other. He was a producer and a showman in search of a stage big enough for his ideas and mega-watt personality. Liverpool were on their knees, urgently in need of somebody to project and propel them back to football's top table where they belonged. When Shankly arrived, Liverpool were stagnating down in the Second Division after an unbroken forty-nine year run in the First. He had found his stage. Liverpool had found their saviour. Shankly led them to promotion as Second Division champions in 1962 and laid such solid foundations that they have rarely been out of the hunt for major honours since then.

Just about the time that Shankly was breathing life into Liverpool, four mop-haired Merseyside pop musicians were starting to 'yeah-yeah-yeah' their way to fame. A music and football revolution had started in Liverpool that was to have an enormous impact on the unsuspecting outside world. The Beatles climbed to the top of the pops as the Red Army marched off with two league titles and the FA Cup between 1964 and 1966. The torch has been carried by subsequent Liverpool teams but it was the Shankly-built side of the swinging sixties that lit the flame.

Liverpool boldly clinched the league title in 1963–64 with a crushing 5–0 victory over Arsenal in the final crucial match of the season at Anfield. They left no doubts about their superiority two years later when winning the title by a margin of 6 points from Leeds. In that championship season, Shankly used just fourteen players.

Against Don Revie's Leeds at Wembley in 1965, a memorable extra-time goal by Ian St John lifted Liverpool to their first FA Cup final victory. The following season, they contested the European Cup Winners' Cup all the way to the final, and were defeated in extra time by Borussia Dortmund.

Shankly – Shanks to his devoted fans – left behind not only the legacy of a great team but enough anecdotal material to fill several books when he surprised everybody by retiring in the summer of 1974. Exactly what the beautiful game meant to him is best summed up with what is probably the most famous Shanklyism: 'Some people believe football is a matter of life and death. I'm very disappointed with that attitude. It's much more important than that.'

The rise of Liverpool galvanised their deadly rivals Everton into championship-challenging mood. They captured the league title in 1962–63 by spending heavily in the transfer market and by playing splendidly on their own territory at Goodison Park. Known as the 'Chequebook Champions', all but two of their squad had been bought from other clubs.

Manager Harry Catterick and his predecessor Johnny Carey had spent wisely, as Everton proved by going through the season unbeaten at home and emerging as runaway winners of the championship. They were undefeated in their last twelve matches after signing a human dynamo of a player from Sheffield Wednesday, Tony Kay. Nobody realised the weight of the baggage he was bringing with him from Hillsborough.

In Alex 'The Golden Vision' Young and Welsh skipper Roy Vernon, Everton had two world-class players, and red-headed Kay had the energy and skill to lift them to new peaks of perfection before his pitiful fall from grace.

Three years later, in 1966, Everton won the FA Cup when they came from behind to beat Sheffield Wednesday 3–2, and in 1968 they were gunned down in the final at Wembley by a rifled shot from West Bromwich Albion goal-hunter Jeff Astle. It was quick consolation for West Brom following their humbling 3–2 defeat by Third Division champions elect Queen's Park Rangers when the League Cup final was switched to Wembley for the first time in 1967. Rangers, managed by Alec Stock, had the man of the match in Rodney Marsh, who conjured one of the finest solo goals seen at Wembley to inspire a Rangers comeback after they had gone 2–0 down in the first half.

That was the year the League Cup came of age. Created by league secretary Alan Hardaker in 1961, it had been greeted with widespread indifference. Once it was given a Wembley setting and the incentive of a UEFA Cup place for the winner, it became an established part of the football calendar and attracted a series of sponsors. The Milk Cup, Littlewoods Cup, Rumbelows Cup, Coca-Cola Cup, Worthington Cup and Carling Cup are all the League Cup by any other name.

By the end of the decade, Harry Catterick had put together another championship-winning Everton team but this time it was largely home-grown. Skipper Brian Labone was a tower of strength in defence and the midfield trio of Alan Ball, Howard Kendall and Colin Harvey bossed games with their mix of sophisticated skill and high-octane energy. Hefty centre-forward Joe Royle was the main hammer in attack, and he was leading marksman in Everton's 1969–70 title-winning team with 23 goals.

Catterick, a former Everton centre-forward, had the almost impossible job of competing with Bill Shankly in the media and public-relations contest for attention on Merseyside. Later, he said:

I was very proud of the 1963 championship achievement, but even prouder when we won the title again seven years later. I found developing players from youth level far more rewarding and satisfactory than buying them.

It was always my belief that to be able to play attacking football you first needed to win control of the midfield. That was why I always concentrated on getting exceptional midfield footballers. You can have the greatest forwards in the world, but if they are not getting the service from midfield then they are next to useless.

We were labelled big spenders when we were on the way to
the championship in 1963. What people didn't realise is that I
was giving even more concentration to building for the future,
and the reward came with that second championship.

Leeds United were another club demanding attention in the 1960s.
They were struggling to survive in the Second Division when Don
Revie took over as manager in March 1961. By the time he left to
succeed Sir Alf Ramsey as England manager in the summer of 1974,
Leeds were firmly established as a major European club.

They did not always win friends with football that was often
mean and ruthless, but they influenced many people by setting new
standards of professionalism and a lot of clubs were moved to try to
emulate their organisation and their tactical efficiency.

Leeds had plenty of method to go with their muscle, and it would
be less than charitable for anybody not to concede that for ten years
Don Revie's team was one of the most powerful forces in football.
He had an excellent pair of back-up specialists in coach and scout
Syd Owen – 1959 Footballer of the Year with Luton – and Les
Cocker, a feisty trainer with extensive knowledge of fitness pro-
grammes and a key driving force behind the scenes for both Leeds
and England.

For all but the first year of Revie's reign, Leeds were challengers
for the major titles, but they were second best so many times that
Revie must have felt as frustrated as a groom continually being
jilted at the altar.

They were First Division runners-up in 1964–65, 1965–66,
1969–70, 1970–71 and 1971–72; FA Cup runners-up in 1964–65,
1969–70 and yet again in 1972–73. Leeds were also beaten finalists
in the European Cup Winners' Cup in 1972–73 and the Inter-Cities
Fairs Cup (later renamed the UEFA Cup) in 1966–67.

These painful near misses helped Revie and his players shape and
toughen their outlook and attitude until they were protecting
themselves behind a shield of strength that earned them their
reputation as 'The Mean Machine' of football.

Right from their first year back in the First Division, 1964–65, the
'nearly men' label was hung around their necks like a lead collar.
They failed to win the league championship on goal average and the
FA Cup in extra time. In 1970, they got within goal-shooting

distance of a sensational 'grand slam' treble of the European Cup, FA Cup and league championship, and finished up firing blanks in all three competitions (an historic hat-trick that would have to wait for Alex Ferguson's Manchester United). It was agonising for a Leeds team packed with quality players and led by a manager whose attitude to football and to life was succinctly summed up by the message he pinned to the dressing-room wall on his first day in charge at Elland Road – 'Keep fighting . . . never give in.'

Leeds *did* keep fighting and there were enough triumphs among the debris of disappointment to prove that they could also be winners. They twice captured the league championship (1968–69 and 1973–74) after being promoted as Second Division champions in 1963–64. They won the League Cup in 1967–68 and the Centenary FA Cup final in 1971–72 – both times beating Arsenal in the final – and they were Fairs Cup winners in 1967–68 and again in 1970–71.

That haul of honours is dazzling by any standards but it was nearly so much more impressive. A riddle going the rounds in the 1960s asked 'What do Leeds and a darts champion have in common?' Answer: they are always chasing doubles and trebles.

The Leeds squad was like a roll call of top international footballers from the era – goalkeepers Gary Sprake and David Harvey, defenders Paul Reaney, Terry Cooper, Jack Charlton and Norman Hunter, midfielders Billy Bremner, Bobby Collins and Johnny Giles, and forwards Peter Lorimer, Allan Clarke, Mick Jones, Eddie Gray and Mike O'Grady. Rarely had a stronger squad been assembled by any single club before the start of the foreign invasion.

Don Revie was a born organiser, a thoughtful tactician, a marvellous motivator of players, a master of press and public relations and single-minded to the point of being ruthless. Like Brian Clough, he was born in Middlesbrough – and also like Clough, he could be brilliant, bombastic and bloody-minded. Above all, Don Revie was a proud man and it was professional pride that he instilled into Leeds from the moment he became manager after a distinguished playing career. The Football League has rarely seen a better club manager but the sun does not shine so brightly on him when his international management comes under scrutiny.

When looking back on his achievements at Leeds, Revie said:

It was essential to adopt a 'tight' system of play in our first couple of years in the First Division while we consolidated our position. I could not see the purpose of battling to get into the First Division if we were not going to make a point of staying there. Perhaps I kept the players on the leash for too long, but when I allowed them full freedom of expression there were not many club teams in the world who could touch us.

Our approach to the game was based on a platform of hard work and discipline, but with all the players encouraged to improvise and show imagination. I used to say during our peak years, 'Go out and enjoy yourselves . . . just don't do anything silly.'

I doubt if there has ever been a team to equal our composure under pressure, and we had a lot more individual flair than many critics gave us credit for. Just our second places alone would have satisfied most clubs, but we also won a hell of a lot.

Manchester City would have a lot of backing in a vote for *the* team of the sixties, yet they were as alike to Leeds as grass to granite. Fluency, fun and flamboyance were the keynotes when Joe Mercer and Malcolm Allison were in harness as manager and coach at Maine Road.

At the peak of their partnership, City captured the Second Division championship (1965–66), the league title (1968), the FA Cup (1969) and the double of League Cup and European Cup Winners' Cup (1969–70). In that stunning sequence of success over a five-year span, City rivalled their grand neighbours in the trophy stakes.

Joe Mercer was the wise old man of soccer, cheerful even in a crisis and accustomed to success as a tigerish yet skilful player with Everton, Arsenal and England. While Matt Busby was the Father of Football, Joe was the game's favourite uncle.

The young, ambitious Malcolm Allison was a shrewd selection as his coach. Big Mal was headstrong and an almost compulsive creator of controversy but he was also one of the most inventive and imaginative thinkers in the game. He had been making nation-wide headlines from the West Country with his outspoken statements and often outrageous touchline behaviour as manager of Plymouth Argyle when Mercer came calling.

They brought the best out of each other and out of the Manchester City players. These two extremely likeable characters put a smile on the face of football.

The character and personality of the City team lay somewhere between the canny experience and infectious enthusiasm of Mercer, and the audacity and arrogance of Allison. The secret of the success of their alliance is that they somehow managed to meet halfway with their contrasting temperaments and values. It was a perfect mix, and they passed on to their team what they had put into the melting pot from their own personalities and knowledge of football and life.

The strength of the team was without any doubt its attacking force. 'The Fistful of Aces' – Francis Lee, Colin Bell, Mike Summerbee, Neil Young and Tony Coleman – was a nap hand that could trump most defences when attacking as a pack. Card-school metaphors are appropriate because Big Mal's gambling instinct was strongly in evidence in the way he pushed forward players at the risk of leaving the defence undermanned and overexposed. That the gamble paid off is proved by the parade of prizes collected by City captain Tony Book, whom Allison had brought with him from the West Country. Uncle Joe Mercer said of Manchester's blue period:

> *Malcolm and I had our ups and downs, as you can imagine with such contrasting outlooks on life. But in our good times together and before he began to believe his own publicity, we were the perfect partnership.*
>
> *We knew each other so well that we could easily have picked identical teams without consulting.*
>
> *In all my years in the game, I have never known excitement to match that generated when City were winning everything there was to win. It was a fabulous team effort.*
>
> *We built our team in the shadow of those great Manchester United sides put together by my dear friend, the one and only Matt Busby. For a time, we actually overtook them. Now that is something that gave Malcolm and me more pleasure than anything else.*

Big Mal was a wickedly handsome and engaging character who somehow managed to balance a playboy life with that of a disciplined coach. A cultured centre-half at West Ham, his attitude was shaped by the way his playing career ended. Malcolm was forced into retirement at the age of twenty-eight by tuberculosis that cost him a lung and almost his life. From then on, he seemed to want to live every week as if it were his last. You needed pace, stamina and a huge appetite for nightlife to keep up with him. He always had his foot hard on the accelerator and a glass of champers was never far out of reach.

Yet for all his love of life in the fast lane, football was his number-one priority. Joe Mercer conceded that City would not have cleaned up the major prizes so quickly, so dramatically, and with such verve without Allison's drive, vision and flair for coaching.

Together, they produced a team that combined their own qualities – a blend of youth and experience, arrogance and simplicity, vigour and quiet authority. Above all it had *style* and that was something that Mercer and Allison had in abundance.

Long after the City cheers were behind him, Big Mal looked back for a series he and I collaborated on for the London *Evening Standard* entitled *Allison Through the Looking Glass*:

> *When that City team were really motoring, there have been few better sights in British football. I would have backed them to beat anybody at their peak. The balance and structure of the side was just right.*
>
> *I literally saw red when I first arrived in Manchester. It seemed everywhere I looked there were young fans walking around wearing red Manchester United scarves. There was no blue to be seen. I vowed to change all that, and within two years you could see blue scarves being proudly worn about the city. That's what Joe Mercer and I did with the team that we built. For a while at least, Manchester was blue.*

City pipped their neighbours to the league championship in a drama-packed finale to the 1967–68 season. On the official last day of the season, City stormed to a 4–3 victory at Newcastle while United went down to a surprising 2–1 defeat at home to Stoke City. Just 6 points separated the top five clubs, with the Mercer-Allison combination smiling at the top of the heap.

Manchester City added the FA Cup to their collection in 1968–69. Third Division Swindon shocked Arsenal by defeating them in the

League Cup final, thanks to two spectacular extra-time goals by Wiltshire Whirlwind Don Rogers on a mud-heap of a Wembley pitch, while up in the north east a sleeping giant stirred. Newcastle, who sneaked into the Fairs Cup despite finishing down in tenth place in the First Division the previous season, confounded everybody except themselves by winning the competition. They got into the tournament because of the 'one city, one team' rule then in operation, which knocked Everton, Tottenham and Arsenal out of contention.

The English representatives went down like ninepins until there was only Newcastle left standing. Liverpool and Chelsea went out on a crazy toss of a coin at the end of deadlocked matches. (This was before penalty shoot-outs were introduced.) Leeds lost both their quarter-final games to Hungarian team Ujpest Dozsa, who had the exceptional Ferenc Bene in their side and were considered just about unbeatable on their home turf in Budapest. Finally, Newcastle stood between the Hungarians and the trophy.

Inspired by a goal from skipper Bobby Moncur – his first for the club in seven years – Newcastle won the first leg against Ujpest 3–0 at a St James's Park desperate for their team to revive old glories. Moncur, a master defender, amazingly scored two goals in the second leg when the Magpies won 3–2. The 6–2 aggregate victory rated right up there with the Newcastle FA Cup feats of the fifties.

Even this marvellous performance by Newcastle could not top the two outstanding achievements by British clubs in Europe in those swinging, breathtaking sixties. The adventures of Jock Stein's Celtic and Matt Busby's Manchester United warrant a chapter to themselves.

CHAPTER 12

THE TEAM THAT JOCK BUILT – AND BUSBY'S BEST

J OCK STEIN, the man to whom many bowed the knee as the master of all managers, was first to show British clubs the way to win the major prize in Europe. He achieved it with a very Scottish style and swagger that was like a rush of fresh air just as European football was in danger of being suffocated by blanket defences.

Stein, a former Celtic centre-half and captain, always passionately believed that football should be played with a positive attitude. He demanded an attacking approach at Parkhead where Celtic – the team that Jock built – provided testimony to his enormous talent as a supreme creator.

I wrote the following article for the Associated News world syndication service in 1977 to mark the tenth anniversary of Celtic's history-making European Cup triumph. More than thirty-five years on, I hope it still captures the match and the moment:

Celtic's record under Jock Stein's mesmerising management was remarkable to the point of miraculous. In his first six full seasons in charge at Parkhead, the Glasgow club won six Scottish League titles and lost only 17 of 204 league games while scoring 597 goals. They reached five Scottish FA Cup finals, winning three, and they won five out of six League Cup finals. It was consistency on a Bradmanesque scale.

Amazingly, the eleven players who brought home the European Cup – the first British triumph in the tournament – were all born within a thirty-mile radius of Glasgow. [Imagine that happening in today's multi-passport environment!]

There were dismissive remarks heard south of the border that the Scottish League was not a real test of a team's quality, but these sort of sniping comments were silenced as Celtic set out to achieve new standards in Europe.

They barnstormed into the final with a brand of exciting, attacking football that put to shame those clubs becoming addicted to the drug of defensive football that paralysed so many games in the mid-to-late sixties.

In the final in Lisbon they came head-to-head with the great architects of defence-dominated football, Internazionale Milan, who captured the European Cup in successive seasons in 1964 and 1965 from the springboard of their stifling *catenaccio* defensive system.

Argentinian coach Helenio Herrera had built a human fortress around the Inter goal and then relied on three or four jet-paced forwards to make maximum capital out of carefully constructed counter-attacks. It was ruthlessly efficient, mind-numbingly boring.

Celtic's style and attitude was the exact opposite. They were geared for flair and adventure. The simple tactic was attack, attack and then attack again.

Every journey has to start with the first step, every revolution with the first bullet, every romance with the first kiss.

Jock's first step was to create a team in his own image – that of a larger-than-life character who liked to entertain and be magnanimous in victory and defeat. The first bullet in the revolution was fired at the heart of the teams who were frightened to try anything daring on the pitch. And the first kiss was that metaphorically delivered to the thousands who packed Paradise Park every week to start a love affair that reached an extraordinary peak in Lisbon.

Jock's team was to become as well known and as greatly admired south of the border as north. There was not an English manager who did not take at least one opportunity to watch them play to see what they could learn.

Ronnie Simpson, son of a former Rangers captain, was Celtic's man-for-all-seasons goalkeeper. He provided a safe-as-houses last line of defence, and torpedoed the slur that Scottish goalkeepers cannot even catch colds. Ronnie had won two FA Cup-winners' medals with Newcastle in 1952 and 1955. Over a decade later at the age of thirty-six he was still as agile and alert as ever.

Jim Craig, iron-man skipper Billy 'Caesar' McNeill, John Clark and power-shooting left-back Tommy Gemmell made up a formidable back line in front of Simpson. They were all encouraged to keep pushing forward as auxiliary attackers. Their tackling was man's game tough but rarely strayed towards the cynical or violent.

Taking responsibility for the supply of passes from the midfield engine room in Celtic's 4–2–4 formation were the skilful and competitive Bertie Auld and the industrious and inventive Bobby Murdoch. Bertie had left Parkhead to become an unsung Anglo with Birmingham City until called back home by the shrewd Stein, who knew he could produce the passes that would help make the team tick. Bobby Murdoch, later to ply his trade with Middlesbrough, was the heart of the team, a driving, determined player who appeared to have been equipped with an extra set of lungs.

The four-man firing line was one of the most effective goal machines in football. Jinking Jimmy Johnstone was unstoppable on his day as a quick and clever right-winger who could destroy defences with his dribbling, darting runs. Bobby Lennox patrolled the left wing with a mixture of cunning and power, cutting in to shoot or to feed delicate passes to central strikers Willie Wallace and Steve Chalmers.

The 1967 European Cup final was a contest between Inter Milan's negative, smothering tactics and the up-and-at-'em cavalier charges of Celtic. Neutrals hoped that the positive would beat the negative.

The Inter Milan method was tried and tested. They liked to

search for a quick score and then sit back and barricade their goal behind a fortress defence. So it was no surprise to Celtic when the Italians opened with a burst of attacking football that could have come out of the Jock Stein manual.

Sandro Mazzola, Inter's key player following the late withdrawal of injured schemer Luis Suarez, headed against Ronnie Simpson's legs in the opening raid.

Then, in the seventh minute, Mazzola triggered an attack that led to the early goal on which Inter had set their sights. He put Corso clear on the left with a penetrating pass. The wingman released the ball to Cappellini, who was in the process of trying to shoot when a crunching Jim Craig tackle knocked him off the ball. It was judged a foul by German referee Tschenscher, and Mazzola deftly scored from the penalty spot.

It had been a magnificent opening spell by the Italians, but by force of habit they shelved their attacking talents and pulled all but two forwards back to guard their goal. It was an invitation to Celtic to attack. This was like asking Nureyev to dance or Tommy Docherty to tell a joke. They simply could not resist the invitation.

The Scottish champions pushed full-backs Craig and Gemmell forward on virtually permanent duty as extra wingers, and the Inter defensive wall buckled and bent under an avalanche of attacks.

Goalkeeper Sarti made a procession of brilliant saves, and when he was beaten, the woodwork came to his rescue as first Auld and then Gemmell hammered shots against the bar. Any other team might have surrendered with broken hearts as the Milan goal miraculously survived the onslaught, but skipper McNeill kept brandishing his fist as he urged his team-mates to greater efforts. The word 'surrender' was not part of the Celtic vocabulary.

At last, after an hour of sustained attack, the spirited Scots were rewarded with an equaliser and it was the exclusive creation of overlapping full-backs Craig and Gemmell.

First of all, Craig brought the ball forward along the right side of the pitch. The retreating Italian defenders tightly marked every player in a green-hooped shirt, but there was one man that they missed. Craig spotted Gemmell coming through on the left like the Flying Scot express train and angled a pass into his path. Sarti had managed to stop everything to date, but no goalkeeper on earth could have saved Gemmell's scorching shot that was smashed high into the net from twenty yards.

Propelled by panic, Inter tried to get their attacking instincts working but they were so accustomed to back-pedalling that they could not lift the pace or alter the pattern of their play.

Celtic, urged on from the touchline by the composed figure of Big Jock, maintained their momentum and created the winning goal they so richly deserved six minutes from the end of a nerve-shredding match. Gemmell came pounding forward along the left touchline. The Italians were not sure whether to mark his team-mates or to try to block his route to goal in case he was tempted to take another pot shot.

Caught in two minds, they gave too much room to Bobby Murdoch, who accepted a pass from Gemmell and unleashed a shot. The diving Sarti was confident he had the ball covered, but Steve Chalmers managed to deflect it out of his reach for a winning goal that made Celtic the first British winners of the premier prize in club football.

At the final whistle, thousands of Celtic fans came chasing on to the pitch to parade their heroes like trophies. The magnificent McNeill battled a way through them to collect the enormous European Cup. Jock Stein then waited anxiously in the dressing room, counting his players as they emerged one by one from the green and white sea of supporters on a night when Lisbon belonged to Glasgow. Scottish football folklore has it that half the pitch was carried home to Glasgow as delirious fans collected souvenirs of what was then the greatest club triumph in British – let alone Scottish – football history.

Following on behind the last of the Celtic players was Liverpool's beaming manager Bill Shankly, one of the few people who could put his record up against his old Scottish pal Stein. As he entered the dressing room, Shankly summed up Stein's achievement with one of his typically direct and appropriate statements. 'John,' he boomed, using Stein's Christian name, 'you've just become bloody immortal.'

For six years, Celtic were the Great Untouchables, winning every-thing in sight apart from an infamous world club championship match with Racing Club of Buenos Aires in which tempers and tantrums overruled the talent of both teams.

A niggling, neurotic encounter at Hampden – won 1–0 by Celtic – was followed by an even nastier second leg in Buenos Aires. That ugly encounter in Argentina could have been staged under world professional wrestling rules except there was nothing fake about the feuding and the fouling. For a start, as Celtic filed out on to the pitch behind a piper, goalkeeper Ronnie Simpson was knocked unconscious by a stone thrown from the crowd. Reserve Sean Fallon had to take over in goal. Racing put two unanswered goals past him and that left the World Club trophy unclaimed – the competition was decided by games won rather than aggregate scores. Jock Stein, to his lasting regret, agreed to a play-off in Uruguay three days later.

It was one of the most violent games ever, more of a war than a football match. Celtic, harbouring grudges from the previous two games, were as guilty as the Argentinians with their retaliate-first tackling. Three Celtic and two Racing Club players were sent off, and armed police had to come on to the pitch to break up brawling players. A fourth Celtic player, Bertie Auld, was ordered off but the referee waved play on when he could not confirm which player should have been marching. The brutal farce, which ended with Racing Club 1–0 winners, was televised around the world – the worst possible advertisement for the Beautiful Game. Jock Stein fined his players £250 each and issued an apology on behalf of the club. The Racing players each got a new motorcar as a bonus.

In 1970, Celtic became the unofficial champions of Britain when they conquered formidable Football League winners Leeds United in the semi-final of the European Cup. In the final, they were beaten 2–1 by Feyenoord after extra time, with Gemmell scoring their goal.

Celtic mastermind Jock Stein was an amiable yet exhilarating person to meet. He was known throughout the game as the 'Big Man', and the description sat comfortably on his broad shoulders.

Visiting him in his Parkhead office was an experience to treasure, and he put himself out to be friendly and forthcoming to quote-hungry journalists, be they Scottish or English. He had a wide, rouge-cheeked face that had a rugged warrior quality about it. That face would have looked at home on the shoulders of a heavyweight boxer. His thick black hair was combed back in tidal waves that baldies such as Jimmy Delaney and Archie Gemmill would have killed for. A crushing handshake signalled sincerity, and he would instantly offer visitors a drink from a well-stocked cocktail cabinet although he never ever touched a drop. 'I've never seen the point in drinking alcohol,' he once said. 'Life provides enough of an adrenaline rush for me.'

Like his close friends Matt Busby and Bill Shankly, Jock grew up in the coal-mining area of the West of Scotland that was a gold mine of footballing talent. He was born in Burnbank, Lanarkshire, on 1 October 1922, and had to work harder than most before he escaped the misery of the coalfields. He was a part-time footballer and a full-time coal miner up until he was twenty-seven years old when he signed for Llanelli in the Welsh League. Then Celtic invited him to join their squad as a reserve, helping the youngsters along with coaching advice.

He got into the Celtic first team because of injuries to the two first-choice centre-halves, and made such an impression that he was appointed captain. In 1953–54 he led Celtic to the league and Cup double before an ankle injury forced his retirement. He never completely recovered from the injury and had a slight limp for the rest of his life.

Stein started his managerial career with Dunfermline in 1960, and within a year he had steered them to a shock victory in the Scottish Cup final against, of all teams, Celtic. He moved on to Hibernian before being summoned back to Parkhead in 1965 as manager.

When asked how confident he had been that Celtic could beat mighty Inter Milan in the 1967 European Cup final, this was his reply:

I don't wish to sound big-headed, but I had no doubts whatsoever. There was not a prouder man on God's earth than I was the night we won the Cup in Lisbon. Winning was important, aye, but it was the way that we won that filled me with satisfaction. We did it by playing football – pure, beautiful, inventive, positive football. There was not a negative thought in our heads.

> *Inter played into our hands. It was so sad to see such gifted players as they had, shackled by a system that restricted their freedom to think and to act. Our fans would never accept that sort of sterile approach. Our objective has always been to win with style.*

Celtic's great European Cup triumph was a victory for football. The game started to come out of the dark tunnel of defence, down which it had been taken by Inter and scores of (or should that be scoreless?) impersonators. Now they all started to try to play the Celtic way.

Sadly, the Stein reign at Parkhead ended in acrimony. The board tried to move him upstairs when he wanted only to be among his players, and in 1978 he at last gave in to one of many overtures to move south, agreeing to take over from Jimmy Armfield at Leeds. Anyone who knew him well realised that it was the right move at the wrong time. He joined the English League at least eight years too late. Jock was fifty-five. He had survived a car crash that almost killed him in the summer of 1975 and there had been warning signs that his heart was not as strong as it used to be – bad news for a man who was all heart.

Stein had been at Elland Road for an uncomfortable couple of months when he was enticed back to his beloved Scotland to take charge of the national team. He had immediate success by steering them to the 1982 World Cup finals in Spain where they were eliminated on goal difference.

Three years later he died tragically, in harness, aged sixty-two, collapsing by the bench moments after Scotland had eliminated Wales from the World Cup in a qualifying match in Cardiff. The spectators were still applauding the teams off as he passed away. He died with the roar of the crowd in his ears. A light had gone out in British football. The game had lost one of its most majestic managers.

Twelve months after Celtic had shown the way, another proud Scot with a coal-mining background became the second British manager to lift the European Cup. He was, of course, Matt Busby.

Manchester United's European Cup final against Benfica at Wembley Stadium had deep significance. The whole of Britain, and the sympathies and good wishes of most of Europe, too, were behind Matt Busby and his team as they set out to fulfill a dream that had been shattered in the Munich air disaster ten years earlier.

It had taken Busby a decade to rebuild a squad of the quality and craftsmanship displayed by the pre-Munich team. The side he was sending into action against Benfica was almost in the class of the Busby Babes. Perhaps the most important piece in the jigsaw, as he put together a mix of outstandingly skilful and physically powerful players, was goalkeeper Alex Stepney, whom he signed in the summer of 1966.

Stepney started his league career with Millwall and had played just four first-team matches for Tommy Docherty's Chelsea when Busby bought him for what was then a goalkeeping transfer record of £50,000. At £500,000 he would have been a bargain. Stepney brought stability and confidence to a United defence that had been giving away goals like a charitable organisation. This carelessness was cancelling out the creative work of a stunningly gifted attack that had three shining jewels in Irishman George Best, Scotsman Denis Law and Bobby Charlton, the favourite son of English football. Law was European Footballer of the Year in 1964, Charlton in 1966 and Best in 1968.

A knee injury forced Law out for this game of a lifetime, which he watched from a hospital bed following an operation. It was like an orchestra losing its lead violinist. Sir Matt visited him in hospital on the eve of the final and told him, 'We will bring the Cup to you. Consider yourself as much a part of the team as if you were playing. We could not have got this far without you.'

Law's place went to Manchester-born prodigy Brian Kidd, who was celebrating his nineteenth birthday on the day of the final. Stepping into the boots of a legend may have been daunting but Kidd gave a performance of which Law himself would have been proud.

Providing the passes from midfield alongside Charlton was master tactician Paddy Crerand, and operating like a mine sweeper in front of the back line of the defence was the 'Toothless Tiger' Nobby Stiles. He had, of course, been one of England's heroes in the 1966 World Cup finals along with Charlton. Now United needed a repeat of his impressive semi-final performance against Portugal when he stifled the menace of striker Eusebio because The Black Panther was the inspiration behind Benfica's climb to their fifth European Cup final in eight years.

Also in the Benfica team from that Portuguese side were midfield marshal Mario Coluna and quick and clever forwards Jose Torres, Jose Augusto and sparkling left-winger Simoes.

With the towering 6ft 4ins Torres leading the attack, the United defence was going to be severely tested and all hearts went out to veteran United centre-half Bill Foulkes, another Munich survivor, who was coming to the end of a long and distinguished career at Old Trafford.

He was flanked by Irish international full-backs Shay Brennan and Tony Dunne, and utility player David Sadler was delegated to drop back from an attacking role to fill in alongside Foulkes whenever there was pressure from Benfica.

Few teams had been under such mental strain as United when they walked out on to the Wembley pitch and into a sea of emotion. The publicity spotlight had been turned on them as never before because of the link with Munich, and the bellowing 100,000 crowd were in a frenzied grip of hope and anticipation.

As was only to be expected in the circumstances, both teams struggled to settle into their stride and the ball was moved quickly from player to player as if it were an unexploded bomb. Nobody wanted the responsibility of trying to force the first opening for fear of making a mistake.

All eyes were on United wonder winger George Best, but he was taking a severe buffeting from the Portuguese defenders, who recalled the way he had destroyed them almost single-handedly in a European Cup tie two years earlier.

Eusebio was getting similar harsh treatment from the unyielding Stiles, and the only forward who was making any sort of impression was United's unsung outside-left John Aston, whose father had won an FA Cup winner's medal with United on this same pitch almost exactly twenty years earlier. Aston was racing past Benfica's defenders in Best fashion, but his team-mates were unable to capitalise on his stunning running in a goalless first half that was wrecked by nervous tension.

Benfica came closest to breaking the deadlock when Eusebio, free for a split second from the fervent attention of Stiles, clipped the United crossbar with a drive from twenty yards.

The half-time break seemed to steady United's nerves and they began the second half with a spurt of the sort of football with which this Busby team continually lit up matches during the 1960s.

The one and only Bobby Charlton, as graceful as a gazelle, gave them the lead that the crowd were baying for when he sprinted away from his marker to meet a cross from Sadler with a perfectly placed glancing header.

Aston created a procession of chances for United to seal victory, but the finishing never matched the brilliance of the winger's foundation work. Nine minutes from the end you could almost hear the intake of breath from the suddenly hushed United fans when Graca equalised for Benfica in a breakaway raid.

With just seconds left and extra time looming, Eusebio looked certain to destroy United's dream. The deadliest marksman in the world broke free from Stiles and had only Stepney to beat, but somehow the United goalkeeper managed to parry his rocketing shot with a sensational save.

United were still shaking from this heart-stopping escape when the final whistle blew, and Charlton and Stiles found themselves facing another bout of extra time, just as they had in the World Cup final.

Matt Busby, the years suddenly heavy on his shoulders, walked urgently on to the pitch and told his players, 'You are being too careless with your passes. Just take a little care and you can win it. Don't throw it away now. Make every pass count and when you get into their box steady yourselves. You are snatching at your shots.'

It was going to take a moment of inspiration and invention to lift the worn-out United players, and it was the genius Best who provided it early in the first period of extra time. He at last managed to escape his Benfica jailers to run on to a headed through ball from Kidd, following a long punt upfield by Stepney. Best side-stepped a tackle and nonchalantly dummied his way past onrushing goalkeeper Henrique before side-footing the ball into the net as if in a training match. George – who always receives enormous support in any argument about who is Britain's most gifted footballer of all time – said later that he was disappointed with his goal.

'I had wanted to make it something unique,' he commented. 'I was going to chip it up and nod it into the net – passing to myself and then scoring. I just wanted to give the fans something to remember. In the end, I chickened out and settled for just making sure I got the ball into the net. Very dull.'

The Best goal – hardly dull to the United supporters – virtually settled the match. The spirit and fight disappeared from Benfica like air leaving a punctured balloon, and birthday boy Kidd put the icing on his cake with a determined smash-and-grab goal. He headed the ball against the bar and then beat everybody to the rebound to nod it into the net.

As if the match was being plotted by the great scriptwriter in the sky, Charlton – who had survived the Munich air crash, aged nineteen – gave the game a fairytale finish, volleying a centre from Kidd high into the Benfica net from the narrowest of angles.

Wembley was wild with excitement and awash with tears as Charlton led his team-mates forward to collect the prize of the European Cup. He had tried to talk Matt Busby into receiving it, but the modest manager said, 'No. This is your night.'

Later, away from the emotion-charged atmosphere of Wembley, Matt – soon to be knighted for his services to football – said, 'A lot of very special people are in our thoughts tonight. We won this Cup for them. We have played a lot better than we did against Benfica, but in view of all the circumstances, the team performed magnificently. I am particularly thrilled for Bill Foulkes and Bobby Charlton. They came through the ordeal of the crash, and this victory will mean so much to them.'

Eusebio, who hugged Bobby Charlton at the final whistle, said, 'I consider Bobby Charlton a friend and, as disappointed as I was to be on the losing side, I had the consolation of seeing him collect the Cup. He is a gentleman as well as a great player and is a credit to our game.'

Charlton's name was on everybody's lips and the victory added to his legend. Ask football fans to name the greatest player they have ever seen and Bobby Charlton is unlikely to be the answer. Ask them who is their *favourite* footballer of all time and there is every chance that Bobby Charlton will be nominated instantly. Charlton was the player everybody loved to love. George Best had more tricks, Denis Law had more dynamism, but Charlton had an indefinable charisma that put him ahead in the popularity polls.

Football followers have three faces and three phases of Charlton deposited in their memory banks. There is the teenaged pre-Munich Busby Babe with his shock of blond hair and the bombing shots from the left wing. His performances dipped and soared like an

English weather barometer, sometimes hot with sunshine brilliance, other times caught in the wild wind of inconsistency. Never, ever was he dull – from his opening goals in league football scored on his debut against, of all teams, Charlton in 1956, and from his first match with England, against Scotland at Hampden Park in 1958. He marked his international debut with a gem of a goal, crashing a shot in on the volley from a pass by one of his schoolboy idols, Tom Finney.

The second, more serious, face, lean and frowning under a rapidly thinning thatch, appeared post-Munich, when his game began to gather maturity, consistency and style. He had lost some of his early impudence but showed greater variety and verve as he switched to an inside-forward role.

The third and – for many people – favourite face of Bobby Charlton shone from the mid-sixties when, with his famous comb-over hair-style, he became a strolling midfield player. Wearing the No. 9 shirt, but rarely as a conventional centre-forward, he plotted openings for team-mates and created goals for himself with sudden sprints at the heart of defences, climaxed with rifled shots from either foot.

His greatest moments came in this deep-lying role, plundering vital goals and supplying a succession of measured passes for England's 1966 World Cup winning team, and providing the same service for the magnificent United side of that golden era. Neither team could have succeeded without him.

Knighted and revered around the world as an ambassador for the sport, Sir Bobby remains the only British footballer to win the grand slam of honours – World Cup, European Cup, league championship and FA Cup winners' medals. He was European and English Footballer of the Year in 1966 and his collection of 106 England caps is topped only by Bobby Moore and Peter Shilton.

Born in Ashington, Northumberland, on 11 October 1937, Bobby came from a mining and footballing family that included the talented Milburn brothers. He and his elder brother Jack played together for England in 35 international matches.

Bobby scored 198 league goals for United in 606 games, and added eight more to his collection when playing 38 times for Preston as player-manager. Later, he became a director of his beloved United. He remains England's top scorer with 49 goals, one ahead of Gary Lineker and five ahead of Jimmy Greaves.

The European Cup final was a special highlight in Sir Bobby's vast gallery of great games. He reminisced, 'We had lived with the ambition of winning the European Cup for so long that this time we knew we had to do it. When the game went to extra time it was like the 1966 World Cup final all over again. We had to be professional and not let emotion take over, as it so easily could have done. We owed it to too many people, particularly Matt Busby, not to fail after all the club had been through.'

In the spring of 2003, at the Laureus World Sports Academy Awards of the Year show in Monte Carlo, which I scripted, Sean Connery was due to make a presentation. He was on stage rehearsing when Bobby's name came up on the autocue screen – Bobby is one of the leading members of the Academy, made up of sporting legends. A young French stage assistant asked, 'Who is Bobby Charlton?' Sir Sean, shaken *and* stirred, replied in that inimitable James Bond voice of his, 'Only one of the greatest footballers that ever lived. He gave us hell.'

Connery was talking as a Scot, of course. Bobby had given *most* teams hell, and in doing so had brought a little bit of heaven to many a football field.

After the joy of winning the European Cup, Bobby had another international challenge to face – he would be a key man in England's attempt to defend the World Cup in far-off Mexico. One of the most delightful and devastating teams in history was waiting there. Bring on the Boys of Brazil.

ve English football's finest hour – Bobby Moore holds
t the number one prize after England's 1966 World Cup
l victory over West Germany at Wembley. Something
Nobby Stiles (*extreme left*) to get his teeth into.

ht Pele touches his toe. For mere mortals, he was
Great Untouchable. He shared the FIFA Footballer
he Century award with Maradona in 2000.

ow Perhaps this Maradona prayer was answered
n his Hand of God goal against England in the 1986
rld Cup quarter-final in Mexico City.

Even the famed and feared Ron 'Chopper' Harris (*left*) could not deter George Best from making progress for Manchester United. Along with Denis Law (*below, centre*) and Bobby Charlton (*right*), Best was the pride of Matt Busby's great 1960s team. Best, Law and Charlton were the Holy Trinity of Old Trafford.

Shankly points the way for his Liverpool team, and by following his directions they ...t the foundations for the all-conquering achievements under his successor Bob ...ley. The glory goes to the head of two more Scots, Kenny Dalglish (*below left*) and ...my Docherty, looking every inch the Kaiser under the lid of the FA Cup won by his ...nchester United team in 1977. Then he fell in love with Mrs Brown, the wife of the ...ted physiotherapist, and the Doc was on his way out as he continued to collect, as he ...ously said, more clubs than Jack Nicklaus.

Above left Brian Clough could b
saying, 'Listen to me, young ma
I'm number one and don't you
forget it.' And Kevin Keegan (*ab
right*) just might be disagreeing
he tries on a beret while on a
playing trip to France. Cloughie
had the last laugh on Keegan w
his Nottingham Forest beat Kev
Hamburg to retain the European
Cup in 1980, in the same season
that Keegan completed back-to-
back European Footballer of the
Year awards.

Left How would Alan Hansen
summarise this on television? 'T
defending here by the Liverpool
player is diabolical, but he is
handicapped by having only on
and a half legs. He's too slow a
cumbersome to catch the young
Everton whippet Gary Lineker.'
There's just no way that these t
will be able to work together.

ve German skipper Lothar Matthaus may be
ng Chris Waddle after his penalty shoot-out
 in World Cup 90, 'Think of the pizza
mercial.' For Paul Gascoigne (*right*) there are
 on the face of the clown.

y Villa completes one of the all-time great goals for Tottenham in the 1981 FA Cup
 replay against Manchester City at Wembley. For this Argentinian, it took just one to
o.

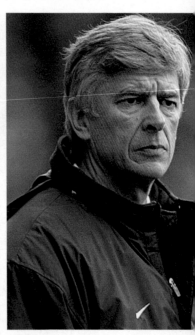

Three of the great modern managers – Alex Ferguson (*above left*), the Guv'nor of Old Trafford; Arsene Wenger (*above right*), the French master of Highbury; and Sir Bobby Robson (below *left*), the Jovial Geordie who has become football's senior statesman. They are all as solid and reliable as the, uh, Rock of Gibraltar.

...undo is taking the name of Butt perhaps too literally in the defensive wall as they ...are to face a free kick from deadeye David Beckham. Along with Alan Shearer (*below ...e*) and Michael Owen (*right*), Beckham (*left*, playing for Real Madrid) is one of the few ...ern English players who can look the Old Masters in the eye without feeling humbled.

Three French Musketeers who have illuminated the soccer stage – Eric Can (*left*), Thierry Henry (*above*) and Zinedi Zidane (*bottom left*). They all have that certain va-va-voom.

Below Roman Abramovich, who starte a Russian revolution at 'Chelski', could saying, 'And who should I make this cheque-ski out to?'

CHAPTER 13

THE BEAUTIFUL GAME

C AN ONE save warrant a game being included in this history of
football? Yes, when it is made by one of the finest goalkeepers
of all time against the most phenomenal player of them all and in
the most important of all the tournaments.

England were playing Brazil in a vital 1970 World Cup group
match in the suffocating Jalisco Stadium in Guadalajara, in front of
a capacity crowd. The game was staged in the heat of the midday
sun on a scorching Sunday that was ideally suited for a siesta rather
than soccer. Only mad dogs and footballers would have gone out in
such sweltering 98-degree conditions, and at a thin-air altitude that
made walking, let alone running, a challenge.

The match was just ten minutes old and goalless when the master
of all strikers came face to face with a genius among goalkeepers –
Pele versus Gordon Banks in a *High Noon* duel.

Carlos Alberto, Brazilian right-back and captain, pushed a carefully calculated pass down the right wing into the path of the skilled
Jairzinho, who suddenly and dramatically accelerated past Terry
Cooper to the byline. He stabbed a centre that seemed to hang
invitingly in the goalmouth for Pele, who had instinctively read the
situation as only he could. He was perfectly positioned beyond his
marker, Alan Mullery, to meet the ball.

The master climbed above the ball and headed it down with
ferocious power into the net – or so he thought. Mullery later

reported that Pele shouted 'Goal!' as the ball flew off his head. So did most spectators in the stadium, including the commentators sending their descriptive phrases around the world to millions of television viewers and radio listeners.

Banks looked rooted on the wrong side of the goal but suddenly, with the blurring speed of a panther, he sprinted and dived to his right and somehow managed to get an outstretched hand under the ball, flicking it up and away over the bar. Pele stopped dead in mid-celebration, hardly able to take in what he had just seen.

This moment of astounding gymnastics from Banks inspired England to give the eventual world champions their hardest match of the tournament. After a magnificent battle, they finally succumbed to a superbly drilled shot by Jairzinho on the hour. He cut in from the right to score after an arrowing Tostao pass and a deft, perfectly delivered pass from Pele had ripped open the middle of the England defence.

Jeff Astle had a gilt-edged chance to equalise within moments of coming on as a substitute but – yes, even in those heatwave conditions – he was caught cold and shot tamely wide.

Evidence that the England players had given their all is that several of them lost up to ten pounds in weight, running round in the midday sun so that the World Cup organisers could satisfy the deadline demands of the great god of world-wide television. The millions who tuned in to the match will always recall it for having seen one of the saves of the century. This is how Pele described the moment that was the talk of football:

> *I just couldn't believe it when Gordon stopped my header. It was incredible that he got to it and even more incredible that he managed to push the ball over the bar. It was the biggest surprise I have ever had on a football pitch. No doubt about it, this was the greatest save I've ever seen.*

England skipper Bobby Moore, who gave one of the most accomplished individual defensive performances of his life, said:

> *I was getting ready to pick the ball out of the net when Gordon appeared from nowhere. He swooped across the goal like Superman and must have set some sort of world speed record*

getting from his near post to the far post. Was it a bird? Was it a plane? No, it was Banksie! What a pity we lost the game, because Gordon didn't deserve to be on the losing side after making a save like that. It was out of this world.

In his autobiography, *Banks of England*, which I ghosted just a few years later, the great man devoted a whole chapter to *that* save, although he confessed he knew less about it than any of the awestruck spectators:

> *I was too involved in what was happening on the pitch to give a second's thought to the save against Brazil. It was only later when I saw it on television that I realised it was a bit special. It was an instinctive save, but if Pele says it was the greatest he has ever seen, who am I to argue with the king? Now every time I see a replay I wonder how I got to it.*
>
> *Somehow I managed to make the 'impossible' save.*

England, with victories over Romania and Czechoslovakia, reached the quarter-finals in a decent defence of the trophy won four years earlier in the relatively cool climes of Wembley Stadium. Without a suddenly unwell Banks at the back, they lost 3–2 to West Germany after extra time, surrendering a 2–0 lead – echoes of '66 but with a painfully different outcome.

This was the first World Cup tournament in which substitutions were allowed and Alf Ramsey made a complete mess of it in this vital game. He rarely had to consider match-time changes and it wasn't one of his strengths. Ramsey was usually caution personified and not one to take anything for granted, yet he convinced himself that as England were leading 2–0 he could afford to save Bobby Charlton's energy for the semi-finals, despite Charlton being one of the mainstays of the team.

While Ramsey was on his feet preparing to take Bobby off, the Germans scored through Franz Beckenbauer – an unexceptional shot that went under Peter Bonetti's dive. Nevertheless, Ramsey carried on with his decision to send on Colin Bell for Charlton, much to Bobby's undisguised frustration. He was making his 106th England appearance, beating Billy Wright's all-time record.

Then came substitute blunder number two. Ramsey sent on Norman Hunter for Martin Peters – chalk for cheese, a bulldog for a poodle – and suddenly, with no midfield playmaker, the team seemed unbalanced.

It was clear to most people that if anybody needed to be substituted it was Hunter's Leeds United team-mate Terry Cooper, who was being run to the edge of exhaustion at left-back by fresh German substitute Jurgen Grabowski. Following a series of twisting, turning runs by Grabowski, a freak header from Uwe Seeler sent the ball on an arc over the wrong-footed Bonetti and the game went into extra time.

Geoff Hurst had what looked a perfectly legal goal disallowed (and the irony was not lost on the Germans after his 'goal that should not have been' in the 1966 final). The great escape lifted the Germans, and it was Gerd '*Der Bomber*' Muller who rammed in the winner after Grabowski had again beaten Cooper. England's reign as world champions was over, as was the stupendous international career of Bobby Charlton.

All eyes were on Bobby Moore as he trudged off at the end, looking like a man who had been to hell and back, which he had. Just two weeks before the tournament started he was sensationally arrested on a jewel-theft charge in Bogota while on a stopover with the England squad heading for Mexico. The accusation was later proved to be false and Moore won an army of admirers for the dignified way he handled the nightmare situation.

When Bobby arrived in Mexico to rejoin the England squad after four days spent under arrest, I was among a posse of press photographers and reporters gathered on the tarmac of Mexico City airport to meet him (can you imagine the press being allowed on the tarmac today?). Prominent among us was Geoffrey Green, Corinthian football correspondent of *The Times* and arguably the greatest football writer of any time. He had a habit of using lines from songs when he talked, and he always greeted people with such phrases as 'Younger than springtime . . .', delivered in a cut-glass Oxbridge accent. Geoffrey was using the phrase 'I'm over the moon' long before it became the cliché crutch of tongue-tied footballers.

As Bobby Moore stepped out from the plane into the dazzling light of hundreds of flashbulbs, he spotted the tall, willowy figure of Peter O'Toole-lookalike Geoffrey among the hordes at the bottom of the steps, punched the air and shouted, 'Over the rainbow, baby . . .!' Foreign reporters, anxious to record Bobby's first words on his return to freedom, scratched their heads as they tried to decipher what the England captain had said.

The next day Jimmy Greaves arrived in Mexico City in a battered Ford Escort at the end of the *Daily Mirror*-sponsored 16,400-mile London to Mexico World Cup rally in which he and his co-driver Tony Fall finished a creditable sixth. Jimmy's first concern as he climbed out of his car was for his West Ham team-mate and good pal Bobby Moore. 'Mooro wouldn't take a liberty, let alone a bracelet,' he said.

Jimmy was whisked off to the home of a British embassy official where Bobby was staying, out of sight of the press pack. He didn't go in by the front door but climbed over the back garden wall to avoid prying eyes. Some hours later, he described how he had been caught by the embassy official's wife, given a bollocking and then allowed in to see Bobby. Jimmy's first words were, 'Show us the bracelet then, Mooro.' The embassy official's wife went ashen – when it came to humour, she and Greavsie were from different planets.

Greavsie and Mooro – as they were affectionately known throughout the game – sank half a dozen bottles of beer, and Bobby said later, 'Seeing Jimbo was the best medicine I could have had. We didn't stop laughing from the moment he came through the French windows until he left three hours later. It was just the relaxation I needed. I would not wish my ordeal on my worst enemy.'

Alf Ramsey was convinced he had a stronger squad for the defence of the World Cup than when England won it, and he was shell-shocked by the quarter-final exit in which he played a part with his ineffective substitutions. The media inquest into England's defeat by West Germany delivered the verdict that they had taken their own World Cup life while the balance of their defence was disturbed.

Goalkeeper Bonetti, a late deputy for Banks – who swore he had been nobbled by a doctored drink – was blamed for two of the German goals, with little allowance given for the fact that he had hardly played any competitive football since the end of the English season.

England were the only team to stretch the Brazilians on their way to the final. Waiting for them there was an efficient and often enterprising Italian team that had beaten West Germany 4–3, again after extra time, in a sensational, seesawing semi-final. Both Brazil and Italy had won the World Cup twice, and the extra incentive was that the winners would keep the Jules Rimet trophy for all time (or until thieves decided they would have it outright!).

The Azteca Stadium in Mexico City became a roaring inferno as Brazil took the lead after eighteen minutes, the one and only Pele soaring above the Italian defenders to score with a tremendous header from Rivelino's high, swirling cross.

Clodoaldo, whose linking play with Gerson had been one of the outstanding features of the tournament, had a rare lapse of concentration seven minutes before half-time and carelessly back-heeled the ball into the path of Boninsegna. Rarely has a goal been given away with such elegance. The lightning-quick Italian striker gleefully accepted the unsolicited gift and raced away to beat oncoming goalkeeper Felix for an out of the blue – out of the azure – equaliser.

Now it was the turn of the Italian fans to hope that, as with all the previous post-war finals, the team that scored first finished second. They had the most disciplined defence of any team, under the baton of skipper Giacinto Facchetti, and in Luigi Riva possessed a player in the class of the Brazilian forwards. Yes, the Italian fans had hope.

But, proficient and full of pace and power as Italy were, they could not contain what many good judges consider to be the greatest attacking force ever gathered together in one team. Even now, more than thirty years on, the names roll so easily off the tongue: Jairzinho, Tostao, Pele, Rivelino, with Gerson tucked just behind, feeding them with probing, positive passes. To see them in action truly was poetry in motion.

Gerson is the one most likely to escape people's minds and memories when trying to name that Brazilian attack, yet he was the master lyricist who made the poems rhyme. Throughout his career, he was said to have smoked forty cigarettes a day. He should have carried a public stealth warning for the way he could dismantle a defence with disguised passes that always carried the correct weight and pace.

It was Gerson, engineer turned executioner, who restored Brazil's lead in the sixty-sixth minute as he rifled in a left-foot cross shot from just outside the penalty area, with the Italian defenders all anticipating a pass that never came.

The Italian defence, famed for its togetherness and solidarity, was now opening up like a crop-circled cornfield but not as mysteriously. Everyone could see that the damage was being done by a Brazilian team in full flight – and what a sight to behold!

Five minutes later the scampering Jairzinho, always a highly mobile menace down the right wing, sprinted on to a delicate pass from Pele and buried the ball in the net with an angled shot for goal number three.

Far too late, the Italians summoned 'Golden Boy' Gianni Rivera to try to pick up the pieces. Strangely, the midfield maestro was sent on as a substitute for out-and-out striker Boninsegna. He arrived on the pitch just in time to be a witness to the *piéce de resistance*, the final course in the Brazilian banquet.

The move started deep in midfield in the eighty-seventh minute, with Clodoaldo performing step-over tricks as if this was an exhibition match. The ball was transferred to Rivelino, who sent Jairzinho away with a precision pass down the touchline. Next on the conveyor belt of brilliance came a strolling Pele, who thankfully had changed his mind after vowing in 1966 never to play in a World Cup finals again after being physically kicked out of the tournament. As casually as if playing on Copacabana beach in Rio, he stroked the ball into the path of right-back and captain Carlos Alberto, who was thundering down the right wing full of goal intent. He powered the ball past goalkeeper Enrico Albertosi for a fourth goal that deserved to be captured on canvas.

Cue pandemonium. When East German referee Rudi Glockner blew the final whistle, the Brazilian players were engulfed in a tidal wave of fans, many of them photographers and radio interviewers wanting to celebrate rather than capture the moment. An impromptu *mardi gras* carnival broke out on the Azteca pitch.

Rivelino collapsed under the weight of the celebrations and had to be carried to the dressing room on a stretcher. The huge crowd waited for Carlos Alberto and his team-mates to battle through to the awards ceremony. The Brazilian skipper did not notice as he paraded the Jules Rimet Trophy – now the property of Brazil – that a gold attachment to the Cup had fallen to the ground. Brazilian reserve Dario retrieved it just as a young spectator was making for the exit with his unexpected souvenir.

Tostao, Pele's plundering partner in attack, refused to swap his shirt with any Italian player. He had promised to give it to the surgeon in Houston, Texas, who had performed two operations on a detached eye retina during the year immediately before the 1970 finals. Five years later, Tostao himself qualified as a medical doctor.

There was deserved applause for Italy, who had played so well in this finest of finals. Despite all the fears that this would be a violent tournament, not a single player was sent off – which has happened twice only, in 1970 and 1950.

'It was,' said Pele, '*a beautiful game*,' and the world had a new description for football. In fact, those words were first uttered by poet, journalist and author Joao Saldanha, who briefly managed Brazil in the build-up to the 1970 finals. Saldanha, a former revolutionary, produced a river of flowery prose. He described the ball as a precious diamond to be treated with loving care, and football as 'the beautiful game'. However, he was too much of a free spirit, even for Brazilian tastes, and when he talked seriously of leaving Pele out of his squad for the finals in Mexico – not such a beautiful thought – he was sacked to make way for Mario Zagola.

The peerless Pele collected 12 goals in four World Cup final tournaments and is the only player to have been a member of three World Cup winning teams, although he missed the final stages in 1962 because of a pulled muscle.

Born in near poverty in Tres Coracoes, Bauru, on 23 October 1940, Edson Arantes do Nascimento – Pele – became one of the most famous people in the world. Arguably, Muhammad Ali is the only other sportsman to equal his international fame.

Pele came under the influence of former Brazilian World Cup player Waldemar de Brito at Bauru, the club where Pele's father, known as Dondinho, had played. De Brito recommended him to Santos where he quickly emerged as an international star, making his debut for Brazil at the age of sixteen and receiving world-wide acclaim at seventeen for his stunning performances in the 1958 World Cup finals.

When European clubs came hunting for the young Pele in the early 1960s, the Brazilian government listed him as a 'national treasure' to prevent him leaving the country. His 92 hat-tricks remain an all-time record.

After a brief retirement, he was persuaded to make a comeback with New York Cosmos in 1974. Among his team-mates was Bobby

Moore. Pele's 65 goals for Cosmos were watched by record crowds in the North American Soccer League, and when he retired, Cosmos also retired his No. 10 shirt, following an emotional final match against his old Santos club in New York.

He was appointed Minister for Sport by the Brazilian government, a job he gave up to follow business interests that turned sour when he accused a former partner of stealing $10 million from his company.

In 1997 he received an honorary knighthood from the Queen at Buckingham Palace.

Pele never played a competitive match at Wembley, but once scored a goal there while making a television commercial! Since then, he has earned more money than he ever did as a player from a world-wide television campaign about a cure for impotency. One thing is for sure, Pele was never ever impotent on the pitch.

Into his mid-sixties, Pele was still describing the Gordon Banks' save of 1970 as the best he had ever seen. Banks would just pip Peter Shilton in my ratings of the top post-war England goalkeepers, but both would be a fingertip behind Northern Ireland's Pat Jennings, who had hands like buckets and a gymnastic ability that would have earned praise from Olga Korbut.

My top twenty post-war British goalkeepers are (in order): Pat Jennings, Gordon Banks, Peter Shilton, Frank Swift, Ray Clemence, David Seaman, Bob Wilson, Jack Kelsey, Bert Williams, Neville Southall, Peter Bonetti, Alex Stepney, Ron Springett, Sam Bartram, Ted Ditchburn, Jim Leighton, Gary Sprake, Eddie Hopkinson, Phil Parkes and, equal twentieth, Gordon West and Malcolm Finlayson – but they would all have to bow the knee to the great Dane, Peter Schmeichel.

CHAPTER 14

TOTAL FOOTBALL AND TOTAL MAYHEM

N ow's THE TIME to put on the flared trousers, the kipper tie and the platform shoes – *de rigueur* for footballers in the glam-rock seventies – for a trip back to a decade when the domestic game was as bubbly as a Kevin Keegan perm.

At the dawn of the 1970s, Britain had an 'old' Labour government, with Huddersfield Town supporter Harold Wilson at Number 10, and 'Tricky Dicky' Nixon was in the White House – the Watergate scandal still to break. The average price for a three-bedroomed semi-detached house in the south east was £5,250. A gallon of petrol cost 6s – 30p in the decimal currency that was still a year away – and a pint of bitter would set you back 1s 10d (9p). You could buy a Jaguar XJ6 for £2,690, but probably not if you earned your living as a factory worker, where the average wage was £23 per week.

Lester Piggott was unbeatable on Nijinsky and Joe Frazier was just about to knock out Jimmy Ellis to become the undisputed heavyweight champion of the world during Muhammad Ali's suspension for refusing to fight in the war that was still raging in the killing fields of Vietnam. Led Zeppelin had taken over from the Beatles and the Rolling Stones as the biggest draw in the music business, and Rolf Harris was about to storm the charts with 'Two Little Boys'.

For just 5s (25p) you could stand on the terraces at most First Division grounds, an eight-page programme would set you back 6d (around 2p) and £9 would buy you a season ticket at Old Trafford to watch George Best, Bobby Charlton and Denis Law.

In 1970, it would have cost you £7 for the best seat in the house to see Chelsea win a dramatic FA Cup final replay against Leeds at Old Trafford. The game was played in Manchester because poor old Wembley was not in any condition to host the match. The pitch had been in an appalling state for the first game. The turf had been wrecked when, crazily, an international horse show was staged on the hallowed ground shortly before the crucial date. The Cup final, which ended 2–2, turned into a farce, played on a rain-saturated, sand-covered pitch that looked more like Blackpool with the tide out than the national football arena.

At Old Trafford, David Webb headed the extra-time goal that gave Dave Sexton's multi-talented Chelsea victory over Leeds. That win opened the way to the 1971 European Cup Winners' Cup final triumph against Real Madrid in Athens, again after a replay. Peter Osgood, the leaning tower of Stamford Bridge, was the main instigator of Chelsea's Cup successes. He scored in every round, including the final, in the 1970 FA Cup run, and the silky skilled centre-forward's goal clinched victory over the Spanish giants in the Cup Winners' Cup final replay.

However, despite the efforts of couple-of-cups Chelsea, Arsenal stole the early seventies show. Ten years earlier, Tottenham had become the first team of the twentieth century to win the league and FA Cup double, which they did at a canter. Their great rivals Arsenal, managed by Bertie Mee, coached by Don Howe and coaxed by inspiring skipper Frank McLintock, did it the hard way. They came from behind to pip Leeds for the 1970–71 championship on the last day of the season, and came from behind again in the FA Cup final against Liverpool five days later, Highbury idol Charlie George winning it for them with a blistering extra-time shot.

Frank McLintock, who had been a four-times loser at Wembley, said, 'I was beginning to hate the place. It was the lowest point of my life when we lost at Wembley to Swindon in the 1969 League Cup final, but that defeat gave us the determination to win. Forget the profit we were making. It was all about pride. We won the

European Fairs Cup in 1970 and that was the springboard for our double year.'

Goalkeeper Bob Wilson, who went on to build a fine career for himself in television, commented, 'It was my privilege to be voted Player of the Year by the Arsenal fans in that double season, but if ever an award should have been shared between a whole squad of players it was that one. We epitomised what teamwork and team spirit were all about. We really did believe in the all-for-one-and-one-for-all principle. There were better footballing teams around, but none that could match our togetherness.'

Meanwhile, a force of nature was gathering pace, roughly in the direction of the Peak District. 'Hurricane' Clough arrived at Second Division Derby County in the summer of 1967, determined to instil a lot of ambition and a little amnesia into the sleeping Midlands giant. The Rams had not achieved anything of note since the Raich Carter/Peter Doherty-stirred FA Cup exploits of the immediate post-war years. On the day that he took over, Clough warned, with a frankness that was to make him the talk of football and a godsend for quote-hungry reporters, 'I will personally punch on the nose anybody who mentions what this club did in the past. From now on we think only of the present and the future. I will not be content until we've got a championship trophy to show off along with a team that will be a delight to the eye. Any player who pulls on a Derby shirt without being prepared to give blood, sweat and tears will be out on his ear before you can say Sam Longson.'

Sam Longson was the chairman of Derby with whom Clough would eventually have a mega fall-out, but in the early days of the revolution at the Baseball Ground they were a team that not only talked but acted big.

Clough bought swashbuckling Dave Mackay from Tottenham to shepherd his young defence and, together with right-hand man Peter Taylor, guided Derby to the Second Division championship. Then, in 1971–72, Derby captured the league title, clinching it with a victory over closest rivals Liverpool in their last match of the season. Clough was just thirty-six years old and full of himself.

'I ought to be able to hold up the England team to my bunch,' he remarked, 'and say, "That's it – that's how to play the game." Alf Ramsey's team should reflect all the good things in English football. It doesn't. Things are the other way around. He'd be better off getting England to try to play like Derby. If that sounds conceited, so be it. Take a look at the First Division table. I've got a right to make my point. We play the game the way it should be played.'

We would hear a lot more from Mr Clough before the final shots of the decade had been fired.

The most romantic football story of the early seventies was the long-awaited success of Stoke City and their Peter Pan of the game, George Eastham. It took Stoke – founded in 1863 and the second oldest league club after Notts County – 109 years to win their first major trophy. Managed by the enterprising Tony Waddington, they beat Chelsea 2–1 in the 1972 League Cup final at the end of a marathon series of matches rarely equalled in any Cup competition.

On their way to Wembley, Stoke were taken to a third-round replay by Oxford United, and they played Manchester United three times before mastering them in the fourth round. Then they got locked in an exhausting four-match semi-final with West Ham.

Stoke would have gone out at the first time of asking against the Hammers but for a startling penalty save by Gordon Banks against his England team-mate Geoff Hurst. In their second replay, West Ham skipper Bobby Moore went in goal for injured Bobby Ferguson, and he managed to save a Stoke penalty before being beaten in the follow-up rush.

To complete the Stoke City fairytale, their winning goal at Wembley was scored by George Eastham, the frail-looking thirty-five-year-old former England inside-left, and the man most responsible for kicking away the soccer slavery shackles. It was his only goal of the year.

At the end of the season, Eastham was beaten to the Footballer of the Year award by his Stoke City team-mate Gordon Banks. Tragically, that was Gordon's final season in top-flight football. The following October he was involved in a car smash that cost him the sight of his right eye and finished his 73 cap international career. Gordon made his last saves in the United States Soccer League where, incredibly – with one eye – he was voted their Most Valuable (best) goalkeeper.

In a sad paradox, one of the greatest performances in the long and proud history of Rangers Football Club is also one that is considered best forgotten by many Scots. A brilliantly engineered 3–2 victory over Lev Yashin-managed Moscow Dynamo in the

1972 European Cup Winners' Cup final in Barcelona was over-shadowed by rioting Rangers fans, who heaped shame on the Ibrox club. They fought full-scale running battles with Spanish police, who reacted with excessive brutality. The trophy presentation had to be made behind closed doors and Rangers were banned from Europe for two years.

Skipper John Greig, who gave noble service to Rangers and Scotland, said later, 'It should have been one of the proudest days of our lives. Instead, we were left feeling as if we had been kicked by our own fans. We won the match on merit but all the headlines went to a stupid minority who spoiled it for everybody else.'

Over the next fifteen years the cancer of hooliganism was to cut even more deeply into British football, and scarred the face of the Beautiful Game.

It was a much brighter story on the pitch, particularly at Anfield where Bill Shankly's Liverpool equalled the Arsenal record of eight league championship successes in 1972–73. The season had an astonishing climax in the FA Cup final at Wembley.

A Second Division team had never won a post-war FA Cup final and few people gave Sunderland a hope of beating Don Revie's mighty Leeds. The Yorkshire club were the Cup holders, and ten of the side that had conquered Arsenal 1–0 a year earlier were on duty again. All but one of their twelve-player squad were internationals. According to the experts, Sunderland were there to make up the numbers.

One man in particular was convinced that Leeds could be beaten. Sunderland manager Bob Stokoe, who had been in charge for just five months and was already being hailed as the 'Messiah of Roker Park', sensed an air of complacency emanating from Elland Road. He quietly built up the confidence of his players on the foundation of the old saying 'We've got nothing to lose'.

Far from being overwhelmed in midfield by one of the most talented partnerships in football, Billy Bremner and Johnny Giles, it quickly became obvious that Sunderland's driving captain Bobby Kerr and the tenacious Mickey Horswill were effectively containing them.

After thirty minutes of deadlocked action in which neither team could gain the ascendancy, Wembley suddenly erupted with a roar that might have been heard all the way up at Roker. The thundering noise came from the throats of Sunderland fans celebrating a goal that left Leeds feeling as if the ground had been cut away from under them. Ian Porterfield, renowned for his left-footed skill, had scored from a corner delivered by fellow Scot Billy Hughes. Porterfield caught the ball on his left thigh before firing it high into the Leeds net with a rare shot from his 'swinger' right foot.

Leeds were like giants being shaken out of a deep slumber. They struck back with top-quality football but to no avail against a Sunderland team suddenly believing that they could achieve the impossible.

They were protected at the back by Jim Montgomery, one of the best uncapped goalkeepers in the game. He knocked the heart out of Leeds with an astonishing double save in the seventieth minute. A diving header from Trevor Cherry looked a certain goal but Montgomery pushed it out at the near post. The breathing of Sunderland supporters was suspended as the ball dropped at the feet of Peter Lorimer, the man with the cannonball shot. From just six yards he fired in what seemed to be the equaliser, but Montgomery had other ideas. He threw himself across the goal and somehow, unbelievably, managed to divert the ball with his left wrist on to the bar. That save ranks with the one that Banks made from Pele. When 'The Greatest Save of All Time' is the topic of debate, Montgomery's is one of the few that challenges Gordon for the top spot. Bob Stokoe raced fifty yards from the touchline at the final whistle to embrace his goalkeeper.

In the dressing room after the game, Jim Montgomery declared, clutching the Cup all the while, 'When I die I shall have my left hand and wrist embalmed. I have never been prouder of a save than that one from Peter Lorimer. Poor old Peter could not believe it, and to be honest, neither could I. All the critics wrote us off without a chance. From the moment I managed to make that double save, all of us knew that this was going to be *our* day.'

Sadly, Bob Stokoe, once a Cup final hero with Newcastle in the 1950s, passed on in the winter of 2004.

Victory in '73 was Sunderland's second triumph at Wembley. Raich Carter had collected the Cup for them in '37 – a coincidence that really figured with the famously superstitious men of Leeds. Manager Don Revie now had the difficult job of trying to pick up his dejected players for a European Cup Winners' Cup final against

AC Milan just eleven days later – to no avail. Once again Leeds finished a treble-chasing season with nothing to show for it but bruised hearts. A spiteful, hate-filled match in Salonika was won by a goal from Luciano Chiarugi in the fourth minute, after which the 'Misers of Milan' closed up the game and hid their goal behind a mass defence.

A new phenomenon caused widespread controversy in the New Year of 1974 – Sunday professional football. Britain had been reduced to a three-day week by a strike in the power industry, which meant no floodlit games. The fixtures were getting in such a jam that the Football Association reluctantly gave the go-ahead for FA Cup ties to be played on the Sabbath. Four games were played on 6 January 1974. Cambridge against Oldham was the first with an 11 a.m. kick-off. Millwall played Fulham on 20 January in the first league match to be played on a Sunday, but it was not until 1981 that Sunday games became a regular part of the football programme.

Another radical change in English football came in the final month of the 1973–74 season when Sir Alf Ramsey was sacked unceremoniously after a reign that had lasted eleven years. The World Cup brought him his greatest glory and his greatest grief. He was knighted as reward for leading England to victory in 1966, but the Football Association axe came down on his neck after England failed to qualify for the 1974 finals in West Germany.

England had to beat Poland to qualify and how they failed will always remain a mystery to everybody who watched the game at Wembley on 17 October 1973. Poland took the lead in the fifty-fifth minute, completely against the run of play, after Norman Hunter, of all people, the most famed and feared tackler in the game, mistimed a challenge out on the right touchline. Lato quickly played the ball into the path of Domarski, whose low shot threaded into the net under Peter Shilton's diving form. 'Bites Yer Legs' Hunter missing a tackle and 'Safe as Houses' Shilton missing the ball? It was difficult for spectators to believe what they were seeing.

Poland had two shots only while England forced 23 corners and had no fewer than 35 goal attempts! It was one of the most one-sided matches ever seen at Wembley. Poland's eccentric but effective goalkeeper Jan Tomaszewski made at least six blinding saves, reducing to nonsense TV match summariser Brian Clough's dismissal of him as a clown. The only time he was beaten was when Allan Clarke nervelessly tucked away a penalty in the sixty-third minute after Martin Peters had been fouled.

In the closing moments of the match the looming outcome briefly turned to *Carry On* farce. Kevin Keegan, on the substitutes' bench, related the classic story in our book *The Seventies Revisited*:

> *Alf Ramsey proved yet again that he was uncomfortable with the substitute rule when he left it until the eighty-fifth minute before he decided to make a change. He called over his shoulder to the substitutes sitting in a row behind him, 'Kevin, get stripped.'*
>
> *It was panic stations as goalkeeper Ray Clemence tugged at my tracksuit bottoms to help me get ready for action. My Liverpool team-mate was so eager that he pulled down my shorts as well!*
>
> *My embarrassment was complete when Alf then made it clear that his command had been meant for Kevin Hector, not this Kevin! Talk about 'Don't panic, Mr Mainwaring.'*

There were just ninety seconds left when the Derby County striker at last got on to the pitch, and he was desperately unlucky not to score with his first and only touch of the ball. The game finished 1–1 and England were out of the World Cup. By the end of the season, Ramsey was out of a job.

It was the end of an era for English football. Ramsey had put his indelible stamp on the international game, and his record will be a lasting testimony to the fact that he was an exceptional manager – played 113, won 69, drawn 27, lost 17, goals for 224, goals against 99.

The man chosen to succeed him, after a brief caretaker spell with Uncle Joe Mercer, was Don Revie, who bowed out of Leeds with a second league championship. Leeds started the 1973–74 season with the then most successful First Division run in post-war football, playing 29 matches without defeat and finally winning the title by 5 points from Liverpool.

Wembley was a happier place for Kevin Keegan six months after the débâcle against Poland. He scored two fine goals as lively Liverpool strolled to a 3–0 FA Cup final victory over a Newcastle side that never looked like living up to the pre-match boasts of Malcolm 'Supermac' Macdonald.

However, that summer was anything but happy for Keegan. In June he managed to get himself roughed up by security guards at Belgrade airport while travelling with Joe Mercer's England squad. They arrested him when completely over-reacting to his clowning around while he collected his luggage.

More *Carry On* farce followed when Bernard Joy, one of the few journalists who witnessed the incident, raced to a telephone to give his newspaper, the London *Evening Standard*, the hot exclusive. When he finally got through to the newspaper switchboard, after the frustrating delays that were common in those pre-direct dialling days, the operator started with pleasantries.

'Nice to hear from you, Mr Joy,' she said. 'What's the weather like out there?'

Bernard, the last amateur to play for England, was in urgent deadline-beating mode.

'I've got no time for small talk,' he snapped. 'Put me through to the copytakers immediately. I've got an exclusive story here.'

'Uh, but Mr Joy,' the operator said. 'It's Sunday. There's no paper today.'

Keegan was back in the headlines for the wrong reasons on his next appearance at Wembley, two months after his nightmare in Belgrade.

Nobody could have predicted that the 1974–75 season would kick off with the two top clubs, Liverpool and Leeds United, under new management. It was widely anticipated that Don Revie would take over as England manager but the retirement of Bill Shankly caused shocks of earthquake proportions throughout football.

Shankly handed over the reins to his faithful right-hand man Bob Paisley, a pleasant, unassuming Geordie who was as different from Shankly as a pint of Newcastle Brown from a shot of Scottish malt whisky. Shankly would lead out Liverpool for the last time in a competitive match in the Charity Shield against Leeds. The traditional curtain-raiser had been switched to Wembley for the first time as a shop window of all that was best about the Beautiful Game. What could the odds have been that while Shankly was leading out Liverpool for the last time, none other than Brian Clough would be leading out Leeds for the first time?

Clough had been the shock choice as successor to Don Revie, an appointment that was greeted in the village world of football with almost as much disbelief as Shankly's retirement.

After a bitter fall-out with Derby, during which his players threatened a rebellion, Clough had very briefly taken his tongue and his talent to the south coast with Brighton before answering the call to take charge at Elland Road. He had been an outspoken critic of the, at times, cynical style of play that had made Leeds such a power in the game, and so the gossip in football was that he would be about as welcome with some of the Leeds players as pneumonia. Sure enough, the wounds caused by Clough's hard-hitting comments over the years could not be healed and he was on his way out of Elland Road, with a hefty compensatory bag of gold, after just forty-four days in the job, moving on to Nottingham Forest. The 'great motivator' had failed to get the vital 100 per cent cooperation of the Leeds players and he became the victim of what many in the game interpreted as player power.

Kevin Keegan and Leeds skipper Billy Bremner showed a different kind of player power in the Charity Shield match. Keegan lost his temper after challenges in quick succession from first Johnny Giles and then Bremner. In reflective mood some years later, Kevin admitted, 'I allowed myself to be provoked by the infamous Leeds tactics, first an off-the-ball whack from Giles followed soon afterwards by a crafty dig from Bremner that brought on the red mist of temper. I went after Bremner and we were both ordered off after swapping wildly aimed punches. To this day, neither Billy nor I could explain why, as we walked off, we both pulled off our shirts in disgust.'

The incident was seen by millions on television at a time when the game was under the microscope because of increasing violence on the pitch and the escalating hooliganism problem. The establishment, more upset by the disrespectful shirt-stripping than the swapped punches, were determined to make an example of both players. What was then a massive £500 fine was imposed on each of them, plus five-week suspensions.

Football louts followed Tottenham to Rotterdam for their 1974 UEFA Cup final second leg against Feyenoord after a 2–2 draw at White Hart Lane. When the Dutchmen went into a 4–2 aggregate lead, so-called Tottenham supporters started an ugly riot that led to seventy arrests and 200 spectators being treated for injuries. Bill

Nicholson, Tottenham's long-serving and highly respected manager, appealed over the public-address system for sanity. Tears in his eyes and his voice breaking with emotion, he said, 'You hooligans are a disgrace to Tottenham Hotspur and a disgrace to England. This is a game of football – not a war.'

England's six-year stranglehold on the UEFA/Fairs Cup, including an unprecedented all-English final between Tottenham and Wolves in 1972, had been broken, but who cared at a time when some people loosely described as English supporters were kicking football into the gutter.

An invasion by the Tartan army helped to hasten the end of the Home International Championships. A great swathe of Scots spilled on to the Wembley pitch at the end of the 1977 England-Scotland match, demolishing the goalposts and digging up chunks of turf as souvenirs of their 2–1 victory. That particular tournament was finally buried without ceremony in 1984 after England and Wales refused to play in Belfast during the Northern Ireland troubles. Ah, the Beautiful Game!

Across the North Sea in Holland, a much brighter picture of the game was being painted. Ajax had perfected a system of 'total football', with all their outfield players able to support and cover for each other in defence or attack. The system revolved around the two Johans – Cruyff and Neeskens – who decorated every game with their stunning skill, and decimated defences with their pace, shooting power and passing accuracy. For three successive years from 1971, Ajax carried off the European Cup.

The Dutch international team – vastly talented but with tinderbox temperament – became the nearly men of the World Cup, finishing runners-up in 1974 and 1978.

The 1974 final against West Germany in Munich got off to an extraordinary start when English referee Jack Taylor, a master butcher from Wolverhampton, awarded a penalty in the first minute. From the kick-off, Holland played a stunning series of fifteen passes before Johan Cruyff made a dash for goal. Uli Hoeness tripped him and Taylor had no hesitation in awarding a penalty, which Neeskens put away.

Just as it looked as if West Germany were going to be paralysed by the strolling players of Holland, they got back into the game, thanks to a penalty. Paul Breitner, an artist at left-back, scored from the spot to make it 1–1. Breitner, incidentally, was a highly intelligent and dedicated Maoist.

The Germans put their foot down on the accelerator and it was the turn of the Dutch defenders to be stretched on the rack of uncertainty. The pressure reached its peak in the forty-third minute when ace opportunist Gerd Muller swept the ball into the net for his sixty-eighth international goal.

Holland, inspired by the cultured Cruyff, played some stunning football in the second half, but were continually denied by the goalkeeping of Sepp Maier, he of the huge gloves and daredevil spirit.

Franz Beckenbauer, the imperious 'Kaiser' who was the driving force behind Bayern Munich's hat-trick of European Cup wins from 1974, collected the new World Cup trophy, as he had the European Nations Cup in 1972. He commented, 'It was a brave decision by the referee to give that penalty so early in the match, but I instinctively felt that we too would get a penalty at some stage. We did not lose our composure or our concentration, and well as Holland played, I think you have to give us credit for having the character to overcome such a disastrous start.'

Leeds were the team beaten by Bayern in the 1975 European Cup final in Paris. By then they were managed by 'Gentleman' Jimmy Armfield, former England right-back and captain, and a true sportsman. Before the game, Jimmy invited Eric Morecambe (with me in Paris for our *Daily Express* column) into the Leeds dressing room and he had the players in fits of laughter with his inimitable brand of humour – 'I had a trial at Leeds once . . . got a six-months suspended sentence. They hung me from the crossbar by my suspenders. Not a pretty sight.'

Nobody was laughing by the end of the evening. A mindless minority of so-called fans could not stomach Leeds United's 2–0 defeat and the *gendarmes* were kept busy dealing with fighting in the crowd. Seats were ripped up and thrown towards the pitch and extra police had to be drafted in to try to bring the hooligans under control. Their behaviour brought more shame on English football in general and Leeds in particular. Hooliganism was now known throughout Europe as 'the English disease'. England had given football to the world. One hundred years on, the gift was hooliganism.

Two weeks before the shame of Paris, an unlikely hero emerged at Wembley in the shape of twenty-one-year-old Alan Taylor, who started the season down in the Fourth Division with Rochdale. Taylor scored two goals for West Ham in the sixth round of the FA Cup and in the semi-final. Then he did it again in the final against Fulham, in the process disappointing three elder statesmen of the game – Fulham manager Alec Stock, skipper Alan Mullery and Bobby Moore, who was winding down his career at Craven Cottage after sixteen glorious years with the Hammers.

Malcolm Macdonald made up for the frustration of his sterile show in the 1974 FA Cup final on a return visit to Wembley on 16 April 1975. He scored all five England goals – four with his head – in a crushing 5–0 defeat of Cyprus in a European Championship qualifier. That feat equalled the five-goal haul by Tottenham's Willie Hall for England against Northern Ireland in 1938 but Macdonald was the first player to accomplish it at Wembley.

At this point, halfway through the decade, Liverpool's domestic domination was about to grow into an international monopoly. After bidding a fond farewell to Bill Shankly, the Anfield club came under the baton of Bob Paisley and the Red Revolution was now set to spread across Europe.

CHAPTER 15

A BRITISH BLANKET OVER EUROPE

B OB PAISLEY moved reluctantly into Bill Shankly's seat as manager of Liverpool. He was content living in the shadow of the great man, quietly planning the team's playing pattern while Shanks did all the shouting.

At the first team meeting after the shock of Shankly's retirement, Bob told the players in his soft, almost apologetic Geordie tones, 'I never wanted this job in the first place, and I'm not even sure that I can do it. I need all the help I can get from you players. There will be no disruptions to the team. Let's just keep playing it the Liverpool way.'

Paisley was underestimating himself. He not only filled the large Shankly shoes into which he had stepped, but managed to take even bigger strides than the old Scottish master. Over a span of eight years, he became one of the most successful managers in the history of the game. At first, sensibly, he stuck with the team and the tactics that he had inherited from Shankly. He implanted his own ideas slowly, gradually developing the Paisley Pattern that was to make Liverpool masters of Europe.

It took the Liverpool players some time to get used to calling him 'Boss' after having affectionately known him as 'The Rat'. This nickname was hung on him because of his wartime service as a Desert Rat with Montgomery's victorious El-Alamein troops.

Born in the football hotbed of Hetton-le-Hole in County Durham, Paisley had joined Liverpool as a player just before the outbreak of war in 1939, after winning an FA Amateur Cup medal with Bishop Auckland. He had served Liverpool as a player, trainer and coach before finally getting the summons to be manager at the age of fifty-five.

A man of great common sense rather than deep intellect, Paisley did not make the mistake of trying to become Bill Shankly the second. He knew there would only ever be one Shanks. He could not have competed with him in the communications business, but he got his ideas and theories across in a quiet, down-to-earth way. A tough, stubborn streak lurked inside him and he was as single-minded and determined as Shankly when it came to wanting to be a football winner.

Proof that his methods worked is there for all to see in the record books. Between 1974 and 1983, under Paisley's management, Liverpool won thirteen major trophies – six league championships, three European Cups, three League Cups and one UEFA Cup.

Tommy Docherty could not match Paisley for winning trophies, but he outstripped him and every other manager for newspaper coverage, not always to do with football. After a spell as an excellent Scotland manager, when he gave English-born players Bob Wilson, Bruce Rioch and Alex Cropley their first caps, along with a certain very Scottish Kenny Dalglish, the Doc gave it all up for his dream job – boss of Manchester United.

In what were frantic and fascinating years at Old Trafford, he took them down and then straight back up again as Second Division champions. The goal that helped send them down was back-heeled into the net by Denis Law, who had surprisingly been allowed a free transfer to his old club, Manchester City. Law scored in the closing moments of the last Saturday of the 1973–74 season, and the game was abandoned as frustrated Manchester United fans came flooding on to the Old Trafford pitch. The match result stood and United were relegated. Popular myth has it that Denis Law was responsible for sending United down but, because of other results, United would have been relegated anyway, regardless of the outcome of their derby with Manchester City.

Docherty survived as United manager and in 1976 and 1977 he led them to successive FA Cup finals. They lost the first one to

Second Division underdogs Southampton, which was a tremendous personal coup for Saints manager Lawrie McMenemy, who built his team around tried and trusted veterans Mike Channon, Jim McCalliog and former Chelsea idol Peter Osgood.

The goal that won it for Southampton, beautifully taken by Hampshire-born Bobby Stokes, turned him into a local hero although to this day the Doc will tell you that the linesman should have waved Stokes offside. Sadly, Bobby died young but his name will always live on in Southampton football history.

Bobby was the toast of a huge party after the shock victory, and leading the celebrations was the old king of the King's Road, Peter Osgood, calling on all his partying experience from his Chelsea days.

For some reason, Ossie was entrusted with the job of making sure the FA Cup got back safely to Southampton, which was a bit like giving the keys to the jungle to Johnny Rotten. So it was that at three o'clock in the morning, a seriously sozzled Ossie was showing off the FA Cup to astonished Southampton supporters having a coffee at a mobile snackbar on the A3. Then Ossie took the Cup home and slept with it, as you would!

'It was the best way of looking after it,' Ossie explained later, with the sort of logic that made sense only to him. There don't seem to be wonderful characters like Ossie in the game any more.

A year later Tommy Docherty, who brought Osgood into football at Chelsea, steered Manchester United to Wembley again. This time they got it right with a deserved 2–1 victory over favourites Liverpool, who had clinched the league championship in the first leg of a hoped-for treble.

Bob Paisley picked up his bruised and bemused players and just four days later, in Rome, they ran out to play Borussia Moenchengladbach in the European Cup final. Liverpool and Borussia were no strangers to each other. They had met in the two-leg UEFA Cup final in 1973, the Merseysiders winning an encounter of the close kind 3–2 on aggregate.

Now, in their thirteenth successive season of European football, Liverpool had finally made it into *the* major final. Veteran winger-turned-schemer Ian Callaghan had played in every one of those seasons and was recalled for the match of a lifetime after being relegated to the substitutes' bench for the FA Cup final against

Manchester United. A switch in tactics from the 4–3–3 formation used at Wembley to 4–2–4 in Rome loaded extra responsibility on Kevin Keegan. The buzz-saw player was moved to the heart of the Liverpool attack where his injured partner John Toshack usually patrolled. For Keegan, the game had double meaning. He was not only playing for a European Cup victory but also to clinch a proposed record £500,000 transfer to Hamburg, Borussia's rivals in the Bundesliga.

Liverpool were in control from the opening minutes, with Callaghan bossing the midfield in Napoleonic mode and Keegan running the Borussia defence – and his marker, Berti Vogts – to the point of panic with a staggering display of perpetual motion.

In a rare raid, Rainer Bonhof hit a post with a snap shot in the twenty-seventh minute. Liverpool responded immediately with a classic goal, Callaghan and Steve Heighway combining to create an opening for Terry McDermott. The midfield man raced fifty yards to arrive in the penalty area at the same time as Heighway's pass and scored with a low shot on the run.

Liverpool's travelling army of ee-aye-adioing fans managed to transfer the sight and sound of the Kop to Rome's Olympic Stadium, responding to the goal with an increase in the volume and passion of their chants. They got even louder after a goal from Dane Allan Simonsen brought Borussia level.

The Red Army went ballistic in the sixty-fifth minute when defender Tommy Smith, of all people, bulleted in a header from a Heighway corner to make it 2–1. A Tommy Smith headed goal was as rare as a Penny Black on a postcard from Siberia, and it helped push the thirty-two-year-old Anfield Assassin deeper into the land of Liverpool legend.

Fittingly, it was man of the match Keegan who settled it for Liverpool seven minutes from the end. He outpaced the stocky Vogts, one of the world's greatest defenders, and sprinted through the middle of the Borussia defence. In his desperation to stop his tormentor, Vogts tripped Keegan from behind just as he had opened up the path to goal. That run of sheer brilliance by the Yorkshire terrier convinced the watching Hamburg officials that they should tie up his transfer immediately after the match.

The penalty responsibility was left to deadeye Phil Neal, who successfully put away thirty-eight penalties during his Anfield career. Neal powered the ball into the net to complete what was then the greatest triumph in Liverpool's history. It was just the start of the Red monopoly.

Match hero Keegan, born in Armthorpe, Yorkshire, on 14 February 1951, was a late developer who was overlooked by the major clubs early in his career. Coventry City rejected him after a trial and he kicked off his professional footballing life down in the bargain basement with Scunthorpe United before being spotted by Bill Shankly's scouts. He went to Liverpool for the bargain price of £35,000 and now he was off on an adventure that would turn him into not just the best player in England but in Europe. Later, Keegan said of the European Cup final triumph against Borussia:

The nice thing is that I became close friends with Berti Vogts after that match in Rome. He is one of the most pleasant men in football, and never once did he try to resort to foul tactics to get the better of me. The penalty was not a malicious foul. He was just trying too hard to catch me.

I was under enormous pressure because the deal with Hamburg was all but complete. This was common knowledge in Liverpool and quite a lot of the fans turned against me, as if I was some sort of traitor, choosing to ignore the fact that I had run my legs off for the club for six years and that they had got me for what Bill Shankly described as a pittance.

I had the satisfaction of knowing I had not let a soul down at Anfield, and I was able to leave with my head held high for a new exciting challenge in Hamburg.

Bob Paisley was manager and deserved the praise that came his way, but we all knew that it was the team that Shanks had built and I am so pleased he was in Rome to see his dreams come true. For me, Shankly was the greatest manager of them all.

Meantime, back home, all hell was breaking loose at Old Trafford where Tommy Docherty got himself sacked for falling in love with Mary Brown, the wife of the club physiotherapist, Laurie Brown. The affair ended his marriage to his wife of twenty-seven-years, Agnes, and propelled him into a second marriage with Mary.

At the time, the irrepressible Tommy and I were collaborating on a book called *The Rat Race* and he told me: 'When Mary and I gave the news to her husband Laurie that we had fallen hopelessly in love, he was standing in his kitchen with a bread knife in his hand. I decided to lighten the moment by saying, "While you've got that in your hand, Laurie, do us a favour and cut me a sandwich." '

Only the Doc could be that outrageous and only the Doc would have shared the story. He just could not resist being the conduit for anecdotes that were usually hilariously, sometimes hideously, funny. He went on to become a successful after-dinner speaker, virtually a stand-up comedian. He should have been on stage at the Glasgow Empire because he was a non-stop joke machine. Now in his seventies, he is still one of the funniest after-dinner speakers in the land. Catch him if you can. You will not hear his like again.

In common with others before and after him, Tommy Docherty failed to control the genius of George Best. The Doc tried to bring him back into the Old Trafford fold after Best had fallen out with Frank O'Farrell, Docherty's short-lived predecessor as manager. O'Farrell found the United seat too hot, just as Wilf McGuinness had when promoted from trainer to boss.

Neither McGuinness nor O'Farrell could solve the enigma wrapped in a riddle that was George Best. He caused continual headaches not only to defenders but also to a procession of managers. It seemed only Matt Busby could handle him.

Best started the 1970s with a four-week suspension for deliberately knocking the ball out of referee Jack Taylor's hands at the end of a League Cup semi-final against Manchester City – a rare case of a player being sent off *after* the final whistle. On his return on 7 February 1970, George produced a stunningly impudent six-goal solo show against Northampton in an FA Cup fifth-round tie that translated as his two fingers to the establishment. Kim Book, brother of Manchester City skipper and later manager Tony Book, was the unlucky goalkeeper on the receiving end.

Born in Belfast on 22 May 1946, Best inherited his sporting prowess from his mother, who was a star player with the Queen Park Hockey Club. He made his league debut for Manchester United against West Bromwich Albion in the autumn of 1963. Marking him was Welsh international Graham Williams, who was given a rare old chasing by the seventeen-year-old unknown youngster. Years later, George was walking along minding his own business when a middle-aged man tugged him by the sleeve and stood directly in front of him. It was Graham Williams. He said, 'Stand still you bugger and let me look at your face. All I saw of you on the pitch was your arse disappearing down the touchline!'

Best had ten sensational years with Manchester United, his exceptional skills with a ball at his feet and his controversial behaviour off the pitch ensuring that he was rarely out of the headlines. He scored 137 goals in 361 league games for United, and won two league championship medals and a European Cup winner's medal. In 1968 he was voted both Footballer of the Year in England and also the European Footballer of the Year.

Best retired in 1973 following a series of altercations at Old Trafford, where he missed the guiding hand of his mentor, Sir Matt Busby. However, the pull of the game that he played better than almost anybody else on earth proved too great, and he came back to play for a string of clubs, including Stockport County, Cork Celtic, Los Angeles Aztecs, Golden Bay, San José Earthquakers, Brisbane Lions and Hibernian. His most memorable return was for Fulham in a Golden Oldies double act with Rodney Marsh, while Bobby Moore was sweeping up behind them. They were enjoying the last of the summer wine – and, in George's case, he went on drinking into the autumn and through to winter. He was a drinking man for all seasons. The trouble with George was that there always had to be a next drink.

He had another team that is rarely mentioned in the record books – the Ford Open Prison XI, after he had been sent to what he called 'one of Her Majesty's hotels' after a drink-driving conviction and an assault on a policeman.

One of George's stories – funny yet sad – is that when playing in America and living in a house by the sea, he had to pass a bar to get to the beach and throughout his stay he never actually made it to the water.

Since hanging up his boots, he has remained in the public eye as a SkySport television panellist, and with a popular road show, first with Rodney Marsh and then with Jimmy Greaves. His well-publicised battle with the bottle led to a liver transplant, and just when we all thought he had at last learned to live an almost ordinary life, he returned to his old drinking ways and his domestic affairs became the daily diet of the gossip and news reporters. Another drink-driving ban brought him to a new low in early 2004 and even his closest friends began to doubt whether he would ever beat his demons.

Regardless of what he got up to off the pitch, the fact remains that few players have ever touched the Everest peak of skill that Best reached in his finest years with Manchester United. Here's how George explained it:

> *I always had a little imp inside me wanting to get out and make me try outrageous things on the pitch. When everything was just right, I felt as if I could have taken on any number of defenders and got the better of them.*
>
> *If you tie me down to my greatest game, I guess it would have to be the European Cup quarter-final against Benfica in Portugal. The Boss [Matt Busby] had told us to keep things tight for the first twenty minutes. I went against instructions, scored two goals in the opening few minutes and we went on to a fantastic 5–1 victory.*
>
> *Afterwards Matt said, 'Uh, George, in future can you at least pretend you are listening to my pre-match talk.'*
>
> *I accept I sometimes do things that are pretty self-destructive. It's a price I have had to pay for whatever the gift is that I was given. Just as I always wanted to try to outdo everyone when I played, I have also wanted to outdo everyone when out on the town.*

George was the first player to score from the spot in a penalty shoot-out. This was during a trial for the system in the pre-season Watney Cup tournament in 1970. United won the trend-setting penalties decider 4–3 at Hull City, and the first player to miss was the one and only Denis Law.

Red and yellow cards were introduced in the 1970s and the first player to see red was Blackburn winger David Wagstaffe. He was sent off in a Second Division match at Leyton Orient on 2 October 1976, beating George – sent off for swearing at the referee – by a few minutes.

The season Best finally quit Manchester United, after that abortive comeback under Tommy Docherty, was the season Bob Paisley took charge at Anfield.

When Kevin Keegan moved to Hamburg in 1977, the Liverpool boss immediately spent £440,000 – all but £60,000 of the fee – on his replacement, a Scot by the name of Kenny Dalglish. He is still considered by many to be Liverpool's greatest ever buy.

Dalglish, taking over Keegan's No. 7 shirt, proved his talent with the exquisitely chipped goal that retained the European Cup for Liverpool against Bruges at Wembley in 1978. That was just the down payment on what was to become a golden decade of service with the Anfield club.

The biggest sensation in English football in the seventies came off, rather than on, the pitch. Don Revie shocked the Football Association hierarchy to their foundations by quitting as England manager to take over as the richly rewarded soccer supremo of the United Arab Emirates. 'Deserter Don' screamed the headlines in the politer papers. What upset many people was not so much Revie's resignation as the furtive manner in which he chose to make the break after 29 matches, of which 14 were won, eight drawn and seven lost.

He sneaked off in disguise for his job interview while the England team were on their South American summer tour, and then sold his story exclusively to the *Daily Mail*'s exceptional sportswriter Jeff Powell. That turned the rest of Fleet Street against Revie like a pack of savaging wolves. Hell hath no fury like an FA committee man scorned or a Fleet Street reporter scooped. The FA reacted by banning Revie from holding any job in British football for ten years, and many football reporters wrote spiteful articles about him. You would have thought he was a mass murderer rather than a man trying to set himself up for life with a contract in (and worth) a million. Revie fought the Football Association's ban in the High Court and won, but had to sit and listen to the judge describing him in his summing-up as 'deceitful, greedy and selfish'.

Ron Greenwood was Revie's replacement, which was like a dictator making way for a preacher. Ron was one of the game's great gentlemen, a dedicated Christian who prided himself on his high principles, but it was clear that despite being one of the best tacticians in the game, he was going to find the pressure of the job hard to handle.

Greenwood inherited a team that had no chance of qualifying for the 1978 World Cup finals, which featured some exceptional football from Argentina and Holland and a disappointing exit for Scotland, who failed to live up to the ludicrously bold promises of their likeable but blinkered manager, Ally MacLeod.

In the fiercest of all World Cup finals – scarred by more than fifty fouls – Argentina took a first-half lead against Holland through the tournament's top marksman, Mario Kempes. Holland, missing the drive and invention of the absent Johan Cruyff, scored the equaliser they were always threatening seven minutes from the end when tall substitute Dirk Nanninga headed in a cross from Rene Van der Kerkhof. In the last minute, Robbie Rensenbrink fired a shot against a post. Argentina came that close to defeat, but they recovered in extra time to take command and the trophy thanks to goals from Kempes and Daniel Bertoni. Eerily, the front row of the main stand was filled with one long line of Argentinian generals. This was not the sort of image that FIFA wanted to portray for the Beautiful Game.

The bad feeling between the two sides erupted even before a ball was kicked in the final. Holland threatened a walk-off protest when Argentina captain Daniel Passarella objected to Italian referee Sergio Gonella about a small plaster on Van der Kerkhof's hand, which was protecting a bruised bone. Passarella claimed it was dangerous. Spanish-speaking Dutch midfielder Johan Neeskens told the Argentine captain, 'If Rene goes, we all go.' Gonella finally persuaded Van der Kerkhof to return to the dressing room to have soft bandaging put on his injury and delayed the kick-off until his return, much to the hair-tearing frustration of deadline-dictated television directors from across the globe.

Two of the Argentine World Cup squad turned up in Europe a month later – at White Hart Lane. Tottenham pulled off an amazing double transfer coup when they bought Osvaldo Ardiles (from Huracan) and Ricardo Villa (from Racing Club) in a £700,000 investment that staggered the football world. Spurs were making the most of the Professional Footballers' Association's decision to lift the ban on foreign players, and the newly introduced freedom of contract suddenly made the Football League an attractive proposition for overseas players.

The story of the seventies would not be complete without mention of the late 'Fat Stan' Flashman, who was the king of the ticket touts – he called himself an 'entertainment broker'. Stan could get his hands on anything from a Buckingham Palace garden party ticket to a seat at the Last Night of the Proms but his richest harvest came from football Cup finals. Allegedly, players and managers used to provide Stan with tickets under the counter in return for notes in the hand. Just before the 1971 Arsenal-Liverpool final, in which the Gunners were going for the double, a Sunday newspaper claimed that police were investigating his business. The game was the hottest ticket in town, and Stan was in his element. When two police cars pulled up outside his King's Cross flat, which doubled as an office, sirens blaring, and four officers got out, he panicked and started to flush the tickets down the toilet. After a commotion outside Stan's front door, the police went off holding on to a neighbour they had come to nab on a hit-and-run charge.

Stan went 'legit' as the wildly eccentric chairman and owner of Barnet Football Club and remains one of the unforgettable characters of the English football scene.

The face of British football was changing rapidly. The beautifully elegant Nottingham Forest right-back Viv Anderson became the first black player to win a full England cap when he made his debut against Czechoslovakia at Wembley on 29 November 1978.

In another first for Forest, Brian Clough made Birmingham City striker Trevor Francis British football's first £1 million footballer in February 1979. Francis repaid a large slice of the fee three months later when he scored the goal that won the European Cup for Forest against Malmo, an unheralded Swedish team managed by Englishman Bob Houghton.

It was a remarkable feat by Clough and his quieter but just as creative partner Peter Taylor, as they worked even bigger miracles than those they had produced together down the road at Derby. They won the League Cup for a second successive year following their double of league championship and League Cup in 1977–78.

On the way to the European Cup in 1979, Forest conquered holders Liverpool in a magnificent first-round tie, but they could not prevent the Merseysiders regaining the First Division championship during a season in which ever-present goalkeeper Ray Clemence was beaten just sixteen times, a First Division defensive record.

That same year, in one of the most dramatic climaxes to any FA Cup final, Terry Neill-managed Arsenal beat Dave Sexton's Manchester United 3–2 at Wembley. Three goals came in the last five minutes, with United pulling back from 2–0 down only to see Alan Sunderland score a last-minute winner. The winning goal was created by Liam 'The Claw' Brady, who was compensated for a below-par performance in the 1978 final when Arsenal were beaten 1–0 by Bobby Robson's beautifully balanced Ipswich Town. In that game, Ipswich's seventy-seventh minute goal was scored by twenty-eight-year-old Roger Osborne with what turned out to be virtually his last kick for the club in a first-team game. He collapsed with the excitement and emotion of it all and was never the same force again. The son of a farm labourer from a Suffolk village of 500 people, Osborne moved on to Colchester and out of the publicity spotlight that, he admitted, he hated.

The irrepressible Clough and Forest marched on. They retained the European Cup the following year, beating Kevin Keegan's Hamburg in the final thanks to a goal from Scottish wing wizard John Robertson. It was a bright start to a decade that became the most tragic in the history of the game.

CHAPTER 16

A DECADE OF DARKNESS AND THE HAND OF GOD

I N WHAT IS INTENDED as a light look at the history of football, it is impossible to cover the 1980s with anything but a heavy heart. Three appalling disasters plunged the decade into a darkness that continues to haunt those caught up in the terrible aftermath. These three events led to a revolution in the game that was to change the face of football forever.

The nation was sent into mourning first of all by the Bradford City fire of 1985 that cost fifty-six lives when a stand at the antiquated Valley Parade ground went up in flames during a Third Division match against Lincoln City.

This was followed three weeks later by the horror of Heysel Stadium. Thirty-nine mainly Italian spectators died from crushing and suffocation during the European Cup final between Juventus and Liverpool in Brussels on 29 May 1985, a day that will go down in infamy.

The catastrophe generated an international debate on hooliganism and scarred the reputation of English football supporters. Subsequent investigations into the tragedy laid the blame on Liverpool fans, and the repercussions were felt throughout the

English game. All league clubs were banned by UEFA from taking part in European competitions, leaving English football to stagnate. By the time the ban was lifted in 1990, English teams were trailing their European rivals both tactically and technically. How ironic that the country that had been so reluctant to join the world and European bandwagons was now suffering from enforced isolation.

Just as the nightmares of Bradford and Heysel were beginning to settle, a third devastating tragedy struck. Ninety-six Liverpool supporters were killed and 170 injured on overcrowded terraces during the Liverpool-Nottingham Forest FA Cup semi-final at Hillsborough on 15 April 1989. The disaster was witnessed by millions on television and led to a whirlwind of change. All-seater stadiums were demanded, which brought an end to the terrace culture. The game would never be the same again.

The decade had got off to a flying start with Forest, Aston Villa and Liverpool leading the way in Europe. It was, of course, expected of Liverpool and Forest by now, but Villa were the surprise packet. They made it six European Cups in succession for English clubs when they beat Bayern Munich 1–0 in the 1982 final in Rotterdam with a goal from Peter Withe.

Ron 'Sergeant Major' Saunders had led them to an unexpected league championship a year earlier and then quit mid-season after one of the managerial disputes that became commonplace at Villa Park. Novice manager Tony Barton took over and he had to send on a novice goalkeeper in the eighth minute of the European Cup final. Regular goalkeeper Jimmy Rimmer came off injured and twenty-three-year-old Nigel Spink came on for just his second taste of first-team football. He played a blinder and kept Villa in the game with a series of saves as the thoroughbreds of Bayern threatened to tear them apart.

While their old boy Kevin Keegan was winning two successive European Player of the Year awards with Hamburg, Liverpool dominated the domestic scene. They won the league championship six times during the decade, including a hat-trick between 1982 and 1984. Bob Paisley handed over the manager's baton to Joe Fagan before the remarkable Kenny Dalglish took over in the shadow of Heysel to keep alight the red flame first ignited by Bill Shankly.

The Football League was becoming truly international, laying the foundations for the mass foreign invasion of the 1990s. As well as

Tottenham's Ossie Ardiles and Ricky Villa, Dutchmen Arnold Muhren and Frans Thijssen were displaying their passing skills with Ipswich Town as overseas players began to rejuvenate what had become a stereotyped English game.

Ricky Villa scored one of the goals of the century in a 1981 FA Cup final replay against Manchester City at Wembley to give Tottenham a dramatic 3–2 victory. It deserves a full description.

Tony Galvin, patrolling Tottenham's left wing with imagination and flair, released a seventy-sixth minute pass to Villa on the left-hand side of the pitch some fifteen yards outside the heavily populated City penalty area. The score stood at 2–2 in what was the 100th FA Cup final, and the thought of extra time – as in the first match five days earlier – was beginning to come to mind. The only thing that had distinguished the first drab game was that City's giant-hearted Scot Tommy Hutchison had managed to score for both teams.

There was nothing drab about the replay. What followed as Villa took possession of the ball from Galvin was the stuff of which fairytales are made. Villa, who had sulked off the pitch when substituted in the first deadlocked match on the Saturday, was now the bright and alert Thursday man. He set off on a diagonal run towards the City goal but as there were five defenders ahead of him it seemed a pretty useless exercise. Most people assumed that he would be passing the ball to a better-positioned colleague, but that was to discount an artist's invention.

Suddenly, Villa changed direction and started running across the face of the City goal, side-stepping tackles with the casual grace of a Fred Astaire flying down to Rio, or perhaps Buenos Aires. There was certainly something of a tango rhythm to his movement as he went this way and that past bemused and confused defenders. Two City players were so befuddled by his unorthodox progress that they ran into each other as they tried to block his path.

The bearded and hefty Argentinian, suddenly a wild bull of the pampas yet as light on his feet as a spring lamb, showed strength to go with his skill. He survived buffeting challenges before unbalancing the oncoming goalkeeper Joe Corrigan by pretending to shoot and then sliding the ball right-footed into the net from eight yards for a goal in a million.

Then it was South American carnival time, and Villa raced

around Wembley on a wild dance of delight with his diminutive countryman Ossie Ardiles trying to catch him. The celebration was as unique as the goal.

A match that had almost died on its feet on the Saturday had been given the kick of life and it guaranteed that the 100th FA Cup final would be remembered through the following century of matches. Villa, who usually had to operate in the shadow of his more illustrious colleague Ardiles, said afterwards, 'On Saturday I was so unhappy. Now I am the happiest footballer in the world. When I ran towards the goal the ball seemed to stick to my feet. I did not think of passing because I enjoy running with the ball. My big thanks to the manager Mr Keith Burkinshaw for picking me. I did not think he would ever select me again after the way I left the field when I was substituted. But now I have repaid him with the greatest goal of my life.'

Tottenham, who had carried on their tradition of winning a major trophy when there was a '1' at the end of the year, returned to Wembley the following season and again went to a replay before beating Terry Venables' Queen's Park Rangers 1–0 thanks to a Glenn Hoddle penalty. Venables and Hoddle – how their careers were to become entwined in the years ahead.

This was the second all-London final in three years. West Ham United beat holders Arsenal 1–0 in 1980, the winning goal headed from just a foot off the ground by, of all people, Trevor Brooking. The man with the bucket load of education certificates usually used his head for thinking.

Terry Venables was rarely out of the headlines in the 1980s – in fact, he was rarely out of the football news from the 1960s onwards. The occasionally swaggering, often amusing and always entertaining Londoner soon left QPR for a spell in Spain. While in charge at Loftus Road, he supervised and encouraged the laying of the first synthetic pitch, which became reality in 1981 – and he wrote a novel about it called *They Used to Play on Grass* – but his vision of the future proved blurred. Luton, Oldham and Preston were the only other clubs to follow Rangers into the plastic revolution and by 1993 they were all back on grass. Uneven bounces of the ball and skin-burn injuries made most people reject the surface. Football was not in need of plastic surgery – yet.

During his reign in Spain, El Tel – as Terry Venables became

affectionately known – won *La Liga* with Barcelona before returning home to manage Tottenham, where he had a mega fall-out with
club owner Alan Sugar that ended in legal fisticuffs. Venables, who
never seemed happy unless he had at least three balls in the air at
once, claimed he was the victim of a witch hunt when a BBC
investigative team turned his private life inside out to try to prove
that he was, in the Venables vernacular, 'on the fiddle'.

He became one of the most popular of all England managers and
later flirted with club management again with Crystal Palace, Middlesbrough and Leeds. He then became a respected ITV summariser
before returning Down Under in 2004 as a consultant to Newcastle
United in New South Wales, where he had been based during a brief
but successful reign as Australia's national team manager.

Gary Lineker, Chris Waddle and Paul Gascoigne, to name just
three, have gone on record in praise of El Tel's coaching skills.
Nevertheless, Venables is rarely given the credit he is due for being
one of the finest coaches England has ever produced, probably
because of the baggage he carries from all his various enterprises.

While Venables was hogging the headlines in England, a young
manager in Scotland was building a reputation that would eventually lift him into the land of legend. Alex Ferguson was putting
both himself and Aberdeen on the football map.

Ferguson had started out in the game while at the same time
holding down a job as an apprentice toolmaker in the Govan
shipyards, where he was a notorious union activist. He once led
an unofficial walkout over a pay dispute. Born in the Clydeside area
of Glasgow one Hogmanay – 31 December 1941 – he has never
forgotten his working-class roots and socialist principles despite
becoming rich beyond his dreams.

A volcano always seems ready to erupt within Ferguson, and it
was no different in his playing days. He was like a John McEnroe of
the football pitch. He managed to get himself sent off seven times
during an explosive career in which he fell just short of international standard – this in an era when physical contact was an
accepted part of the game. Much of his trouble was self-inflicted as
he verbally lashed referees when he disagreed with their decisions.

Ferguson started playing at senior level with famous amateur
side Queen's Park, and over the next fourteen years was a prolific
goalscorer during football travels with St Johnstone, Dunfermline,

Rangers, Falkirk and Ayr United. He was a galloping centre-forward, scoring 35 goals in 67 games for Rangers, the club he supported as a boy, but Fergie dramatically quit Ibrox following an argument with the manager over who was at fault for a Celtic goal in an Old Firm derby. This was in 1969 when Celtic were the undisputed kings of Scottish football.

After that shock departure, Fergie had a valuable spell at Falkirk where he mixed playing with the side of the game that attracted him the most – coaching. He had always had good tactical sense on the pitch and he began to develop his overall understanding of the nuts and bolts of the game. Outside business interests, including a pub, diverted his attention as he concentrated on providing for his family. He counts a close-knit family as his biggest blessing – over and above anything he has achieved at Pittodrie and Old Trafford. His wife, Cathy, is his number one supporter, closely followed by three sons, including twins.

Ferguson wound down his playing career with Ayr United, a single-season stay during which the succession of injuries he had collected with his barnstorming style of play caught up with him and forced his retirement at the age of thirty-two.

Management was now the magnet and following a debut season in charge at East Stirling in 1974–75, he switched to St Mirren. Showing signs of things to come, he took them into the Premier Division before getting the sack in 1978 after an angry dispute with the directors. The stories coming out of the Paisley club were mixed. According to one, he had been fired following a row over players' bonuses, which would tie in with Fergie's past as a militant shop steward. Another account alleged that he had unleashed 'an unpardonable' swearing tirade in the hearing of a lady on the club premises. Alex can put his tongue to the shipyard language of his youth but is noted for his gentlemanly manners when in the company of women. He lodged a claim for unfair dismissal.

Fergie was quickly snapped up by Aberdeen. The club had not won a Scottish championship for more than twenty years but over the next eight seasons, Ferguson achieved the remarkable feat of interrupting the domination of Scottish football by Rangers and Celtic. Under his dynamic leadership, Aberdeen won three league championships, four Scottish Cups, one League Cup, and in 1983 – the one that really took the eye – the European Cup Winners' Cup.

Gordon Strachan, his main motivator at Aberdeen, recalled, 'They were unbelievable times. Alex had this almost demonic will to win and managed to instil it into the team. He had us playing out of our skins. He asked for – no, demanded – total effort, and he also liked us to do things with a certain style. He wanted inspiration with the perspiration.'

Aberdeen beat mighty Real Madrid 2–1 in the Cup Winners' Cup final in Gothenburg and suddenly Alex Ferguson was the name on the lips of ambitious club chairmen looking for their next manager. A queue of clubs tried to entice him away from Aberdeen, including Rangers, Arsenal, Aston Villa, Tottenham, Wolves and Barcelona. He turned down all approaches until Manchester United came calling in November 1986, just after he had finished a spell as part-time manager of Scotland following the death of Jock Stein. Ferguson conceded, 'United are the only club I would consider leaving Aberdeen to join. I remember the late, great Jock Stein once telling me that the biggest mistake he ever made was turning down Manchester United. I am not about to make the same mistake.'

On 4 March 1951, in Dalmarnock in the East End of Glasgow, one Kenneth Mathieson Dalglish was born. Brought up in the docklands area of Govan where Fergie was making his living, Kenny Dalglish spent his youth a goalkick away from the Ibrox home of his favourite team, Rangers.

He had a trial at Liverpool as a fifteen-year-old schoolboy in August 1966, playing for the 'B' team in a 1–0 victory against Southport reserves in the Lancashire League. Shankly had his mind focused on the upcoming season and took no notice when his training staff sent Dalglish home without signing him. A few seasons later, though, when he saw Dalglish playing for Celtic, he nearly blew a gasket as he realised Liverpool could have had him for nothing. Eleven years after the trial, Dalglish finally became a Liverpool player for a fee of £440,000, by which time Shankly had put himself out to grass.

Like the great Hughie Gallacher before him, Dalglish started out as a goalkeeper, playing between the posts for his Milton Bank primary school team – yes, a classic case of a goalkeeper turned poacher. By the time he was capped as a Scottish schoolboy international, he had moved forward to right-half, scoring twice on his debut in a 4–3 victory over Northern Ireland schoolboys.

His ambition was to play for Rangers but they did not seem to realise he was on their doorstep. After failing to impress Liverpool, he showed his wares to West Ham, again with no interest. So it was back to Glasgow for young Kenny, and the Protestant son of an engineer signed as a part-time professional for Jock Stein and the very Catholic Celtic. Assistant manager Sean Fallon clinched the deal, leaving his wife outside in the car while he popped into the Dalglish home. 'Just be a few minutes,' he said to his wife. Three hours later he returned with the Dalglish signature safely on a contract. His wife pointed out the little matter that it was their anniversary and he was supposed to be taking her out.

Between playing for Celtic's nursery side, Cumbernauld United, Dalglish worked as an apprentice joiner, which could explain why he later showed he knew all the angles on a football field.

A year later, with Celtic the newly crowned kings of Europe, he became a full-time professional and played in a Parkhead reserve team that became known as the Quality Street Gang. Just imagine walking casually into the ground to watch a reserve match and finding Dalglish, Lou Macari, Danny McGrain and Davie Hay performing on the field in front of you.

Jock Stein, never one to shoot his mouth off, caused folk to sit up and take notice when he said, 'I've got a couple of forwards who are going to become the talk of the game, Kenny Dalglish and Lou Macari. They're a bit special. I'll wager they become two of the best forwards of this or any other generation.'

In Aberdeen one night, Tommy Docherty sent twenty-year-old Dalglish on as a substitute for his international debut in a 1–0 1972 European Championship victory over Belgium. 'He will develop into one of the all-time greats, take my word for it,' the Doc said later, as he celebrated the news that the win at Pittodrie had clinched his appointment as full-time manager of Scotland. He went on, 'I've got the job at just the right time. It's years since we have been so rich in young talent. As well as Dalglish, I can call on Alan Hansen at Partick, Danny McGrain and Lou Macari at Celtic and Martin Buchan at Aberdeen. The future's bright.' What would Berti Vogts give for players of that calibre coming through?

Dalglish went on to win a record 102 caps and scored a record-equalling 30 goals, the total Denis Law reached in 55 matches for Scotland. In truth, Kenny was rarely as impressive for his country as his club. He was one of the great British club players but there are many ahead of him on the international stage.

Anfield was plunged into mourning when Kevin Keegan decided to take the Deutschmark and transfer his talent to Hamburg in 1977 but the modest, unassuming Dalglish would prove himself just about the finest player in the club's history. He continually comes out top in the polls despite support for Keegan, Ian St John, Billy Liddell, Roger Hunt, Ian Rush and Graeme Souness.

There is not a British player who can match Kenny's honours collection. He has won more medals than Montgomery. Just look at what he achieved on top of his 102 caps for Scotland.

With Celtic, in the course of scoring 167 goals, he won:

League championship 1972, 1973, 1974, 1977
Scottish Cup 1972, 1974, 1975, 1977
Scottish League Cup 1975.

With Liverpool, while scoring 118 goals, he won:

European Cup 1978, 1981, 1984
League championship 1979, 1980, 1982, 1983, 1984, 1986, 1988
League Cup 1981, 1982, 1983, 1984
FA Cup 1986.

He was voted Footballer of the Year in 1979 and 1983 and the PFA Footballer of the Year in 1983.

Dalglish plundered his goals with the cold professionalism of an assassin gunning down a victim. The only player to have topped a century of goals in both the English and Scottish Leagues with just two clubs, he had a great awareness of what was happening around him, and no forward can match him as a shielder of a ball. He would frustrate defenders into committing themselves to a tackle, side-step them and then either dart for goal or bring a team-mate into play with a perfectly weighted pass. Kenny was an unselfish team player who was quite happy to share the goal glory with colleagues. His partnership with Ian Rush was a joy to behold, provided you were not one of the defenders trying to obstruct their double act. They seemed to have a telepathic understanding, and Kenny made dozens of goals for his Welsh partner.

'I knew that if Kenny was in possession and I ran into space,' said Rush, one of the greatest strikers to come out of Wales, 'the ball would arrive just where and when I wanted it. There was nobody to touch him for making an accurate pass in a packed penalty area. He was a perfectionist who was not happy if anybody messed things up. Kenny wanted the ball in the back of the net and did not mind who put it there. A great individualist, yet a team player.'

Dalglish was appointed player-manager in the wake of the Heysel Stadium tragedy, and put the smile back on Liverpool faces by capturing the league championship and FA Cup double in his first season. Kenny repeated the championship success in 1988 and 1990, making his final league appearance in May 1989.

Bob Paisley, reaching down into his long memory, said, 'Of all the players I have played with, coached and managed in more than forty years at Anfield, I have no hesitation in saying that Kenny is the most talented. You will struggle to name any British forwards who have been better than him. His consistency is just unbelievable.'

Following the Hillsborough disaster, Dalglish was magnificent in the way he carried the city's grief on his shoulders. He worked tirelessly to try to ease the pain of survivors and the distressed relatives of those Liverpool fans who lost their lives so senselessly on the terraces of an outdated football ground. Dalglish was dignity personified. He attended as many funerals as possible, read lessons, helped out with counselling and tried to bring solace to the bereaved.

Kenny never made an issue of the stress and strain he was under but it must have taken its toll. In 1971, he had witnessed the catastrophe at Ibrox during the Old Firm match between Rangers and Celtic when stairway thirteen at the decaying stadium collapsed, killing sixty-six fans. Then, in 1985, he saw the horrors of Heysel as a member of the Liverpool team. No man should have such nightmares to haunt him and it is no wonder that following the Hillsborough disaster he began to look haggard and drawn.

A true professional of enormous character, he got his mind back on football and lifted the FA Cup after a 3–2 extra-time victory over Everton at Wembley in 1989. Liverpool were beaten to the league championship – and another double – in the last seconds of the 1988–89 season when Michael Thomas scored a dramatic injury-time goal that clinched the title for Arsenal.

Liverpool regained the championship the following season, and were going for another hat-trick – following the treble of the early 1980s – when Dalglish astonished everybody by announcing that he was quitting. The Quiet Man was walking out with the club top of the table and locked in a fifth-round FA Cup saga with Everton. The tie had ended 4–4 the day before Kenny decided to leave.

As many guessed, Dalglish's health was suffering as a result of the enormous pressure he had been under. He admitted that he was 'a person pushed to the limit' and on match days he felt as if his head was exploding – but he would rise again.

There was a Merseyside blanket over English football in the eighties. Everton refused to be overshadowed by all-conquering Liverpool and had the silverware to prove it. Under the rousing management of former Goodison player Howard Kendall, they won the FA Cup in 1984 by beating Graham Taylor's Watford. Everton collected the league championship in 1984–85 and also won the European Cup Winners' Cup, and they took the league title again in 1986–87 before Kendall was enticed away to Bilbao.

In 1984–85, in fact, they came tantalisingly close to a treble. They had already clinched the league championship when they arrived in Rotterdam for the Cup Winners' Cup final against Rapid Vienna. Just three days later they were due to meet Manchester United in the FA Cup final at Wembley.

In Rapid Vienna, Everton were facing a team that specialised in Houdini-style escapes. They had been eliminated by Celtic in the second round but produced medical and video evidence to prove that one of their players had been injured by a flying bottle in the second leg in Glasgow. A replay was ordered and Rapid won.

The Austrians came from three goals behind to conquer Dynamo Dresden in the quarter-finals, and they beat Moscow Dynamo in the semi-finals after being a goal down and missing a penalty. Their most prominent player was Hans Krankl, a vastly experienced international striker who had helped Barcelona win the Cup Winners' Cup in 1979.

Everton were fired by the ambition of keeping pace with their neighbours and archrivals – just the previous season, Liverpool had completed the treble of league championship, European Cup and League Cup.

With Andy Gray as a battering-ram centre-forward, assisted by the subtle touches of his plundering partner and fellow Scot Graeme Sharp, Everton hammered Rapid 3–1 after a goalless first-half in which they might have had another three. They did not give the outgunned Austrians a chance to exert their amazing powers of recovery.

The treble target looked a distinct possibility three days later when Manchester United defender Kevin Moran became the first player to be sent off in an FA Cup final. His reckless tackle on Everton midfielder Peter Reid in the seventy-eighth minute moved referee Peter Willis to flourish the history-making red card. Unfortunately for Everton, feeling the strain of their long, hard season, they were unable to capitalise on having an extra man, and the game was without a goal after ninety minutes. The ten men of United won the Cup thanks to Norman Whiteside's superbly struck extra-time goal. Three years earlier, Whiteside, at seventeen, had become the youngest ever World Cup player when appearing for Northern Ireland in the 1982 finals.

The victory over Everton was the second of two FA Cup successes that were the major achievements of Ron Atkinson's four and a half years in charge at Old Trafford. United won a replay 4–0 against brave Brighton in 1983, only surviving in the first match after Gordon Smith had missed a late open goal. BBC radio commentator Peter Jones made Smith part of Brighton folklore with his doomed prophecy '. . . and Smith MUST score.'

Everton were back at Wembley for a third successive FA Cup final in 1986, facing the old enemy Liverpool, who comfortably won this first all-Merseyside final 3–1. Ian Rush scored two goals to top a magnificent individual performance. Everton's goal was scored by Gary Lineker – soon to join El Tel in Barcelona. Shortly after the game, Rush moved to Juventus but he hated it in Italy and was soon back on Merseyside. 'I couldn't settle. It was like living in a foreign country,' was his classic remark.

Tottenham made a third FA Cup final appearance in six years in 1987, and lost a five-goal thriller to Coventry City in extra time. The Sky Blues were at Wembley for the first time in their 104 year history, while Spurs were bidding for their eighth victory in eight FA Cup finals.

It would have taken a brave or foolish man to bet against Tottenham continuing their winning streak when in less than two minutes Clive Allen scored his forty-ninth goal of the season for Spurs. In the end, it all came down to glory and heartbreak for Tottenham's marvellous defender Gary Mabbutt, who played at the top level throughout his career despite being a chronic diabetic. He scored Tottenham's second goal to put them 2–1 in the lead but it was cancelled out on the hour by a diving header from Coventry marksman Keith Houchen. For the fifth time in seven years, the final drifted into extra time and in what was the ninety-seventh minute the unfortunate Mabbutt turned a cross into his own net to give Coventry a victory they thoroughly deserved.

Wimbledon, nicknamed the Crazy Gang, brought some romance to the domestic arena – if a little ruggedly – by battling their way from the Fourth Division to the First and then shocking mighty Liverpool by defeating them in the 1988 FA Cup final. With English clubs barred from Europe, the FA Cup took centre stage, just like the old days. Lawrie Sanchez scored the only goal of the match and Dave Beasant became the first goalkeeper to save a penalty in an FA Cup final at Wembley. The usually spot-on John Aldridge was the man who suffered the misery of the miss. With Vinnie Jones and John Fashanu prowling the pitch, it was hardly the Beautiful Game but it was fun and exciting to watch.

Arsenal, under the command of their former strolling player George Graham, were beginning to make their powerful presence felt right across the soccer canvas, embarking on a period of supremacy that bridged the eighties and nineties.

On the World Cup stage, Italy were the winners in Spain in 1982 with a two-faceted performance. Cautious and cynical in the first three matches, they concentrated purely on qualifying for the later rounds. Then they produced a flood of free-style football to beat defending champions Argentina, tournament favourites Brazil, Poland (who finished third) and, in the final, European champions West Germany. The tournament's top scorer with six goals was Paolo Rossi, restored to the Italian team after a ban for his alleged involvement in a bribery scandal had been lifted.

In the semi-finals, the Germans won the first World Cup penalty shoot-out when they beat France 5–4 after a 3–3 draw. The controversial penalty deciders, hated by many purists, had now been given complete approval and a dressing of respectability.

England had the frustration of coming home after the second

phase without having been beaten, just as happened to Scotland in 1974. They needed to beat host nation Spain by two clear goals to edge out West Germany, but were unable to break down the Spanish defence in a goalless draw. Manager Ron Greenwood's plans were handicapped by injuries to key players Trevor Brooking and Kevin Keegan. They were sent on as late substitutes and both missed chances to win the game in the final frantic minutes.

Bobby Robson succeeded Greenwood, and he led England to the finals in Mexico in 1986 (they were originally scheduled for Colombia but financial problems meant a late switch). After a stuttering start, England fought their way through to the quarter-finals, with six-goal Gary Lineker the hot shot of the tournament.

The barrier between England and a semi-final place was Argentina, the only unbeaten team left in the topsy-turvy competition. Watched by a crowd of 114,580 spectators in Mexico City's Azteca Stadium, the match was heavy with tension because of the overspill of feeling from the Falklands War. Squads of military police brandishing white batons patrolled the ground, but apart from a few isolated skirmishes, the rival fans gave all their attention to a game that was electric with action and atmosphere.

All eyes were on Diego Maradona, who was in the form of his life and forcing good judges to reassess whether Pele really was the greatest footballer of all time. He might have been the shortest man on the field at 5ft 4ins, but the chunky, wide-shouldered Argentinian captain paraded across the pitch with the assured air of a giant among pygmies. England's defenders noticeably quivered every time he took possession, which was often because he was continually demanding the ball the moment it reached the feet of any team-mate. When he had the ball on his left foot, he would glide past tackles with the ease of a Rolls-Royce overtaking a Reliant Robin. When he did not have the ball, he was still a menace because of the speed with which he ran into areas of space to make himself available for a pass.

England defender Terry Fenwick, out of the retaliate-first school of football, decided that a physical assault might be the best way to keep Maradona quiet. Wrong! All he got for his clumsy effort was a booking and a cold stare from the Master that could be interpreted as meaning that he would eventually pay for his attempted ambush.

Maradona would pick his moment to provide action to go with that look.

England might have fared better in a goalless first forty-five minutes had they been more adventurous but they were so conscious of Maradona's match-winning ability that they cautiously kept players back in defence. They would have been better employed supporting raids against an Argentinian back line that looked vulnerable under attack.

The second half belonged almost entirely to Maradona, and the two goals that he scored became the major talking point of the entire tournament. The first will always be remembered for the controversy it caused – many would say Maradona cheated – and the second for its quite astounding quality.

Six minutes had gone when Maradona swept the ball to the feet of Valdano, and raced into the penalty area for the return. As he made his break, some England defenders were appealing for offside but the linesman's flag stayed down as Valdano's centre was deflected across the face of the England goal by Steve Hodge. Goalkeeper Peter Shilton came off his line prepared to punch clear. There seemed no way the stocky Maradona, dwarfed by the powerfully built England goalkeeper, could outjump Shilton but spectators looked on in amazement as the ball cannoned into the net off Maradona with the airborne Shilton stretching out to thrash empty air.

All eyes in the press box swivelled towards the action replay on the television screen as journalists sought confirmation of what they thought they had just seen, and there was the instant evidence. No doubt about it – Maradona had pushed the ball into the net with his left hand.

Outraged, Shilton led a posse of protesting players trying to persuade referee Ali Ben Naceur that the goal had been illegal but, from the angle that the Tunisian saw it, Maradona appeared to have scored with his head. He pointed to the centre-circle and the little man from Buenos Aires went on a dance of celebration that should have been a skulk of shame.

Four minutes later, with the aggrieved England players trying to regain their composure, the Jeykll and Hyde character that was Maradona unveiled the genius in his game. He produced the sort of magic that had prompted Napoli to buy him from Barcelona for a world record £6.9 million in 1984. To say he ran rings round England would be too simple a description of a goal that stands comparison with the very best scored anywhere and at any time. Indeed, it was voted Goal of the Century in 1999.

Running with the ball at his feet from close to the halfway line, Maradona drew England defenders to him like a spider luring its prey. Kenny Sansom, Terry Butcher and then Terry Fenwick – he who tried a physical assault in the first half – all came into the Maradona web and were left in a tangle behind him as he accelerated past their attempted tackles.

Again, it was Maradona versus Shilton, this time on the ground. Maradona did not have to cheat his way past the England goal-keeper. He sold him an outrageous dummy that left Shilton scrambling for a shot that never was, and then nonchalantly prodded the ball into the empty net for a goal of breathtaking beauty. It was a moment of magnificence that sweetened the sour taste left by Maradona's first goal – well, almost.

England, to their credit, battled back and substitute John Barnes laid on a goal for the razor-sharp Lineker in the eightieth minute but it was Argentina who went through to the semi-finals.

As they walked off the bakehouse of a pitch, exhausted after their 2–1 defeat, the England players, led by Shilton, found the energy to continue their complaints to the referee about the first Maradona goal. Most of the capacity crowd were talking only about his second goal as they filed out of the ground at the end of an eventful quarter-final that would always be remembered as 'Maradona's match'.

The man in question had a mix between a smile and a smirk on his face as he said later, 'Yes, the ball did go into the England net off my hand. It was the hand of God. It was not deliberate and so I do not in any way feel guilty claiming it as a goal. Would an England player have gone to the referee and said, "Don't award the goal. The ball hit my hand?" Of course not. Anyway, why all the controversy? Surely my second goal ended all arguments.'

Argentina duly won the thirteenth World Cup final at the Azteca Stadium on 29 June 1986 when they beat West Germany 3–2, and it was Maradona who collected the trophy as captain.

The European Championship – formerly the Nations Cup – had now come of age and was contested with the same concentration and ferocity as the World Cup. In 1980, West Germany, with Karl-Heinz Rummenigge in full flow, became the first team to win the trophy for a second time. France, inspired by Michel Platini, captured the championship with great flair in 1984, and Holland were the 1988 victors, thanks to the goalscoring of Marco van Basten and the silky skill of Ruud Gullit.

Seven-figure British transfers became commonplace in the 1980s. Bryan Robson set a new record in 1981 with his £1.5 million move from West Bromwich Albion to Manchester United and by the end of the decade United had lifted the record to £2.3 million for Middlesbrough central defender Gary Pallister.

Mark Hughes (£2.3 million to Barcelona), Gary Lineker (£2.75 million to Barcelona), Ian Rush (£2.8 million to Juventus) and Chris Waddle (£4.25 million to Marseille) were among the big-money exports. All four would eventually return to the English game, which was getting its act together after a decade that, sadly, will be remembered for all the wrong reasons.

CHAPTER 17

ALL BE SEATED
FOR THE PREMIER

G ROUNDBREAKING would be an accurate way to describe football's next decade. There was not so much a wind of change as a hurricane, and it brought with it some unsavoury business. It is tempting to call them the naughty nineties. The word 'sleaze' became part not only of the political vocabulary but also of soccer speak.

The triple tragedy of the Bradford fire and the horrors of Heysel and Hillsborough provided the springboard for a football revolution in England. If you have been paying attention at the back, you will recall that in the immediate post-war years there was standing room only at the Football League's packed grounds. Now there was to be no standing room at all.

All-seater stadiums gradually replaced the Victorian mausoleums that had become a blot on the football landscape. More than metaphorically, a huge demolition ball was swinging through the game, and with the new look came a brand new competition – the Premiership. In fact, the FA Premier League was actually the old First Division dressed up in bright new clothes, disguising familiar faces but not managing to hide all the old faults and warts.

'Loadsamoney' – a catchphrase from Thatcher's eighties – travelled first class into the nineties on the football gravy train.

Millions were poured into what was then the FA Carling Premier-ship by the satellite television company BSkyB in return for wall-to-wall coverage, dished up for their growing army of subscribers. Suddenly, clubs did not have to rely on bums-on-seats at their grounds to keep them afloat. Couch potatoes were important new customers.

The revolution came at a price. The lower division clubs of the old Football League scratched a living while the Premiership fat cats made money – and in many cases, ran up debts – like never before. Football stopped being a sport and became big business. Mega-rich owners, such as Jack Walker at Blackburn, virtually bought success, and tycoons, such as Sir John Hall at Newcastle United, floated their clubs on the Stock Exchange. Shareholders now had to be satisfied along with the supporters. Chelsea was not yet even a glint in the eye of Roman Abramovich, but Ken Bates was digging deep to lay the foundations for a new-style Stamford Bridge.

The Bouncing Czech Robert Maxwell had fun in football, secretly using his employees' pension money first to fund Oxford United and then Derby County. The 'Swindler of the Century' became part of a different sort of floatation when he slipped off his yacht and died in the warm waters off the Canary Islands in 1991. Goodness knows what he would have got up to with football club accounts had he been around when the Sky money came pouring in.

When Tommy Lawton moved from Chelsea to Notts County for £20,000 in 1947, everyone said that the game was going crazy. Fifty-one years later, Alan Shearer, the Lawton of his time, was sold by Blackburn to Newcastle for what was then a world record £15 million. Players earning £10,000 per week were suddenly common-place, and the superstars were raking in more than £40,000 per week as clubs competed to attract the best talent. England had almost overnight become a gold mine for overseas stars, attracting prospectors of the quality of Klinsmann, Bergkamp, Cantona, Gullit, Juninho, Zola, Ravanelli and Asprilla. Those who had grown up with the maximum wage of £20 a week watched with open mouths. The phrase 'it can only end in tears' was often heard, but the footballers – and a contagious rash of agents – were laughing all the way to the bank.

With the money came controversy and stories of betting and bung scandals dominated the headlines. Liverpool goalkeeper Bruce

Grobbelaar was the best known of a group of players accused in court of throwing games for money. It gave a whole new meaning to a fistful of dollars.

The biggest managerial casualty was phenomenally successful Arsenal manager George Graham. In eight electrifying years in charge at Highbury – a ground he graced as a player in Arsenal's 1970–71 double side – Graham had claimed six trophies: the League Cup (1986–87), league championship (1988–89 and 1990–91), League Cup and FA Cup (1992–93) and European Cup Winners' Cup (1993–94). He pieced together, coached and cajoled one of the finest club defensive combinations of any time – goalkeeper David Seaman, safe as houses behind the famous back four of Lee Dixon, magnificent skipper Tony Adams, Steve Bould or Martin Keown, and Nigel Winterburn as an enterprising left-back. Then in 1995, George was investigated for allegedly taking kick-back money from transfer deals – euphemistically described as 'bungs' – dismissed by the Highbury hierarchy and banished from all football for a year. The scandal reverberated throughout the game.

To his credit, Graham did not try to protest his innocence. He was prepared to own up to naivety and determined to come through the ordeal a stronger and better person. Lesser men would have crumbled under the pressure, much of it self-inflicted. In the book we wrote together, *The Glory and the Grief,* he says:

> *If I could turn back the clock, there is little that I would do differently in my eight years as Arsenal manager. The only definite change would be that I would say 'no, no, no' when Norwegian agent Rune Hauge decided he wanted to thank me for all I'd done to help him open doors for transfer business in England. The fact that he wanted to show his appreciation with two generous cash gifts put a temptation in my way that I was unable to resist. It is no defence, but I am sure that few people could have resisted accepting the money. I have never claimed to be some sort of shining knight, and I am as weak as the next man when it comes to life's temptations. I concede that greed got the better of me, but only temporarily.*

George eventually handed the money – a little matter of £425,000 – to Arsenal. He came out of it all empty handed, without a job, his career in ruins. He remains the only manager to have been caught and punished for what those close to the game allege is a common occurrence in football – George Graham, scapegoat.

George served his suspension with dignity and, in 1996, bounced back as Leeds manager. He took over from Howard Wilkinson, who had guided Leeds to the final First Division championship, in 1991–92, before it morphed into the Premiership.

In 1998, Graham surprised everybody – probably even himself – by leaving Elland Road to take charge of Tottenham, the club he had dwarfed while winning everything in sight down the road at Highbury. After just four months in the job he lifted the Worthington Cup, but a faction of the crowd saw Arsenal red every time they looked at him and he was never allowed to feel at home at White Hart Lane. He was just beginning to put the spur back into Spurs when he was dismissed in March 2001 for being too open with the media about his budget restrictions at Tottenham.

Now a regular expert summariser with Sky television, George still has a lot to give the game if the right challenge comes along.

Scandal was not exclusive to the English game. Across the Channel in France there was turmoil when Marseille were kicked out of the European Cup they had won in 1993 after it was proved they had bribed their way to the French championship. Ah, yes, the Beautiful Game!

Meanwhile, in Belgium, the touchpaper was just being lit for the biggest revolution in the game since J.C. Thring wrote the first rules.

A favourite after-dinner game is to name five famous Belgians. Well, here's one who deserves a statue built to him by Europe's money-saturated professional footballers – Jean-Marc Bosman. He, more than anybody, is responsible for their huge earnings after single-handedly moving the goalposts so that players had total freedom of contract. His battle was similar to the one fought by the unsung George Eastham against the soccer barons running – I almost said ruining – the English game in the 1950s, but the difference was that Jean-Marc was fighting on a huge international stage.

A moderate midfield player with Liège in the Belgian Second Division, his contract had expired and he wanted to play for Dunkerque in France. However, Dunkerque could not afford to pay the fee that Liège were demanding. The stubborn, twenty-six-year-old stood his ground and told the club. 'You do not own me. I am not your slave. I have honoured my contract and now I should be free to go where and when I please.'

Liège reacted by cutting his wages because he was no longer a first-team player. That was one cut too many for Bosman. With the help of brilliant lawyer Jean-Louis Dupont, he took his case for freedom to the European Court of Justice in Luxembourg and sued for restraint of trade. In an historic ruling on 15 December 1995, the European law lords gave Bosman and all other EU football players the right to a free transfer at the end of their contracts, with the provision that they were transferring from one EU Federation to another.

It was later agreed that out-of-contract players over the age of twenty-four could move without a fee on their heads. Celtic were the first British club to lose out when Scottish international midfielder John Collins moved 'on a Bosman' to Monaco in the summer of 1996 for nothing. A year earlier, he could have fetched around £5 million.

Bosman – a hero to players and agents alike – did not make a fortune out of football. His case took five years to get through the grinding gears of the legal system. He was thirty-one and into the veteran stage by the time he was granted his freedom. His one windfall was a damages pay-out of 16 million Belgian francs (£312,000). Now living comfortably in the suburbs of Liège, he said when reflecting on his momentous court success, 'This was a victory not just for me but for all footballers throughout Europe. It was always beyond my comprehension why players could not be treated in the same way as any other workers. When your contract is over, you either get a new one or you move on. There is no such thing as a fee. The judges agreed with me. If I had not brought this case, somebody else would have done soon because the situation was just farcical.'

The law lords also ruled that there should be no restrictions on the number of European community players in a side, and so it was that on 26 December 1999 Chelsea became the first British club to field a team made up entirely of overseas players.

The downside to the Bosman ruling was that many smaller, weaker clubs started to lose their best players without a hope of financial compensation. While in England fans were suddenly able to enjoy the skills of half the French World Cup winning team, cash-strapped clubs in France – where attendances are small – were losing their best attractions. A survey showed that out of thirty of the top French footballers, five only were earning their daily bread in France. The rest were spread around Italy, Spain, Germany and England, and getting paid at least four times what they could have picked up in their homeland.

England has also benefited from the imaginative input of some of France's finest managers. Arsene Wenger took over from George Graham at Arsenal after Bruce Rioch had a brief spell in charge. Gerard Houllier became a high-profile boss at Liverpool, and the former midfield master Jean Tigana had three hectic years in control at Fulham.

Away from the courtroom, the nineties got off to a roaring start with an enjoyable and eventful World Cup finals in Italy. England made an impressive bid for the trophy, finally going down in the semi-finals to West Germany in a penalty shoot-out.

The tournament turned tearful Geordie Paul Gascoigne into an overnight hero. He proved to have the talent but not always the temperament to cope with the sudden fame.

The finals got off to an unbelievable start with a result that seemed too far-fetched to be true. Reigning champions Argentina, including a weightier but just as skilful Maradona, were beaten 1–0 by 500-to-1 outsiders Cameroon. It was not just the Cameroon victory that caused the shock. What made it even more mind-numbing was the fact that the Africans achieved their win with just nine men left on the pitch at the end of one of the most sensational games ever witnessed at this level.

The magnificently constructed Milan stadium had been alive with the sound of music from La Scala opera house at the grand opening ceremony, but the Argentinians did not know whether they were on their arias or their elbows as Cameroon tore into them with a mix 'n' match blend of subtle skills and stark violence. In a strangely lethargic Argentinian side, Maradona was the only one to look like a world champion and the Cameroon defenders literally left their mark on him with tackles that were right out of the school of thuggery. The little man lost a lot of sympathy, however, by over-acting his agony.

The French referee Michel Vautrot had booked four players before sending off Andre Kana Biyik in the sixty-second minute.

Just four minutes later, Biyik's brother, François Omam, scored the only goal of the match for Cameroon with a downward header that the goalkeeper allowed to screw out of his arms and into the net. Five minutes from the end, the Africans had Benjamin Massing sent off for a flying tackle on Claudio Caniggia that would not have been out of place at Twickenham. Cameroon, known at home as the 'Indomitable Lions', held out for a victory that was as unlikely as any in the history of the World Cup.

England drew with Jack Charlton's redoubtable Republic of Ireland team and held Holland to a goalless draw before beating Eygpt 1–0, a Mark Wright goal booking their place in the second stage. Scotland made an early departure for the fifth successive finals after a 1–0 defeat by Brazil. 'Our players always get home before their postcards,' said Tommy Docherty.

Aston Villa captain David Platt came on as a substitute against Belgium and clinched a place for England in the quarter-finals with a spectacular volleyed winner in the last minute of extra time. The Republic of Ireland also made it through after a dramatic penalty shoot-out victory over Romania but their brave challenge finished with a 1–0 defeat by hosts Italy.

England again had to go to extra time before conquering Cameroon 3–2, with two goals coming from Gary Lineker penalties. They were outplayed for much of the time by an unorthodox Cameroon side in which thirty-eight-year-old Roger Milla was a constant menace with his dribbling skill and cunning running. Milla's World Cup performances inspired a public subscription at home for the building of a statue in his honour.

England saved their finest display of World Cup '90 for an epic semi-final, the first they had reached on foreign soil – but they finished up with empty hands and broken hearts, and tears on Gazza's face, as the old enemy West Germany got the better of them in a torturous penalty shoot-out.

Gascoigne, who had been more productive and prominent in midfield than German skipper Lothar Matthaus, collected a second booking of the tournament in extra time. He knew this would rule him out of the final and he could not stop the tears rolling down his face as the game finished at 1–1 and went to penalties.

The Germans converted all their penalties against outstanding goalkeeper Peter Shilton, while Stuart Pearce and Chris Waddle failed for England. They would later be rewarded for their incompetence with lucrative pizza-plugging TV commercials in which they took the mickey out of themselves – taking the pizza, you might say.

West Germany beat Argentina 1–0 in a best-forgotten repeat of the 1986 final, memorable only because it made Franz Beckenbauer the first man to manage and captain a World Cup winning team. A snarling, spoiling match was settled in the eighty-fifth minute by an Andreas Brehme spot-kick. The Argentinians angrily claimed the penalty should not have been awarded following what looked like a piece of theatrics by Rudi Voeller, who was almost in the Jurgen Klinsmann class as an ace diver.

Maradona whinged throughout and, in an appalling performance, Argentina finished with nine men. Pedro Monzon became the first player to be dismissed in a final in the sixty-fourth minute for a reckless tackle. In the closing stages, with tempers out of control and Mexican referee Edgardo Mendez out of his depth, Gustavo Dezotti was shown the red card after wrestling German defender Jurgen Kohler to the ground. The Beautiful Game? Rather, the Shaming Game.

Bobby Robson's last match as England manager, and Peter Shilton's 125th and final game as England goalkeeper, ended in a 2–1 defeat by Italy in a play-off for third place. Italy took the lead following a rare, sloppy error by skipper-for-the-day Shilton, who had been one of the most reliable last lines of defence ever. He went on to become the first player to make 1,000 league appearances. With a loss of concentration on what was such a special occasion for him, Shilton placed the ball down on the ground without realising that Roberto Baggio was loitering with intent alongside him. '*Grazie*,' said the Italian idol as he accepted the gift.

Then David Platt – one of England's outstanding players of the tournament along with Des Walker, Gary Lineker and Gazza – headed a fine equaliser. The winning goal, almost inevitably in a tournament packed with penalties, came from the spot. Salvatore 'Toto' Schillaci put the eighty-fourth minute penalty wide of Shilton for his sixth goal, which made him top scorer in the finals.

The likeable Bobby Robson, who had survived many assassination attempts by the Rottweilers of the tabloid press, had announced before the finals that he would be standing down as England manager. Surprisingly, the FA had not offered him a new contract and he was about to return to club management with PSV Eindhoven.

After all the shouting was over, he said:

> *I'm sad that Peter Shilton and I could not have gone out on a winning note, but we just didn't get the breaks. Yes, Peter made a mistake, but the fact that you can count his other errors as England goalkeeper on one hand shows what an outstanding player he has been. One of the greatest goal-keepers of all time, and a wonderful inspiration to everybody in the England squad.*
>
> *With a little bit of luck we might have beaten Italy, just as with some luck we might have beaten West Germany. But you have to accept what you get in football. It's swings and roundabouts.*
>
> *On the whole I have been delighted with our performances in the World Cup, and I think in young Paul Gascoigne we have a real star of the future. Mind you, he is as daft as a brush. I wish my successor luck, and I think I am leaving him with a wonderful squad of players with whom to take England forward to a bright future.*
>
> *I just hope some of the press treat him in a more sympa-thetic way than they have me. I became a victim of the tabloid war, with newspapers being sold on the back of stories about me that were often fabricated. This sort of reporting does untold damage and is like a cancer in the game.*

Graham Taylor, Robson's successor with the big grin and a liking for rock 'n' roll, got even worse treatment from the tabloids. He was eventually hounded out of the job by a baying press after England's flop in Euro '92 followed by failure to qualify for the 1994 World Cup finals in the United States. An exceptionally good club manager, he seemed out of his depth in the international arena, and he got stuck with a nickname given to him by the *Sun* – Taylor the Turnip.

The lowest moment of Taylor's England career came in a match that England won 7–1 against San Marino in a World Cup qualifier in Bologna on 17 November 1993. Davide Gualtieri had the ball in the England net for the part-timers of San Marino in 8.3 seconds, the fastest international goal on record.

Paul Gascoigne was crying again at Wembley in 1991, this time in pain. Playing for Tottenham in the FA Cup final against Clough's Nottingham Forest, he made a crazy, scything tackle on Gary Charles in the fifteenth minute. Gazza injured his knee so badly in the challenge that he was carried off and taken to hospital for an operation that delayed his £8 million transfer to Lazio. A month earlier, in the first semi-final to be played at Wembley, Gazza had helped beat deadly rivals Arsenal with a rifled thirty-five yard free kick that beat England goalkeeper David Seaman. 'One of the best free kicks I've never seen,' Seaman said later.

The Tottenham-Forest final went into extra time. Bizarrely, while Spurs manager Terry Venables was out on the pitch coaxing and encouraging his players in the short break, Brian Clough stood passing the time of day with a policeman. Spurs went on to win 2–1 when Forest defender Des Walker deflected the ball into his own net. The FA Cup was the one trophy that always eluded Clough, who later said of the policeman incident, 'He was a very nice chap and I was interested in what sort of day he was having. Trying to crowd thoughts into players' minds at that stage is pretty pointless. If they don't know what to do by then, they should not be professional footballers.' There will never be another quite like Brian Clough.

Kenny Dalglish had not lost his gift for surprise. In October 1992 he was unveiled as the new manager of Blackburn Rovers, with club owner Jack Walker's chequebook as his chief supporter. 'King Kenny' did not disappoint his legions of fans. He guided Rovers back to the top table from the play-offs at the end of his first season, and in 1994–95 turned Jack Walker's dreams to reality when – with a little help from Alan Shearer's thirty-seven goals – he brought the championship back to Blackburn for the first time in eighty-one years. 'Uncle' Jack had backed Dalglish to the tune of £30 million. Who said you cannot buy the title? Perhaps it was Roman Abramovich.

The rule-makers were doing their best to improve the game as a spectacle and to remove the on-field violence that was breeding more violence among the loutish element in the crowd. Professional fouls were made automatic red card offences, and to cut out time-wasting the pass back to the goalkeeper was banned.

For World Cup '94, nobody was quite sure how the Americans would react to the 'soccer' finals being played across the United

States. In fact, Americans supported the matches in record numbers (3,587,538 spectators in total) and deserved much better than the dreary final between Brazil and Italy, which was, inexplicably, decided on penalties rather than with a replay. That somehow cheapened the greatest football show on earth. Brazil emerged winners after Italian idol Roberto 'The Divine Ponytail' Baggio fired his penalty high over the bar in the sad shoot-out in Los Angeles.

This Brazilian team was a pale shadow of their great predecessors who had won the trophy in such scintillating fashion in three previous finals. They had two magnificent forwards in Romario and Bebeto but were poorly served by their midfielders who, unusually for Brazil, were functional rather than flair players.

Miracle worker Jack Charlton – now worthy of being called O'Charlton – once again motivated the Republic of Ireland beyond expectations, and they got through to the second round before being eliminated by Holland.

During the tournament, two scandals rocked the football world, one sad, the other horrific. The old master Diego Maradona, now thirty-four, had been behaving peculiarly from his first kick, punctuating his performances with odd facial gestures and showing astonishing energy for a man who was clearly overweight. He was dope tested following a 2–1 victory over Nigeria and it was announced that his urine contained five different variants of the stimulant ephedrine. The Argentine management team immediately withdrew their flawed genius before FIFA could hand him a suspension. Maradona, of course, protested his innocence but as he had been caught up in cocaine scandals while with Napoli in Italy, the once magnificent footballer was shown little compassion.

This was a minor incident compared with the tragedy that scarred Colombian football. They finished bottom of their group and performed abysmally, including a stunning 2–1 defeat by the United States.

Just days after the team had made an early return home, Colombian defender Andreas Escobar – who had conceded an own goal against the Americans – was shot and killed in his hometown of Medellin. Rumours have never gone away that it was a contract killing ordered by a bookmaker who had lost a fortune to people betting on a United States victory.

Escobar's father Dario still lives in Medellin and continues to mourn for his son. He tours Colombia giving talks in schools about the futility of violence.

'Andreas was more than a good son,' he said. 'He was a good man and a good friend. He felt terrible about the own goal after the game against the United States and I told him it was only a mistake and tried to calm him down.

'Andreas' spirit lives on in the pictures and the videos of him playing. There is also a statue of him in the local stadium. Everyone remembers him as a true gentleman of football.'

Our old friend Terry Venables took over the England management baton from Graham Taylor, and he put together an inventive team that restored English pride with an inspiring challenge as host nation for Euro '96.

England came into the tournament under a cloud of controversy after a few drink-fuelled players got involved in a wild night out in Hong Kong, following a match that was meant as a warm-up for championship action at home. Paul Gascoigne, who often went a prank too far, was at the centre of it all. He and several team-mates were photographed pouring drinks down each other's throats while half lying in a pretend dentist's chair in a nightclub. On the flight home, several players were accused of causing damage to aircraft property. As if it wasn't bad enough having fans as hooligans, now the players were behaving like louts.

Only an exceptional performance in the European Championship could restore their pride and self-respect and that is exactly what they produced, under the influence – you could almost say the intoxicating influence – of master coach Venables.

England were held 1–1 by Switzerland in the opening game at Wembley, a harsh penalty award against Stuart Pearce cancelling out an Alan Shearer goal and costing them a deserved victory. Then came the 'British final' – England against Scotland, who had held Holland to a goalless draw in their first game. It was a cracker.

Trailing 1–0 to a Shearer goal, the Scots were awarded a penalty twelve minutes from the end. David Seaman saved superbly from Gary McAllister, and within a minute the one and only Gazza had scored a gem of a second goal for England. He celebrated by going to a chosen spot at the side of the Scottish goal and, as he lay down, England team-mates poured bottled water down his throat in a send-up of the dentist's chair incident. The crowd loved it and suddenly the England players were forgiven their boisterous behaviour in Hong Kong.

In their next match, again at Wembley, England paralysed Holland 4–1 with football as good as had ever been seen from players wearing the three lions on their shirts. Alan Shearer – in the Lawton, Dean, Lofthouse class – scored two, and so did Teddy Sheringham, the subtle striker who made any team he played for tick with his intelligent positioning and precise passing.

Shearer and Sheringham were described as the 'SAS' partners, and they devastated the Dutch defence with their clever interchanges and sudden injections of pace. They were brilliantly supported by Gascoigne, who was at his impudent best. It was like watching Dutch total football from the 1970s.

'That's as close as you can get to perfection,' said a jubilant Venables as the country went into meltdown, with supporters across the country celebrating in the streets as if England had already captured the European Championship. It was all to prove premature.

To try to get round the spate of penalty shoot-outs that were deciding major matches, UEFA introduced a 'Golden Goal' sudden-death system. The first team to score in extra time would be the winners, but still two quarter-finals went to shoot-outs, including a nervous 4–2 victory by England over Spain after a goalless draw. The brilliant goalkeeping of David Seaman saved England; and man-of-character Stuart Pearce made amends for his penalty miss in Italia '90 with a brave, successful spot-kick against Spain.

The old enemy Germany – not just West, but *Deutschland alles* – were waiting for England in the semi-final. As if in an action replay of their 1990 World Cup encounter, the game was decided by penalties after a 1–1 draw. This time Gareth Southgate missed to leave the Germans 5–4 winners. Cue pizza commercial.

Germany and the Czech Republic slogged their way through ninety minutes of the final at Wembley to end it deadlocked at 1–1. For the first time, a final was decided on a 'Golden Goal' when substitute Oliver Bierhoff scored his second goal of the match five minutes into extra time, with the Czech defenders screaming for an offside flag that never came.

Terry Venables had been unable to agree a new contract with the FA and was allowed to stand down immediately after the tournament to be replaced by another former Tottenham favourite, Glenn Hoddle. Venables said at the close of his England adventure (11 wins, 11 draws and only one defeat):

> *I am disappointed with the way it ended because there is nothing more heart-breaking than to go out on penalties in a semi-final. It's like getting ready to sit down at a wonderful banquet when somebody takes the chair away from under you. But I am immensely proud of the players, and they can go away with heads high. The performances against Scotland and, in particular, Holland provided exactly the football we had planned, and we gave as good as we got against Germany until the lottery of the shoot-out.*
>
> *I have thoroughly enjoyed being in charge of the team and in different circumstances it would have been nice to carry on. But that's not to be. I now hand over to Glenn and I wish him the best of luck. He has some smashing players to work with.*

Two years later Glenn Hoddle had an even stronger squad to take with him into the World Cup finals in France, with the young pass master David Beckham and the boyish but breathtaking striker Michael Owen making their breakthrough into international football.

However, deep concern was being voiced in the media about the way Hoddle was going about the job of managing England. For a man who had been a creative conductor of a player and one of the greatest passers of a ball ever to wear an England shirt, he was strangely cautious and indecisive. He seemed set to disappear in a maze of his own making, plus he had introduced a few oddball procedures, such as consulting his faith healer Eileen Drewery and encouraging his players to go to see her.

He had also secretly entered into an agreement to write his diary of World Cup events in harness with FA spokesman David Davies and told half-truths at tense press conferences. He had an enormous bust up with Paul Gascoigne when dropping him from the squad at the last minute but the facts came out in drips to a press pack desperate for news. The media got behind Hoddle and his team for the finals in France but if anything were to go wrong, they were ready to drop on him with the cutting force of a guillotine.

England got through to stage two with victories over Tunisia and

Colombia despite losing in the last minute to Romania. They had to get past Argentina to win a place in the quarter-finals.

An Alan Shearer penalty and a wonder goal by Michael Owen – running on to a superb pass from David Beckham and outsprinting a pack of chasing Argentinians – gave England hope of victory.

The score was 2–2 when Beckham, with a petulance that would be cured by maturity, got himself red-carded for taking a silly retaliatory flick-kick at Diego Simeone, who had fouled him in a vicious manner.

It took Beckham all of two years to live down that moment of madness and for six months after the World Cup he was pilloried for having sabotaged the team effort. Nobody knew it better than boy David, and he gritted his teeth and got on with giving all his concentration to his game and the love of his life, Victoria Adams, known throughout the world as pop star Posh Spice. Low profile and David Beckham have always been strangers.

Following Beckham's premature departure, the ten men of England battled through to extra time. Hoddle's tactical awareness was scrutinised and criticised when he took off the creative Darren Anderton and replaced him with the toy bulldog David Batty.

The game went to the dreaded penalty shoot-out and who should come up to take the fifth England spot-kick but David Batty, who had never taken a penalty in a major match in his life. His weak shot was saved and out yet again in the Russian roulette of penalties went mortally wounded England. Cancel the pizzas.

The final was a strange affair. Brazil were roasting-hot favourites to beat host nation France and retain their championship but only one team turned up on the day. France, with two-goal Zinedine Zidane in imperious form, virtually cantered to a 3–0 victory.

At the after-match inquest into Brazil's punchless performance it emerged that the gifted Ronaldo – the 'new Pele' – had suffered some sort of fit and had been given tranquillisers. He played like a man in a trance and his team-mates did not seem to be able to get out of second gear. Brazil tried to play down the story that Ronaldo had played only because of pressure put on them by their kit sponsors. Football was now in the throttling hands of commercial companies.

The English media did not forget – or forgive – Glenn Hoddle's almost contemptuous treatment of them. When the FA sacked him in February 1999, after he had made a crass remark about disabled people paying for sins in a previous life, he found few in the press ready to plead his case.

The football roundabout was spinning madly. Kenny Dalglish – suddenly disillusioned at Blackburn – turned up as manager of Newcastle United following the surprise departure of the equally disillusioned Kevin Keegan, who in 1998 brought his exciting brand of no-holds-barred attacking football to Fulham. The exciting possibilities of what could be achieved with a potent cocktail of Keegan's talent and Mohamed Al Fayed's fortune filled the fans with hope and expectation – but after Howard Wilkinson had been in charge of England in a caretaker capacity for one game in 1999, who is this turning up to fill Glenn Hoddle's shoes? None other than Kevin Keegan. Football was entering the new millennium full of surprises.

In August 1998, the Football League unveiled their list of One Hundred League Legends drawn from the first 130 odd years of a game that was growing and developing out of all recognition. The list was compiled by a panel of distinguished football journalists under the chairmanship of the late, lamented commentator and writer Bryon Butler, who commented, 'This was a torturous job, not so much as to who we should put in but who should be left out. We discarded heroes by the dozen for one reason or another until we got down to our final choice. We know it's not going to be a list that satisfies everybody. That would be impossible.

'Can you imagine the pain of having to leave out players of the calibre of Jack Charlton, Trevor Brooking, Ian Wright, Peter Beardsley, David Seaman, and even dear old Ron "Chopper" Harris? But we feel comfortable with the final list. Now let the arguments begin!'

In chronological order, here are the hundred heroes for all seasons. The teams are the ones with which they were most associated, and the periods are approximate:

Pre First World War:
Billy Bassett (West Bromwich Albion), Archie Hunter (Aston Villa), John Goodall (Preston, Derby), Steve Bloomer (Derby), Billy Meredith (Manchester City, Manchester United), Bob Crompton (Blackburn Rovers), Billy Foulke (Sheffield United,

Chelsea), Alf Common (Sunderland, Middlesbrough), Sam Hardy (Liverpool, Aston Villa), Bill McCracken (Newcastle), Vivian Woodward (Tottenham, Chelsea), Clem Stephenson (Aston Villa, Huddersfield), Charles Buchan (Sunderland, Arsenal).

1920s–1930s
Elisha Scott (Liverpool), Dixie Dean (Everton), George Camsell (Middlesbrough), Hughie Gallacher (Newcastle, Chelsea), Harry Hibbs (Birmingham City), Alex James (Preston, Arsenal), Eddie Hapgood (Arsenal), Cliff Bastin (Arsenal), Wilf Copping (Leeds, Arsenal), David Jack (Bolton, Arsenal), Stanley Matthews (Stoke City, Blackpool), Ted Drake (Arsenal), Joe Mercer (Everton, Arsenal), Raich Carter (Sunderland, Derby), Peter Doherty (Manchester City, Derby), Frank Swift (Manchester City), Tommy Lawton (Everton, Chelsea, Notts County).

1940s–1950s
Wilf Mannion (Middlesbrough), George Hardwick (Middlesbrough), Johnny Carey (Manchester United), Stan Mortensen (Blackpool), Neil Franklin (Stoke City), Trevor Ford (Aston Villa, Sunderland), Nat Lofthouse (Bolton), Tom Finney (Preston), Alf Ramsey (Southampton, Tottenham), Len Shackleton (Newcastle, Sunderland), Jimmy Dickinson (Portsmouth), Arthur Rowley (West Bromwich Albion, Fulham, Leicester City, Shrewsbury), Billy Liddell (Liverpool), Billy Wright (Wolverhampton Wanderers), Jackie Milburn (Newcastle), John Charles (Leeds), Ivor Allchurch (Swansea, Newcastle, Cardiff), Danny Blanchflower (Aston Villa, Tottenham), Bert Trautmann (Manchester City), Jimmy McIlroy (Burnley, Stoke City), Tommy Taylor (Manchester United), Duncan Edwards (Manchester United).

1960s–1970s
Cliff Jones (Swansea, Tottenham), Johnny Haynes (Fulham), Jimmy Armfield (Blackpool), Terry Paine (Southampton), Bobby Charlton (Manchester United), Jimmy Greaves (Chelsea, Tottenham), Denis Law (Huddersfield, Manchester City, Manchester United), Gordon Banks (Leicester City, Stoke

City), Dave Mackay (Tottenham, Derby), Bobby Moore (West Ham), Alan Mullery (Fulham, Tottenham), Geoff Hurst (West Ham), Nobby Stiles (Manchester United), Johnny Giles (Manchester United, Leeds), Billy Bremner (Leeds), Frank McLintock (Leicester City, Arsenal, Queen's Park Rangers), Alex Young (Everton), Martin Peters (West Ham, Tottenham, Norwich), Tommy Smith (Liverpool), Norman Hunter (Leeds), Pat Jennings (Tottenham, Arsenal), Alan Ball (Blackpool, Everton, Arsenal, Southampton), Colin Bell (Manchester City), George Best (Manchester United).

1980s–1990s

Peter Shilton (Leicester City, Stoke City, Nottingham Forest, Southampton), Ray Clemence (Liverpool, Tottenham), Malcolm Macdonald (Luton, Newcastle, Arsenal), Kevin Keegan (Liverpool, Southampton, Newcastle), Trevor Francis (Birmingham City, Nottingham Forest), Graeme Souness (Middlesbrough, Liverpool), Liam Brady (Arsenal), Glenn Hoddle (Tottenham), Bryan Robson (West Bromwich Albion, Manchester United), Alan Hansen (Liverpool), Kenny Dalglish (Liverpool), Gary Lineker (Leicester City, Everton, Tottenham), Ian Rush (Liverpool), Ossie Ardiles (Tottenham), Neville Southall (Everton), Paul McGrath (Manchester United, Aston Villa), John Barnes (Watford, Liverpool), Tony Adams (Arsenal), Paul Gascoigne (Newcastle, Tottenham), Alan Shearer (Southampton, Blackburn Rovers, Newcastle), Ryan Giggs (Manchester United), Eric Cantona (Leeds, Manchester United), Peter Schmeichel (Manchester United), Dennis Bergkamp (Arsenal).

On the world stage, FIFA could not split Pele and Maradona, and they were elected joint Footballers of the Century, which was not very satisfactory. Maradona won a website poll and Pele dominated a poll of football coaches and journalists. A lot of bad feeling was generated between the two football-daft nations of Brazil and Argentina, which spilled over into the awards ceremony. After Maradona had collected his trophy he walked out just as Pele was about to receive his award. Pele, preparing to acknowledge his great rival, found himself staring at an empty front-row seat. Pele and

Maradona were as good as each other but Pele always represented the game with dignity. He never needed the hand of God or a nostril full of cocaine.

Johan Cruyff was voted European Footballer of the Century, beating Franz Beckenbauer and Spain's Alfredo di Stefano into second and third places respectively.

Roger Milla, Cameroon's 'dancing destroyer', was elected Africa's Footballer of the Century ahead of Liberian goal hunter George Weah. Both have helped to put African football on the map and it was in Africa that the Beautiful Game was making its biggest strides as the new millennium dawned.

Back in England, where it had all started, looming bankruptcies and growing wage bills heralded a new phrase in football-speak – 'in administration'.

And the Football Association got dragged into, of all things, a sex scandal following the appointment of their first ever foreign manager in the stylish shape of the suave, sophisticated (and some would say over-sexed) Swede, Sven-Goran Eriksson.

Mark Palios, the chief executive, was forced to resign after it was revealed that both he and Eriksson had been scoring away from home with the same FA secretary.

Careful scrutiny of the FA's leadership of the game since its formation in 1863 reveals many bumbling and bungling moments, but this was the first time anybody had been caught with their trousers down. Meantime, at many of the clubs there was a growing crisis of empty trouser pockets.

CHAPTER 18

THE FERGUSON FACTOR

IF THE BIBLE is right ('the love of money is the root of all evil') then football came into the new millennium full of evil intent. Millions of pounds were being thrown around in the search for success on the pitch, much of it obscenely spent by clubs dipping dangerously deep into overdrafts.

Usually sound and sensible clubs such as Ipswich Town and Leicester City (not helped by the collapse of ITV Digital and the millions of pounds that were lost to the game) were among dozens dragged into administration. In Scotland there was hardly a club chairman who could look his bank manager in the eye. Leeds United set the standard for budget madness, almost going out of existence with debts in excess of £50 million.

Amid all this insanity Manchester United were impressively balancing their books as one of the wealthiest clubs in the world. Their appeal stretched far beyond British boundaries, which gave them enormous commercial clout to go with the startling playing success they were enjoying under the remarkable management of Sir Alex Ferguson.

The United side that Fergie inherited from Ron Atkinson when he arrived fresh-faced from Aberdeen in November 1986 was not just a slumbering giant – it was in a coma. They had won just one of nine league games and were living in the shadow of a great past that seemed to be haunting and taunting them. The league championship trophy had not resided in the Old Trafford cabinet since the Busby glory days of 1967.

Like a procession of his predecessors, Ferguson struggled to meet the Busby standards. He battled for three years to make any sort of impressive impact at Old Trafford, and it looked as though it was going to be too big a job for him. The media vultures, swooping and snooping on the sidelines, thought so. In the *Sun*, Jimmy Greaves asked: 'How much longer can United afford to have Ferguson wasting their money?' In fact, he came within one match of being shown the door.

'Fergie out!' chanted the United fans at Maine Road when United were flattened 5–1 by neighbours Manchester City. The following week they lost at home to Crystal Palace and you could almost hear the knives being sharpened in the Old Trafford boardroom.

The decisive make-or-break game came in the third round of the FA Cup at Nottingham Forest on 6 January 1990, a day heavy with sadness for Alex because his mother had just died. United scrambled a 1–0 win and the victory turned their season – and Fergie's fortunes – right around. They went on to win the FA Cup, beating Ian Wright-inspired Crystal Palace 1–0 in a replay. This was the same Palace side that earlier in the season had been beaten 9–0 at Anfield, when eight different players had scored for Liverpool, creating a league record. Who did Palace beat in the FA Cup semifinal six months later? Liverpool.

That stumbling, nervous United win in the Wembley replay, from a goal by defender Lee Martin, triggered a sequence of startling success that put even Sir Matt Busby's great achievements in the shade. By the close of the 2003–04 season, the United trophy haul under Ferguson was eight Premiership titles, five FA Cups, one League Cup, the European Cup Winners' Cup and the European Cup. The top prize of the European Cup came as the last leg of an extraordinary treble in 1998–99 along with the league championship and FA Cup.

By then, the European Cup was a vastly different competition from the one that Manchester United won back in 1968. UEFA had slowly managed to introduce their long-desired European League in the form of a Champions League masquerading as the European

Cup, but without the sudden-death knockout ingredient that gave the old-style tournament such surprise and stature. The original concept had just the winners of the national championships going head to head, so it was a competition for the best teams only. There are those who much preferred it.

In the autumn of 2002, the doom-and-gloom merchants were predicting that United – and Fergie – were past their sell-by date. After a hat-trick of title triumphs, they had slipped miles behind new champions Arsenal but by the end of the season, United had captured the Premiership yet again. The legend of Alexander the Great was stronger than ever.

The first championship victory in 1992–93 was particularly important to Fergie because the man he so admired, Sir Matt Busby, was still alive to see United win the title after a barren spell of twenty-six years. Fergie said at the time, 'This is the greatest present we could have given Sir Matt. He has been a source of inspiration to me ever since I came into football, and he has continually supported me during some uncomfortable times here at Old Trafford.'

Like Sir Matt, Ferguson was rewarded for his triumph in Europe with a knighthood. Also like Sir Matt, he has always put his faith at the feet of flair players. Eric Cantona came from Leeds to light the fire of the team that won the inaugural Premiership title in 1992–93. Fergie was one of the few managers who could control the fiery, temperamental Frenchman, perhaps because – thinking back to his wildman days as a player – he recognised a kindred spirit.

When Cantona had the world falling about his ears after he had infamously kung-fu kicked a Crystal Palace fan in 1995, Alex supported him all the way through his crisis and talked him into not quitting the game. In the same circumstances, other managers may well have turned their backs on the player.

Fergie certainly found a way of communicating with Cantona that was beyond the powers of the press. Hard-bitten reporters, reared on 'over the moon, Brian' and 'sick as a parrot' quotes, looked on dumbstruck when the Frenchman told them after the judge had quashed his jail sentence, 'When seagulls follow a trawler, it is because they think sardines will be thrown into the sea.' That was all he said at the news conference. The press boys were, well, sick as parrots.

There is a stubborn and ruthless side of Ferguson. Ask any of the eight players he sacked in just one day at St Mirren. There has also been plenty of evidence at United that he never allows himself to be blinded by sentiment. For instance, he had no hesitation in moving out two of the players who had served him so well both at Aberdeen and then United, goalkeeper Jim Leighton and Gordon Strachan, when they were showing signs of being past their best.

Mark Hughes and Paul Ince, both favourites with the United crowd, were sold when they might have expected several more seasons at Old Trafford. Dutchman Jaap Stam was on his bike within weeks of mildly criticising Fergie in an autobiography, and the silence from Sir Alex was deafening when he stood back and allowed David Beckham's transfer to Real Madrid to go ahead in the summer of 2003.

Fergie's stubbornness was perhaps best illustrated during the 2003–04 season in an enormous bust up away from the football field. He went to the threshold of the courtroom before settling his differences with mega-rich United shareholders John Magnier and J.P. McManus over the ownership of champion racehorse Rock of Gibraltar. So much mud was thrown from both sides during the dispute that it is inevitable some will stick.

When it comes to losing, Fergie challenges even Bill Shankly as the worst football has known. He can rarely bring himself to be gracious in defeat, and his players fear the 'Ferguson Hairdryer' treatment if he feels they have let him and the team down. He stands close to any United player to whom he wants to make a point and berates them with fire and brimstone that can dry hair from ten paces.

'Goldenballs' Beckham – as he is known to his Posh wife – even got a boot in the eye after a home FA Cup defeat by Arsenal in February 2003. A loose boot kicked in fury by Fergie accidentally cut Becks above the eye, causing journalists to consult psychiatrists to consider if there was something wrong with the United boss. The diagnosis is simple. Ferguson *has* to be a winner. He is out of the Vince Lombardi school of sports psychology. The legendary American Football coach once claimed, 'Winning is not everything. It's the *only* thing.'

Ferguson is a master at winding up rival managers in what he sees as ongoing psychological warfare. Kevin Keegan and Arsene

Wenger are just two who have had unsettling experience of Fergie's mind games. He is a master at manipulating the media to put across his message, and he blatantly used television cameras to force the football authorities to take more care over the timing of matches. The sight of Ferguson standing on the touchline with stopwatch in hand used to be a regular cut-away shot for television directors as he virtually intimidated referees into blowing the final whistle when it suited him. He more than anybody was responsible for the introduction of the sensible and satisfying 'time left' ruling.

There are those who consider Ferguson to be a bully of a manager, but regardless of what anybody thinks of his methods no one can dispute that he is one of the most successful managers of all time. When you add what he achieved at Aberdeen to his trophy collection at Old Trafford, he is simply untouchable – and at Aberdeen he worked on a shoestring budget.

At Old Trafford, with one of the biggest chequebooks in the world of football, he has bought boldly and brilliantly – for example, Peter Schmeichel, Roy Keane, Ruud van Nistelrooy, Fabien Barthez, Juan Sebastian Veron, Ole Gunnar Solskjaer, Dwight Yorke, Andy Cole, Teddy Sheringham and Laurent Blanc. All England and Wales football followers – and the managers – should be grateful that he has insisted on keeping the famous United conveyor belt of youth players going, a system that has produced David Beckham, Ryan Giggs, Paul Scholes, the Neville brothers, Nicky Butt, Wes Brown, John O'Shea and Darren Fletcher.

Beckham buried the bad memories of his red-card embarrassment in France '98, becoming England's golden hero on the way to the 2002 World Cup finals, jointly hosted by Japan and South Korea.

England were led to Asia by Sven-Goran Eriksson, a Swede who appeared to have ice in his blood except when it came to matters of a romantic nature. He was the eventual choice after Kevin Keegan had thrown in the towel following a 1–0 World Cup qualifier defeat by Germany at Wembley in October 2000. Keegan, manager for 19 months and 18 matches, said with wrist-slitting honesty, 'I'm just not up to the job. It's best to admit that I'm not quite good enough and have fallen short of what's required. I have no complaints about the players. I blame no one but myself.'

Keegan had taken England to the Euro 2000 finals in Holland and Belgium, where defeats by Portugal and Romania signalled an early return home. It was a sad way for centre-forward Alan Shearer to finish his international career. The strong-willed England skipper bowed out voluntarily after netting 30 goals in 63 matches. He has resisted all calls to return to the international fold despite a string of stirring performances with Newcastle and a record haul of more than 200 Premiership goals. Shearer is one of the few modern English players who can look the old gods of the game in the eyes and not feel humbled.

France added the European Championship to their World Cup thanks to a 106th minute extra-time 'Golden Goal' from David Trezeguet against a skilful Italian team that was leading 1–0 with just seconds of normal time to go. By the time the next European Championship came round, the 'Golden Goal' had been consigned to the wastebin of history, and Trezeguet had got himself a permanent place in the record books.

England lived dangerously on their way to the World Cup 2002 finals, clinching qualification with an astonishing last-minute free kick from David Beckham against Greece at Old Trafford on 6 October 2001. Just a month earlier they had revived their hopes of making it to the finals with an unbelievable 5–1 victory over Germany in Munich, Michael Owen scoring a scorching hat-trick.

On a personal note, I will never ever forget it for the saddest of reasons. The game was into its last minutes when I got a call from Simon Moore, the son of ITV's exceptional football commentator Brian Moore, telling me that his father, one of my closest friends, had just died. I was honoured to deliver the eulogy for Brian, together with Bob Wilson, and I was able to tell the packed congregation along with thousands listening outside the Kent church where Brian was a regular worshipper:

> *Brian reached the top of his profession without collecting the baggage of arrogance and conceit that weighs on so many who become public celebrities. He was the consummate professional, but much more important, he was a wonderful human being. We mourn the passing of The Voice of Football.*

Brian deserves a mention in this fleeting history of the game in which commentators have played a significant role, going all the way back to the first broadcast by Captain H.B.T. Wakelam in 1927. The Captain and his shouted numbered squares had an audience of a few hundred. Commentators of the quality of John Motson, Barry Davies, Clive Tyldesley, Peter Drury, Martin Tyler and Alan Parry have taken up the microphone in succession to past masters Kenneth Wolstenholme, David Coleman and Brian Moore, and British viewers are better served than most with the standard of television football presentation. The 2002 World Cup was watched on television by an estimated global audience of 60 billion.

England skipper David Beckham was less than 100 per cent fit going into the finals after breaking a bone in his foot in the service of Manchester United. Suddenly, 'metatarsal' was part of everyday conversation as the Beckham foot became a focal point of attention. It developed into much more than just a footnote when he recovered in time to score the penalty that sunk Argentina in the group matches. That finally put to rest the ghosts that had haunted him for four years since his sending-off against the Argentinians at France '98.

England's goalkeeper David Seaman took over from Beckham as the 'Haunted One'. He was beaten from thirty-five yards by a freak free kick – or was it meant? – from Ronaldinho that put Brazil through to the semi-finals. This was a nightmare revisited for Seaman, one of the great goalkeepers, who was deceived by a similar long-range effort from Nayim in the last minute of Arsenal's 1995 European Cup Winners' Cup final against Real Zaragoza.

The Republic of Ireland were the talk of the tournament for all the wrong reasons. Skipper Roy Keane, arguably the most influential midfield player of the decade, was sent home after a vicious verbal attack on team manager Mick McCarthy just before the tournament was due to start. Even without their main player, the Irish battled through to the second stage before going out on penalties to Spain.

Brian Clough had been Roy Keane's first manager in his Nottingham Forest days. Asked if he would have sent the Irishman home following the row with McCarthy, Clough said, 'Yes, I would certainly have sent him home . . . but first of all I would have shot him.'

Brazil went on to win the World Cup for a fifth time, with the revived Ronaldo scoring both goals in a 2–0 victory over Germany to make up for his virtual non-appearance in the 1998 final in Paris.

In February 2003, an upsetting sight brought grown men to the edge of tears – the demolition of Wembley's famous twin towers.

Surely the FA could have ensured the towers were preserved, somehow, instead of turning a million memories to dust, but the world's most famous sports stadium was reduced to rubble to make way for a new dawn and a new Wembley. FA Cup finals were temporarily transferred to Cardiff's magnificent Millennium Stadium. George Cohen, standing in the ruins of the cathedral of English football on the day the towers came tumbling down, acted as a spokesman. England's giant-hearted right-back in the 1966 World Cup winning team on that most golden of Wembley days said, 'The towers have been a beacon for English football, recognised all over the world, and this is an enormously emotional moment for a lot of people. I feel quite tearful, but I am also realistic enough to know that it is time for the old stadium to come down.

'The time is right to rebuild it. The new stadium will be more comfortable for everyone. Nobody will be able to take away the memories we all have of the original ground. It will always have a place in our hearts, particularly we boys of '66! All I hope is that the new stadium will continue the legend of Wembley, and that it will be the start of a wonderful new era for English football.'

Perhaps the biggest revolution of the new millennium was the sudden escalation of interest and participation in women's football. The Women's Football Association was formed in 1969 with forty-four member clubs, and two years later the FA Council at last lifted the disgraceful ban on women playing at the grounds of affiliated clubs. Rarely has grass grown more slowly.

The first official women's international in Britain was played at Greenock in November 1972 – exactly one hundred years after the men started the ball rolling. England beat Scotland 3–2 and the first goal was scored by Liverpool's Sylvia Gore. By the late 1990s, football was the number one participating sport for girls and women. The Dick, Kerr Ladies would be thrilled and amazed if they could see what they had started.

The women's game was growing world-wide with the speed of a forest fire, and nowhere were the flames stronger than in the United States. Sell-out crowds flocked to the third women's World Cup there in 1999, with 90,000 watching their team win the trophy in a 5–4 penalty shoot-out victory over China. The players became nationwide icons, particularly decisive penalty taker Brandi Chastain, winning her 150th cap in the process. She whipped off her shirt in celebration, and became the most famous American stripper since Gypsy Rose Lee.

Among school-aged girls and boys, soccer is phenomenally successful in the United States, as is women's soccer, but the traditionalists continue to cling to gridiron, baseball and basketball as *the* major American men's team sports.

The Europeans got their grip back on the major women's titles at the Olympic Games in 2000, Norway beating the United States in a 'Golden Goal' finish to the final in Sydney. Germany were 'Golden Goal' winners against Sweden in the 2003 World Cup final.

In the men's game, Liverpool started the 2000s with a unique hat-trick of Cups – League Cup, FA Cup and UEFA Cup, playing 63 matches and scoring 127 goals in the process. When completing their treble of European Cup, league title and League Cup in 1983–84, they amassed 118 goals in 67 games. This latest treble was a triumph for the meticulous planning of French manager Gerard Houllier and his right-hand man Phil Thompson.

The following season there was stark evidence of the pressure managers are under when Gerard had a heart scare during a Premiership match against Leeds, and underwent an emergency eleven-hour operation. He was back at Anfield to steer Liverpool to their seventh League Cup success in 2003, a victory made all the sweeter because they beat deadly rivals Manchester United in the final.

Nevertheless, growing unrest rumbled around Merseyside over Liverpool's failure to break the United/Arsenal grip on the Premiership. They had won the old league championship a record eighteen times, but the glittering new prize of the Premier crown continued to elude them.

The relative lack of success finally claimed the head of the popular Houllier. Liverpool, who had considered negotiating a multi-million pound partnership deal with, of all things, the Thai government, replaced Houllier in the summer of 2004 with Spaniard Rafael Benitez, fresh from clinching the Spanish title and UEFA Cup double with Valencia.

Benitez was taking over the reins of a club in danger of being dwarfed by the exploits of Manchester United and Arsenal, where Gerard Houllier's countryman, Arsene Wenger, was setting startling new domestic standards.

CHAPTER 19

ARSENAL INVINCIBLES

T HIS IS WHERE we came in. At the start of our journey through the
domestic history of English football we acclaimed the Invincibles of Preston North End, who went unbeaten through the first
Football League season of 1888–89. How fitting that we approach
the final lap of our story with Arsenal repeating the feat of an
undefeated league season, the first club to achieve this perfection at
the top table in 115 years.

Their Premiership triumph of 2003–04 was even more remarkable than the one that made Preston immortal. There were just 22
games for the Deepdale club to negotiate. Arsenal played 38, won
26 and drew 12. They clinched the championship at neighbouring
Tottenham with four games still to go, finally running away with
the title 11 points clear of runners-up Chelsea.

What made it all the more memorable is that they did it in style,
often playing as fluent and as flamboyant football as has ever been
witnessed on an English field. I speak with – dare I admit it – more
than fifty years as a spectator behind me, and I have rarely seen
football to match what Arsenal produced at the peak of their form.
Only the Busby Babes of the 1950s, the United of Best, Charlton and
Law and Super Spurs of the 1960s have come close.

The conquest owed more to Gallic flair than English pragmatism.

Not surprisingly, French manager Arsene Wenger was elected Manager of the Year and 30-goal Golden Boot winner Thierry Henry retained both his PFA and Football Writers' Player of the Year awards after another season of sensational striking.

Wenger, a quiet, thoughtful and modest man, who shows just occasional glimpses of in-born arrogance, said:

I did not think any team capable of this. It is a remarkable achievement, and one that may never be seen again. To win the championship with 90 points is exceptional in itself, to do it without a single defeat is, well, just unbelievable. It will take time for what we have done really to sink in. Many years from now they will look back at this season and say, 'Goodness, what a team that must have been.' And do you know something, it really is an outstanding team and I am very very proud and privileged to be associated with it.

Yet for all the satisfaction ricocheting off the marble halls of Highbury, there was a tinge of regret because it could so easily have been an even more significant season for the Gunners. They fell at the semi-final hurdle when going for an historic hat-trick of FA Cup final victories, beaten 1–0 by their arch rivals Manchester United. In what was by their sky-scraping standards a disappointing season, United went on to beat plucky Millwall in the final at Cardiff.

Even more painful for Arsenal was defeat in the last moments of their two-leg Champions League quarter-final against Chelsea, a team they had beaten so many times they could almost claim to have won them outright.

But the Chelsea that eliminated them from Europe was a shining new version pulled together by the millions of pounds poured into the club by the recently installed czar of Stamford Bridge, Roman Abramovich.

The south-west London club took on the new nickname of Chelski as Russia's second wealthiest man – with a personal fortune estimated at more than £10 billion – tossed his loose change into the Chelsea coffers, and loose change for the oil baron runs into millions.

For anybody of a certain age it was just mind-numbing what was going on down the old King's Road, where for years Chelsea had been the conduit for comedians' jokes and were suitably known as the Pensioners. Now here was a thirty-six-year-old Russian turning them into his personal toy as he made Chelsea overnight into one of the most prosperous clubs in the world, apparently with no player outside their financial reach.

It seemed like only yesterday that the Berlin Wall was dismantled and Communism hit the capitalist buffers in Russia. Abramovich was just twenty-three when the wall came tumbling down in November 1989, and here he was just fourteen years later, one of the richest men on the planet and buying out one of British football's greatest characters in Ken Bates. What would Comrade Lenin have made of it all? At least if Abramovich had taken over Liverpool, he could have shouted 'Come on you Reds'.

The Russian revolution at Stamford Bridge quickly claimed the neck of likeable Italian manager Claudio Ranieri. Runners-up in the Premiership and semi-finalists in the Champions League? Just not good enough. He was replaced by Jose Mourinho, a supremely confident Portuguese coach whose shock capture of the European Cup with Porto in 2004 suddenly made him football's most wanted man.

Chelsea were linked with just about every major player in the world as Mourinho got his hands on the fattest chequebook in the game. All eyes were on the King's Road. Could the championship be bought? One thing we all knew for certain – English football would never be quite the same, what with the Thai government trying to get a foothold at Anfield, Leeds United ready to take anybody's money to stay alive, foreign managers and players almost everywhere you looked, and here in the heart of London a Russian tycoon waving a golden wand over Chelsea. It was a whole new ball game. Some of us held up our hands and said that we preferred it the way it was, and forecast it would all end in tears, but few were listening. Attention was focused on the revolution knocking down the walls of our game.

Meanwhile, the football statisticians were at work trying to put Arsenal's Premiership performance into some sort of perspective.

Their run of Premiership matches without defeat at the end of the 2003–04 season stretched to 40, just two off the all-time record set by Brian Clough's Nottingham Forest in the old First Division. The Gunners proudly powered past this record early in the 2004–05 season, but they had a long way to go to match the unbeaten 104 game run of Steaua Bucharest, and African statisticians came up with the impressive figure of 108 matches without defeat by ASEC Abidjan of the Ivory Coast. AC Milan were undefeated in the fiercely competitive *Serie A* in the 1991–92 season, part of a 58 match unbeaten sequence. Ajax not only went through the 1994–95 season unbeaten in the more than decent Dutch league, but also – and this will land below Arsenal belts – won the European Cup.

So while Arsenal's was the greatest achievement by an English club, there have been even more impressive performances on the international stage. It should also be mentioned, in fairness to the old timers of Preston, that as well as going through their league season unconquered, the original Invincibles also won the FA Cup without conceding a single goal.

While Preston had an overload of Scots, Arsenal were powered by foreign feet. Supporting the untouchable Henry were Dutchman Dennis Bergkamp, Frenchmen Robert Pires, Sylvain Wiltord and powerhouse skipper Patrick Vieira, Swede Freddie Ljungberg, Brazilians Edu and Gilberto Silva, Nigerian Nwankwo Kanu, Spaniard Jose Reyes and German goalkeeper Jens Lehmann.

The top flight had become a league of nations. On the first Saturday of the Premiership in 1992–93, eleven overseas players lined up for the kick-off. By the summer of 2004 the foreign legion had risen above seventy-five. Those eleven were: Anders Limpar (Sweden) and John Jensen (Denmark), both Arsenal; Andrei Kanchelskis (Russia) and Peter Schmeichel (Denmark), both Manchester United; Jan Stejskal (Czech), QPR; Roland Nilsson (Sweden), Sheffield Wednesday; Gunnar Halle (Norway), Oldham; Michel Vonk (Holland), Manchester City; Eric Cantona (France), Leeds; Hans Segers (Holland), Wimbledon; and Craig Forrest (Canada), Ipswich Town – not a foreigner in sight at Chelsea.

There was strong English influence at Arsenal in their historic, record-breaking season. Ashley Cole blossomed into a class act at left-back, Martin Keown gave his usual 100 per cent effort in his final season at Highbury, Ray Parlour was industrious in midfield, and Sol Campbell was a rock at the heart of the defence.

Both Cole and Campbell continued to show their magnificent club form for their country when helping England's bid for the Euro 2004 championship in Portugal. That tournament will be remembered by England supporters for the rise to international stardom of teenaged sensation Wayne Rooney. At Goodison they had known about Rooney's potential ever since he was a precocious kid of twelve, already with a man's body and a talent far beyond his years. Now, at eighteen, the Everton prodigy stood out head and shoulders above the cream of European footballers as one of the most gifted of all the forwards on show. Rooney, who had already rewritten the record books as the youngest ever England cap (17 years 111 days) and youngest ever England goalscorer, grabbed the attention with a series of stunning individual displays.

He scored four goals and helped propel an at times lethargic England team through to the quarter-finals – despite England losing their opening game 2–1 to France, with two dramatic last-gasp goals from Zinedine Zidane. Ice-man manager Sven-Goran Eriksson melted to the point where he compared Rooney's impact on the tournament to that of Pele in the 1958 World Cup finals in Sven's native Sweden. This statement was taken completely out of context to suggest that Sven was saying Rooney was the new Pele. Let's wait and see. We could re-open that debate when he has reached a haul of, let's say, 500 goals – less than half of Pele's output.

Not only the tabloids but also the broadsheet press got carried away with what became, for the headline writers, Wayne's World.

Significantly, it was when Rooney's tournament came to an abrupt end with a broken bone in his foot after twenty-seven minutes of the quarter-final against host country Portugal that England suddenly lost their drive and direction. Skipper David Beckham, weary after a year of bedding down into his new world with Real Madrid and a constant barrage of revelations about his private life, could not raise his game or his England team-mates.

Thanks to an early goal by a suddenly alert Michael Owen and a late equaliser by the vastly improved Frank Lampard, England battled to a 2–2 draw, despite being outplayed for long periods by a better organised Portuguese team. Screams of robbery resounded when the referee disallowed a last-minute headed goal by Sol Campbell, but clear-eyed neutrals agreed with the decision that John Terry had impeded goalkeeper Ricardo as the ball went into the net.

So it came to a penalty shoot-out, an event that has become a great challenge to England's footballers. It got off to the worst possible start when Beckham, who had missed a penalty against

France, heaved his first kick high and wide. The penalty spot seemed to move as Becks took his kick, and he could be seen to mutter 'Out damned spot!' or words to that effect.

Our eyes had not deceived us. There *was* movement beneath the penalty spot. A crumbling sand foundation was turning the shoot-out into a rollercoaster challenge.

Goalkeeper Ricardo saved the shot from substitute Darius Vassell and then proceeded to belt the next one past the despairing dive of David James to give Portugal a 6–5 victory on penalties. Ricardo was taking the pizza.

So out went England from a mediocre tournament they might easily have won if only Beckham, Owen, Scholes and the usually reliable Steven Gerrard had been anywhere near their best and able to match the contribution and commitment of the phenomenal Rooney.

England were not the only giants to stutter and stumble to an early exit. They were joined on the early flights home by under-performing France, Italy, Germany and Spain. Consolation for French manager Jacques Santini was a highly paid job as manager of Tottenham, where the White Hart Lane faithful were hoping he could do 'a Wenger' for them. Now that *would* be a miracle.

The Euro 2004 finals finished as they had started, with host country Portugal facing Greece, the shock side of the tournament. In one of the biggest upsets in the history of the European Championships, it was 100 to 1 outsiders Greece who emerged the winners.

As they feted their new gods, the delirious Greek supporters could not give one of their figs that the victory had taken the game back into the dark days of negativity. They were magnificently drilled by their German manager Otto Rehhagel, but were more concerned with football that was stifling rather than stimulating.

The ancient Greeks featured in the early part of this story of football and all that. How sad that the modern Greeks took as their philosophy the opening words of the inscription over Plato's door at the Academy of Athens: 'Let no one enter . . .' They could become unbeatable if they add attacking flair to their springboard of deep defence. Then the message on the way to World Cup 2006 would be 'Beware Greeks bearing goals'. Their defence-dominated discipline in Portugal introduced a new phrase to the football coaching manual – winning ugly.

CHAPTER 20

THE TIME TRAVELLERS

A S THE END of this journey through the history of football approaches, let's indulge in a flight of imagination. How would some of the early pioneers react if they could somehow be transported, with the help of H.G. Wells, to a modern Premiership match?

H.G. Wells was from the Victorian generation that laid the foundations for football, and in 1895 – the year when the original FA Cup was stolen from Aston Villa – he produced his first novel, *The Time Machine.* So which trail-blazing characters are to become time travellers, spirited to the here and now? What about good old J.C. Thring, the former Shrewsbury public schoolboy who was the first to write down a set of rules for the game of Association Football. What would he make of it all?

Well, for a start, he would want to know what that netting was on the back of the goal, what all the markings were on the pitch, and why there was a crossbar on top of the posts. The game he envisaged back in 1848 allowed for just a tape between the posts. He would also be puzzled that the goalkeeper was confined to his penalty area, and was the only one handling the ball. In his early version of the game, any player could stop the ball with his hands.

Reverend Thring, who studied theology at Cambridge University, would no doubt cover his ears in shock and embarrassment if he heard the language of the crowd and many of the players. He would wonder why one man on the pitch was dressed differently from all the other players and what he was doing blowing a whistle and holding up yellow and red cards. Some sort of musical magician, perhaps, with two flag-waving assistants. The Thring rules made no allowances for a referee. 'And what, pray,' he might ask, 'does "the referee's a wanker" mean? I have an idea, judging by the tone of the chants, that it is not very complimentary.'

Most of all, Reverend Thring would be appalled to find that the game is played on the Sabbath. 'This is a sin for which everybody involved will be punished,' he would surely venture to say. 'On the seventh day we should rest.'

A modern cynic might respond, 'Well, we're considering a mid-winter break.'

If the aristocratic Lord Kinnaird, nine times an FA Cup finalist with Wanderers and Old Etonians, and a famed and feared hacker in his day, were to become a time traveller, he would undoubtedly watch with mouth agape, unable to believe the evidence of his eyes. 'Why on earth aren't the players kicking each other?' he would ask. 'It used to be a man's game. Physical contact was encouraged and applauded. A load of namby pambies seem to be playing the game now.'

If Norman 'Bites Yer Legs' Hunter and Ron 'Chopper' Harris were there, two sixty-somethings sitting nearby, they would surely nod their heads in agreement.

His Lordship may decide to buy a match programme to see who is playing. 'Two pounds?' Kinnaird would say, his voice going up an octave, when asked for the money by the programme seller. 'That's more than I paid one of my servants for a month's work.' No one would dare tell him a seat in the stand usually costs about £30.

Lord Kinnaird's disbelief would change to contempt should an untouched player fall down as if shot. 'That man would make a wondrous Hamlet,' he might remark. 'When I was playing the game, a player would never go down as if smitten unless well and truly hacked.'

Chopper and Bites Yer Legs would both give thumbs-up agreement. 'Many of today's players should have Equity cards,' Chopper might remark.

Imagine Alf Common talking to Rio Ferdinand. In 1905, Alf was the first player to be sold for a £1,000 fee. If Rio told him that his transfer

from Leeds to Manchester United in 2002 cost around £30 million, Alf
would be speechless – and he certainly wouldn't be able to find his
tongue if Rio carried on to tell him that he earns around £100,000 a
week, even when suspended. The most Alf ever earned was a fiver.

'Tell me,' Alf might ask, eventually, in his strong Geordie tones,
'why do the players have their names on their backs? Don't they
know each other? And why do the numbers not run from one to
eleven? There's a player with thirty-five on his back. Hell, how
many do you have in a team?'

The soft Perthshire accent would quickly identify the next time
traveller. Welcome William McGregor, the founder of the Football
League. Just look at what he started! He would not be able to take in
the fact that the average weekly wage bill for the major clubs is in
excess of half a million pounds.

'Surely to goodness,' he would exclaim, 'you cannot get that back
through gate revenue alone. And by the way, where have all the
terraces gone? Football is a game to be watched standing up. They
will be watching it in armchairs next.'

Then he would be taken to one of the glass-fronted executive
boxes where cigar-puffing, champagne-swilling supporters do indeed lounge in armchairs and a television set mounted on the wall
shows highlights of games being played around the country. 'That,'
William would be informed, 'is where much of the money comes
from to bankroll the players' wages.'

McGregor would stare at the television and wonder if it is some
kind of cash machine, which in a way it is – a cash cow that could
one day be milked dry by the clubs. He would be mesmerised by the
television pictures. 'The nearest I had to that,' he might mutter, 'was
a kaleidoscope.'

If he was taken to the dressing room when the players were
having a half-time team talk, he would be even more amazed to the
point that he would probably wonder if he was hearing things.
These days, the manager's tactical orders have to be translated into
several languages – Portuguese over there, French here, Dutch in
the corner – and the manager often speaks in a language other than
English. If William were introduced to the owner of the club, he
would be nonplussed to find himself shaking hands with a Russian.

'Where are all the English and Scottish players?' he might ask
and be disconcerted to learn that they are mostly in the reserves or

playing in the lower divisions, and that the reservoir of Scottish imports has all but dried up.

'But where,' he would enquire, 'are the youngsters playing with a fitba' at their feet, learning how to dribble?'

Playing with their Gameboys, he would be told. Goodness knows what he would make of that! Perhaps he would content himself with quietly speculating how on earth schoolboy footballers can be motivated to play when all the first-team places have gone to overseas players and there are no more local heroes.

The one and only Mrs Lindon, who virtually gave her life so that players could – as Greavsie put it – have better balls, died of a lung disease caused by blowing up pig bladders. How would she describe the modern laceless, faceless ball? 'Totally lacking in charm and character' possibly? Now that would be a blow for the manufacturers.

Fantasy football will go on forever, but what about the real game? The crisis that threatened to crush Leeds in 2004 could prove to be just the start of a collapse of clubs that over-reach themselves in a bid to stay aboard the gravy train. With all the money being thrown at it and the invasion of foreign talent, is the modern game better than ever? Have we reached the Promised Land?

The quality of football in the Premiership is generally superior to anything played in the old First Division. The individual skill factor is the highest it has ever been, and the penalty area play of Ruud van Nistelrooy and Thierry Henry, to name just two examples, has rarely, if ever, been bettered. However, most of the great skill is displayed by foreign feet.

Before the older generation, clinging to memories of the way the game used to be played, throw in a few tackles from behind, it must be said that the game was more exciting to watch in the good old bad old days when there was shuddering physical contact. It has now been sanitised beyond common sense. Forwards dare not so much as touch a goalkeeper (ask John Terry), and solid tackling has become a lost art because defenders fear the dreaded yellow and red cards. Imagine what would have happened had today's rules applied at the time of the 1958 FA Cup final. Nat Lofthouse scored when he famously shoulder-charged goalkeeper Harry Gregg into the net, ball and all. Today, Nat would have been sent to the Tower.

Only somebody wearing blinkers would not admit that the multi-skilled and creative invaders from overseas are a joy to watch, but how would they have coped with a 'Bites Yer Legs' Hunter, a 'Chopper' Harris or a Tommy Smith hammering them from behind every time they received the ball? The tackle from behind was an evil curse on the game that deserved to be kicked out, but now it seems even breathing down the neck of the player with the ball is outlawed.

What has disappeared from the game is its soul. Most of the mercenaries playing in the Premiership have no real feeling for, or rapport with, their clubs. They have little idea of history and tradition. It is a case of just another day, just another game, just another dollar. Everything now is measured in money terms, and goals have ceased to be the currency of the game that really counts.

In the old days, the transfer money used to circulate around football, bringing much-needed succour and support to smaller clubs. Now the cash disappears from the game – and also from the country – into the pockets of the players (good luck to them) and the agents (mostly parasites).

Perhaps the time has come to reintroduce a maximum wage. In the soccer-slave days, £20 per week was ridiculously low. Now would a £20,000-per-week limit be a good idea? It could help save clubs that have mortgaged themselves up to the hilt trying to keep pace with the Joneses – well, the Fergies and the Wengers, anyway.

Surely £20,000 per week is enough to satisfy anybody. Agents might quibble but they could easily bring football to its knees with their demands unless some sort of control is introduced. The rule would probably be challenged and beaten in the courts, but those with the future of football at heart will know it makes sense.

Another idea is to restrict clubs to paying out a maximum fixed percentage of their income in wages, which would curb those clubs that continually spend beyond their means. The handful of clubs that make a profit would probably fight against any sort of restriction on their expenditure but without something of the sort happening in Scotland, the entire structure is in danger of collapse.

So the time travellers have all returned to their own eras. Throughout a journey that started in China with Tsu'Chu and rattled on all the way into the new millennium, where the football fields are awash with money for the haves and misery for the have-nots, it has been excitement all the way. Despite some disfigurement to the face of football, all in all, it remains the Beautiful Game.

EDWARD III'S PROCLAMATION

In the middle of the fourteenth century, Edward III commanded local authorities to ban all sports, including football, and enforce archery practice. Here's an extract from his proclamation:

> *Whereas the people of our realm, rich and poor alike, were accustomed formerly in their games to practise archery, whence by God's help, it is well known that high honour and profit came to our realm, and no small advantage to ourselves in our warlike enterprises, and that now skill in the use of the bow having fallen almost wholly into disrepute, our subjects give themselves up to the throwing of stones and of wood and of iron, and some to handball and football and hockey, and others to coursing and cock-fights, and even to other unseemly sports less useful and manly, whereby our realm, which God forbid, will soon, it would appear, be void of archers.*
>
> *We, wishing that a fitting remedy be found in this matter, do hereby ordain that in all places in your country, liberties or no liberties, wheresoever you shall deem fit, a proclamation be made to this effect: that every man in the same country, if he be able-bodied, shall, upon holidays, make use, in his games, of bows and arrows and so learn and practise archery.*
>
> *Moreover, we ordain that you prohibit under penalty of imprisonment all and sundry from such stone, wood and iron throwing, handball, football, or hockey, coursing and cock-fighting, or other such idle games.*

RICHARD MULCASTER'S TREATISE IN FAVOUR OF FOOTBALL, 1581

The handball, the football, the armeball

The Football play, which could not possibly have grown to this greatness, that it is now at, nor have been so much used, as it is in all places, if it had not had great help, both to health and strength, and to me the abuse of it is a sufficient argument, that it hath a right use: which being revoked to his primitive will both help, strength, and comfort nature: though as it is now commonly used, with thronging of a rude multitude, with bursting of shins, and breaking of legs, it be neither civil, neither worthy the name of any train to health. Wherein any man may evidently see the use of the game master. For if one stand by, which can judge of the play, and is judge over the parties, and hath authority to command in the place, all those inconveniences have been, I know, and will be I am sure very lightly redressed, nay there shall be no complaint, where there is no cause. The football strengthens and makes brawny the whole body. It helps weak hams by much moving and simple shanks by thickening of the flesh no less than riding doth.

APPENDIX 3

JOSEPH STRUTT'S OBSERVATION OF FOOTBALL, 1801

During its early formative years, football was witnessed by distinguished writer, artist and antiquary Joseph Strutt, who recorded in *The Sports and Pastimes of the People of England from the earliest period* (first published in 1801):

> . . . *an equal number of competitors take the field and stand between two goals placed at a distance of 80 to 100 yards the one from the other. The goal is usually made with two sticks driven into the ground about two or three feet apart. The ball, which is commonly made of a brown bladder and cased with leather, is delivered to the midst of the ground, and the object of each party is to drive it through the goal of their antagonists, which being achieved the game is won. The abilities of the performers are best displayed in attacking and defending the goals. When the exercise becomes exceedingly violent the players kick each others' shins without the least ceremony, and some of them are overthrown at the hazard of their limbs.*

RULES FOR THE SIMPLEST GAME BY J.C. THRING, 1848

1. A goal is scored whenever the ball is forced through the goal and under the bar, except it be thrown by hand.
2. Hands may be used only to stop a ball and place it on the ground before the feet.
3. Kicks must be aimed only at the ball.
4. A player may not kick the ball whilst in the air.
5. No tripping up or heel kicking allowed.
6. Whenever a ball is kicked beyond the side flags, it must be returned by the player who kicked it, from the spot it passed the flag line, in a straight line towards the middle of the ground.
7. When a ball is kicked behind the line of goal, it shall be kicked off from that line by one of the side whose goal it is.
8. No player may stand within six paces of the kicker when he is kicking off.
9. A player is 'out of play' immediately he is in front of the ball and must return behind the ball as soon as possible. If the ball is kicked by his own side past a player, he may not touch or kick it, or advance, until one of the other side has first kicked it, or one of his own side has been able to kick it on a level with, or in front of him.
10. No charging allowed when a player is 'out of play'; that is immediately the ball is behind him.

THE CAMBRIDGE RULES, 1862

The Cambridge committee members, all with public school backgrounds, were: Rev. R. Burn (Shrewsbury), R.H. Blake and W.T. Trench (Eton), W.R. Collyer and W.T. Martin (Rugby), J.T. Prior and W.P. Crawley (Marlborough), H.L. Williams (Harrow) and W.S. Wright (Westminster).

Rule 1
The length of the ground shall be not more than 150 yards. The ground shall be marked out by posts, and two posts shall be placed on each side line, at a distance of 25 yards from each goal line.

Rule 2
The goals shall consist of two upright poles at a distance of 15 feet from each other.

Rule 3
The choice of goals and kick off shall be determined by tossing, and the ball shall be kicked off from the middle of the ground.

Rule 4
In a match when half the time agreed upon has elapsed, the sides shall change goals, when the ball is next out of play. After a change or a goal obtained, the kick off shall be from the middle of the ground in the same direction as before. The time during which the match shall last, and the numbers on each side are to be settled by the heads of the sides.

Rule 5
When a player has kicked the ball, any one of the same side who is nearer to the opponent's goal line is out of play, and

may not touch the ball himself, nor in any way whatsoever prevent any other payer from doing so.

Rule 6
When the ball goes out of the ground by crossing the side lines, it is out of play, and shall be kicked straight into the ground again from the point it is first stopped.

Rule 7
When a player has kicked the ball beyond the opponent's goal line; whoever first touches the ball (touchdown) when it is on the ground with his hands may have a free kick, bringing the ball 25 yards straight out from the goal line.

Rule 8
No player may touch the ball behind his opponent's goal line, who is behind it when the ball is kicked there.

Rule 9
If the ball is touched down behind the goal line and beyond the line of the side posts, the free kick shall be from the 25 yards post.

Rule 10
When a player has a free kick, no one of his own side may be between him and his opponent's goal line, and no one of the opposite side may stand within 10 yards of him.

Rule 11
A free kick may be taken in any manner the player chooses.

Rule 12
A goal is obtained when the ball goes out of the ground by passing between the posts had they been of sufficient height.

Rule 13
The ball when in play may be stopped by any part of the body, but may not be held or hit by the hands, arms or shoulders.

Rule 14
All charging is fair, but holding, pushing with the hands, tripping up and shinning are forbidden.

THE SHEFFIELD RULES, 1857

1. The kick from the middle must be a place kick.
2. Kick Out must not be more than 25 yards out of goal.
3. A Fair Catch is a catch from any player provided the ball has not touched the ground or has not been thrown from touch and is entitled to a free kick.
4. Charging is fair in case of a place kick (with the exception of a kick off as soon as a player offers to kick) but he may always draw back unless he has actually touched the ball with his foot.
5. Pushing with the hands is allowed but no hacking or tripping up is fair under any circumstances whatever.
6. No player may be held or pulled over.
7. It is not lawful to take the ball off the ground (except in touch) for any purpose whatever.
8. The ball may be pushed or hit with the hand, but holding the ball except in the case of a free kick is altogether disallowed.
9. A goal must be kicked but not from touch nor by a free kick from a catch.
10. A ball in touch is dead, consequently the side that touches it down must bring it to the edge of the touch and throw it straight out from touch.
11. Each player must provide himself with a red and dark blue flannel cap, one colour to be worn by each side.

FORMATION OF THE FOOTBALL ASSOCIATION, 1863

The meeting convened to form 'an association of football clubs' was held at the Freemasons' Tavern in Great Queen Street, London, on 26 October 1863. Distinguished Victorian football historian Alfred Gibson described the historic occasion that was to prove a turning point for the game:

> There were present the following ardent pioneers: Mr. F. Day, the Secretary of the Crystal Palace Club, revived after forty years in a guise the original members would have never dreamed. Their colours were blue and white, with blue serge knickerbockers, and the Club was a new one that very year.
>
> Blackheath Club, the obstinate sticklers for hacking and incidentally thereby the founders of the Rugby Union, were represented by the Captain, Mr. T.H. Moore, and Secretary, Mr. F. W. Campbell. The original 'Heathens' were formed in 1858, and played in black knickerbockers, and red and black striped jerseys with stockings to match.
>
> Mr. J. Shillingford, the Secretary of Percival House and Blackheath School, attended, representing a club formed in 1856. Mr. W. Macintosh, the Captain, was the delegate of Kensington Grammar School. Mr. E.C. Morley, the Captain, and Mr. T. D. Gregory, the Secretary, represented the Barnes Club, who played in a field belonging to J. Johnstone, Esq, near the White Hart, and whose blue and white vestments would be seen in many a subsequent Cup tie. Mr Morley it was who had the honour of being appointed the first Hon. Secretary to the

young Association (with the responsibility of drawing up the first Rules after due consultation).

Mr. Hartshorn appeared for Charterhouse, the nursery of so many bright and debonair Internationals of a later period. Blackheath Proprietary School was represented by the Captain, Mr. W. H. Gordon; Forest Club of Leytonstone (later Wanderers, the first winners of the Cup) by Mr. H. F. Alcock and Mr. A. W. Mackenzie (H.F. was the elder brother of C.W. Alcock, who would become the principal driving force of the Association).

The 'No Names' of Kilburn had no less a person than Mr. A. Pember, the Captain and a mighty warrior and legislator, who was elected the Chairman; and the War Office was there in the person of Mr. G.T. Warren. Crusaders and Surbiton were also represented, and there were several unattached gentlemen, players of the game but not affiliated to any club.

But the public schools, save Charterhouse, did not attend, and with their absence began the first troubles.

THE FIRST RULES OF THE FOOTBALL ASSOCIATION

1. The maximum length of the ground shall be 200 yards, the maximum breadth shall be 100 yards, the length and breadth shall be marked off with flags; and the goal shall be defined by two upright posts, eight yards apart, without any tape or bar across them.

2. A toss for goals shall take place, and the game shall be commenced by a place kick from the centre of the ground by the side losing the toss for goals; the other side shall not approach within 10 yards of the ball until it is kicked off.

3. After a goal is won, the losing side shall be entitled to kick off, and the two sides shall change goals after each goal is won.

4. A goal shall be won when the ball passes between the goal posts or over the space between the goal-posts (at whatever height), not being thrown, knocked on, or carried.

5. When the ball is in touch, the first player who touches it shall throw it from the point on the boundary line where it left the ground in a direction at right angles with the boundary line, and the ball shall not be in play until it has touched the ground.

6. When a player has kicked the ball, any one of the same side who is nearer to the opponent's goal line is out of play and may not touch the ball himself, nor in any way whatever prevent any other player from doing so, until he is in play; but no player is out of play when the ball is kicked off from behind the goal line.

7. In case the ball goes behind the goal line, if a player on the side to whom the goal belongs first touches the ball, one of his

side shall be entitled to a free kick from the goal line at the point opposite the place where the ball shall be touched. If a player of the opposite side first touches the ball, one of his side shall be entitled to a free kick at the goal only from a point 15 yards outside the goal line, opposite the place where the ball is touched, the opposing side standing within their goal line until he has had his kick.

8. If a player makes a fair catch, he shall be entitled to a free kick, providing he claims it by making a mark with his heel at once; and in order to take such a kick he may go back as far as he pleases, and no player on the opposite side shall advance beyond his mark until he has kicked.

9. No player shall run with the ball.

10. Neither tripping nor hacking shall be allowed, and no player shall use his hands to hold or push his adversary.

11. A player shall not be allowed to throw the ball or pass it to another with his hands.

12. No player shall be allowed to take the ball from the ground with his hands under any pretext whatever while it is in play.

13. No player shall be allowed to wear projecting nails, iron plates, or gutta percha on the soles or heels of his boots.

BIBLIOGRAPHY

The author has dipped copiously into the waters of previous books by a host of writers, and is happy to acknowledge them here. In particular, he wishes to pick out the works of two hugely respected former press box colleagues, Brian Glanville and David Miller, now the doyens of their profession and always giving a lead in how to write about football with authority, accuracy and ardour.

A History of British Football, Percy M. Young, Arrow Books 1973
Against the Odds, Bobby Robson with Bob Harris, Stanley Paul 1990
Arsenal Official History, Phil Soar and Martin Tyler, Hamlyn 1989
Association Football, Volumes 1–4, edited by A.H. Fabian and Geoffrey Green, Caxton 1960
Association Football and English Society 1863–1915, Tony Mason, Harvester Press 1980
Association Football and the Men Who Made It, Volumes 1–4, Alfred Gibson and William Pickford, Caxton Publishing, 1907
Back Page Football, Stephen F. Kelly, Macdonald Queen Anne Press 1988
Bobby Moore, the Life and Times of a Sporting Hero, Jeff Powell, Robson Books 1993
Book of Football, consultant editor Brian James, Marshall Cavendish 1971–72
Book of World Football, Brian Glanville, Dragon 1972
Boys of '66, Martin Tyler, Hamlyn 1981
Daily Telegraph Football Chronicle, Norman Barrett, Carlton 1993
England, the Complete Post-War Record, Mike Payne, Breedon Books 1993
Famous Sporting Fiascos, Stephen Winkworth, Sphere Books 1984
Football and the Decline of Britain, James Walvin, Macmillan 1986
Football Encyclopaedia, edited by Frank Johnston, Associated Sporting Press, 1934
Football League Players' Records 1888–1939, Michael Joyce, Soccerdata Tony Brown 2002

Football Players' Records 1946–92, Barry J. Hugman and Tony Williams 1992

Golden Age of Football, Peter Jeffs, Breedon Books 1991

Heroes and Villains, Alex Flynn and Lynton Guest, Penguin 1991

History of the Football Association, Bryon Butler, Macdonald Queen Anne Press 1991

History of the World Cup, Brian Glanville, Faber and Faber 1973 and regular updates

Illustrated Encyclopaedia of British Football, Phil Soar, W.H. Smith 1990

Leeds United Story, Jason Tomas, Arthur Barker 1971

Managing My Life, Alex Ferguson with Hugh McIlvanney, Hodder & Stoughton 1999

News of the World Annuals, various and in particular the statistical input of Albert Sewell

Pele: My Life and the Beautiful Game, Pele with Robert L. Fish, New English Library 1977

Puffin Book of Football, Brian Glanville, Puffin Books 1970

Rothman's Football Yearbook later Sky Sports, years 1971 to 2004 and in particular the statistical input of Jack and Glenda Rollin

Soccer, A Panorama, Brian Glanville, Eyre and Spottiswoode 1969

Soccer Companion, David Pickering, Cassell 1994

Soccer Firsts, John Robinson, Guinness Publications 1989

Stanley Matthews, David Miller, Pavilion 1989

Sunday Times Illustrated History of Football, Chris Nawrat and Steve Hutchings, Hamlyn 1997

The Chelski Revolution, Harry Harris, Blake Publishing 2003

The Double and Before, Danny Blanchflower, Four Square 1961

The Football Fact Book, Jack Rollin, Guinness Publishing 1990

The Football League 1888–1988, Bryon Butler, Macdonald Queen Anne Press 1987

The Football Man, Arthur Hopcraft, Sportspages 1988

The Glory Game, Hunter Davies, Mainstream 1972

War Games: The Story of Sport in World War Two, Tony McCarthy, Queen Anne Press 1989

Wembley FA Cup Final, The History, Andrew Thraves, Weidenfeld and Nicolson 1994

We Won the Cup, David Barber, Pan Books 1981

WEBOGRAPHY

The internet has become the greatest library in the universe for fortunate authors and researchers, who now have so many facts and figures at their fingertips that they are, if anything, too well informed. The author wishes to thank, in particular, omniscient web-masters Peter Young www.englandfootballonline.com and Bob Dunning *www.bobdunning.net* for their encouragement and definitive databases. I also recommend the following sites as well worth a visit for in-depth football information:

    www.aboutaball.co.uk
    www.bbc.co.uk/football
    www.dailysoccer.com
    www.englandfc.com
    www.englandstats.com
    www.fifa.com
    www.football365.com
    www.football.guardian.co.uk
    www.footballnetwork.org
    www.itv-football.co.uk
    www.premierleague.com
    www.skysports.planetfootball.com
    www.soccerage.com
    www.soccerbase.com
    www.soccer.net
    soccernet.espn.go.com
    www.sportinglife.com/football
    www.telegraph.co.uk
    www.thefa.com
    www.timesonline.co.uk/football
    www.uefa.com
    www.users.pandora.be/football (links to all the major club sites)

OTHER BOOKS BY NORMAN GILLER

The author has used various of his earlier books to help refresh his memory for the story of *Football And All That*, and has occasionally unashamedly lifted facts and figures previously published under his name. His books output includes the following titles:

Athletics and the Olympics:
The Golden Milers with Sir Roger Bannister
The Marathon Kings
Olympics Handbook 1980
Olympics Handbook 1984
Olympic Heroes Brendan Foster

Boxing:
Crown of Thorns, the World Heavyweight Championship with Neil Duncanson
Eye of the Tiger with Frank Bruno
Fighting for Peace Barry McGuigan biography, with Peter Batt
From Zero to Hero with Frank Bruno
Henry Cooper's 100 Greatest Boxers
How to Box with Henry Cooper
Know What I Mean with Frank Bruno
Let's Be Honest with Reg Gutteridge
Mike Tyson Biography
Mike Tyson, the Release of Power with Reg Gutteridge
My Most Memorable Fights with Henry Cooper
Watt's My Name with Jim Watt

Cricket:
Book of Cricket Lists with Tom Graveney
Cricket Heroes with Eric Morecambe
Denis Compton The Untold Stories
Top Ten Cricket Book with Tom Graveney
World's Greatest Cricket Matches

Football:
ABC of Soccer Sense with Tommy Docherty
Banks of England with Gordon Banks
Billy Wright A Hero for All Seasons
The Book of Football Lists
The Final Score with Brian Moore
The Glory and the Grief with George Graham
Golden Heroes, History of the Footballer of the Year Award with Dennis
    Signy
McFootball, the Scottish Heroes of the English Game
The Rat Race with Tommy Docherty
The Seventies Revisited with Kevin Keegan
World's Greatest Football Matches

In collaboration with Jimmy Greaves: *A–Z World Cup History; Don't
Shoot the Manager; GOALS!; It's a Funny Old Life; Let's Be Honest*
(with Reg Gutteridge); *The Sixties Revisited; Stop the Game, I Want
to Get On; Taking Sides; This One's On Me*; plus novels *The Ball
Game, The Boss, The Final, The Second Half*; and in collaboration
with Jimmy Greaves and Ian St John: *Saint & Greavsie's World Cup
Special*

Other sport:
The Book of Golf Lists
The Book of Rugby Lists with Gareth Edwards
The Book of Tennis Lists with John Newcombe
The Judge Book of Sports Answers
The Judge 1,001 Arguments Settled

Quiz books:
*Big Fight Quiz Book, Sports Quiz Challenge, Sports Quiz Challenge 2,
    Sports Quiz Trivia, TVIQ Puzzle Book, TV Quiz Trivia*

Comedy novels: *Carry On Doctor, Carry On England, Carry On Loving,
    Carry On Up the Khyber, Carry On Abroad, Carry On Henry*
Novels: *A Stolen Life, Mike Baldwin: Mr Heartbreaker, Hitler's Last
    Victim*

Miscellaneous:
Gloria Hunniford's TV Challenge
Lucky the Fox with Barbara Wright

INDEX